Praise for *Web Development with Clojure*

The second edition continues to be an excellent resource for those new to the joy of Clojure web development.

➤ Colin Yates, principal software engineer, QFI Consulting LLP

A key part of building applications in Clojure is knowing how those tools fit together. Which is where Web Development with Clojure comes in: In this book Dmitri Sotnikov takes you through the process of harnessing Clojure to build a functional web application. Along the way he manages to explain just enough of the language, libraries and tools involved to orient the reader while never getting bogged down in technical trivia. Like Clojure itself, Web Development with Clojure is both functional and to the point.

➤ Russ Olsen, vice president, consulting services, Cognitect

Clojure is an awesome language, and using it for developing web applications is pure joy. This book is a valuable and timely resource for getting started with the various libraries of the Clojure web-development toolbox.

➤ Fred Daoud, web-development specialist and coauthor of *Seven Web Frameworks in Seven Weeks*

Sotnikov illustrates Clojure's flexible approach to web development by teaching the use of state-of-the-art libraries in making realistic websites.

➤ Chris Houser, *The Joy of Clojure* coauthor

With this book, you'll jump right into web development using powerful functional programming techniques. As you follow along, you'll make your app more scalable and maintainable—and you'll bring the expressiveness of Clojure to your client-side JavaScript.

➤ Ian Dees, author, *Cucumber Recipes*

Dmitri's book successfully walks a narrow line of introducing language features while also solving real, modern software development problems. This represents a significant return on investment for the time you devote to a technical book.

➤ Brian Sletten, Bosatsu Consulting, author of *Resource-Oriented Architecture Patterns for Webs of Data*

This is a fast-paced, no-cruft intro to applying your Clojure chops to making web apps. From chapter 1 you're running a real web app and then adding databases, security, JavaScript, and more. No dogma, no preaching, no fluff! To the point, productive, and clear. This book gives you all you need to get started and have a real app that you can continue to grow.

➤ Sam Griffith Jr., polyglot programmer at Interactive Web Systems, LLC

Web Development with Clojure, 2nd Edition

Build Bulletproof Web Apps with Less Code

Dmitri Sotnikov

The Pragmatic Bookshelf

Raleigh, North Carolina

Many of the designations used by manufacturers and sellers to distinguish their products are claimed as trademarks. Where those designations appear in this book, and The Pragmatic Programmers, LLC was aware of a trademark claim, the designations have been printed in initial capital letters or in all capitals. The Pragmatic Starter Kit, The Pragmatic Programmer, Pragmatic Programming, Pragmatic Bookshelf, PragProg and the linking *g* device are trademarks of The Pragmatic Programmers, LLC.

Every precaution was taken in the preparation of this book. However, the publisher assumes no responsibility for errors or omissions, or for damages that may result from the use of information (including program listings) contained herein.

Our Pragmatic books, screencasts, and audio books can help you and your team create better software and have more fun. Visit us at *https://pragprog.com*.

The team that produced this book includes:

Michael Swaine (editor)
Potomac Indexing, LLC (index)
Candace Cunningham, Molly McBeath (copyedit)
Gilson Graphics (layout)
Janet Furlow (producer)

For sales, volume licensing, and support, please contact *support@pragprog.com*.

For international rights, please contact *rights@pragprog.com*.

Printed in the United States of America.
ISBN-13: 978-1-68050-082-0
Printed on acid-free paper.
Book version: P1.0—July 2016

Contents

Acknowledgments

In the case of this book, there is no false modesty. I genuinely have to thank a great many folk who have helped make it possible. The volume of feedback I received shaped the book and made it far more useful than it would have been otherwise.

I'd like to thank my my beautiful wife, Linda. She spent many hours helping me refine the book. It simply would not have been the same without her oversight.

The Pragmatic Bookshelf team has my thanks for their guidance and insight. I'd like to call out Mike Swaine and Susannah Pfalzer in particular for their suggestions and constant demand for quality throughout the process. I'd also like to thank Molly McBeath for her thorough copyediting and valuable feedback on the drafts.

I was lucky to have a team of highly experienced technical reviewers who were willing to ask tough questions. The list includes James Reeves, Sam Griffith Jr., Russ Olsen, Colin Yates, Ian Dees, and Kevin Beam.

Finally, I owe a big thanks to the customers who chose to put their trust in me and buy the beta version of the book. Their feedback helped ensure that the book met the stated goals.

I'm proud to put my name on this book thanks to all the people who've taken this journey with me. My sincere respect and gratitude goes out to all of you.

Introduction

The cover of this book has a bonsai tree on it. I chose it to represent elegance and simplicity, because these qualities make Clojure such an attractive language. A good software project is like a bonsai. You have to meticulously craft it to take the shape you want, and the tool you use should make it a pleasant experience. I hope to convince you here that Clojure is that tool.

What You Need

This book is aimed at readers of all levels. While having some basic proficiency with functional programming will be helpful, it's by no means required to follow the material in this book. If you're not a Clojure user already, this book is a good starting point since it focuses on applying the language to solve concrete problems. This means we'll focus on the small number of language features needed to build common web applications.

Why Clojure?

Clojure is a small language whose primary goals are simplicity and correctness. As a functional language, it emphasizes immutability and declarative programming. As you'll see in this book, these features make it easy and idiomatic to write clean and correct code.

Web development has many languages to choose from and as many opinions on what makes any one of them a good language. Some languages are simple but verbose. You've probably heard people say that verbosity doesn't matter—that if two languages are Turing complete, anything that can be written in one language can also be written in the other with a bit of extra code.

I think that's missing the point. The real question is not whether something can be expressed in principle; it's how well the language maps to the problem being solved. One language lets you think in terms of your problem domain, while another forces you to translate the problem to its constructs.

The latter is often tedious and rarely enjoyable. You end up writing a lot of boilerplate code and constantly repeating yourself. There's a certain amount of irony involved in having to write repetitive code.

Other languages aren't verbose and provide many different tools for solving problems. Unfortunately, having many tools does not translate directly into higher productivity.

The more features a language has, the more things you have to keep in your head to work with the language effectively. With many languages I find myself constantly expending mental overhead thinking about all the different features and how they interact with one another.

What matters to me in a language is whether I can use it without thinking about it. When a language is lacking in expressiveness, I'm acutely aware that I'm writing code that I shouldn't be. On the other hand, when a language has too many features, I often feel overwhelmed or I get distracted playing with them.

To make an analogy with mathematics, having a general formula that you can derive others from is better than having to memorize a whole bunch of formulas for specific problems.

This is where Clojure comes in. It allows us to easily derive a solution to a particular problem from a small set of general patterns. All you need to become productive is to learn a few simple concepts and a bit of syntax. These concepts can then be combined in myriad ways to solve all kinds of problems.

Why Make Web Apps in Clojure?

Clojure boasts tens of thousands of users; it's used in a wide range of settings, including banks and hospitals. Clojure is likely the most popular Lisp dialect today for starting new development. Despite being a young language, it has proven itself in serious production systems, and the feedback from users has been overwhelmingly positive.

Because web development is one of the major domains for using Clojure, several popular libraries and frameworks have sprouted in this area. The Clojure web stack is based on the Ring and Compojure libraries.[1,2] Ring is the base HTTP library, while Compojure provides routing on top of it. In the following chapters you'll become familiar with the web stack and how to use it effectively to build your web applications.

---

1. https://github.com/ring-clojure/ring
2. https://github.com/weavejester/compojure

Many platforms are available for doing web development, so why should you choose Clojure over other options?

Well, consider those options. Many popular platforms force you to make trade-offs. Some platforms lack performance, others require a lot of boilerplate, and others lack the infrastructure necessary for real-world applications.

Clojure addresses the questions of performance and infrastructure by being a hosted language. The Java Virtual Machine is a mature and highly performant environment with great tooling and deployment options. Clojure brings expressive power akin to that of Ruby and Python to this excellent platform. When working with Clojure you won't have to worry about being limited by your runtime when your application grows.

The most common way to handle the boilerplate in web applications is by using a framework. Examples of such frameworks include Ruby on Rails, Django, and Spring. The frameworks provide the canned functionality needed for building a modern site.

The benefits the frameworks offer also come with inherent costs. Since many operations are done implicitly, you have to memorize what effects any action might have. This opaqueness makes your code more difficult to reason about. When you need to do something that is at odds with the framework's design, it can quickly become awkward and difficult. You might have to dive deep into the internals of that framework and create hacks around the expected behaviors.

So instead of using frameworks, Clojure makes a number of powerful libraries available, and we can put these libraries together in a way that makes sense for our particular project. As you'll see, we manage to avoid having to write boilerplate while retaining the code clarity we desire. As you read on, I think you'll agree that this model has clear advantages over the framework-based approach.

My goal is to give you both a solid understanding of the Clojure web stack and the expertise to quickly and easily build web applications using it. The following chapters will guide you all the way from setting up your development environment to creating a complete real-world application. I will show you what's available and then guide you in structuring your application using the current best practices.

CHAPTER 1

Getting Your Feet Wet

In the *Introduction*, on page xi, we looked at some of the benefits of the functional style when it comes to writing applications. Of course, you can't learn a language simply by reading about it. To really get a feel for it, you have to write some code yourself.

In this chapter you'll dive right in and build a guestbook application that allows users to leave messages for one another. You'll see the basic structure of a web application as well as the tools necessary for effective Clojure development. And you'll get a feel for how web development in Clojure works. If you're new to Clojure, I recommend you read through Appendix 1, *Clojure Primer*, on page 219, for a crash course on the basic concepts and syntax.

The material I'll cover in this book is based on my experience and personal preferences. It's worth noting that there are other equally valid approaches. The libraries and methodologies that we'll explore are just one way to structure Clojure web applications, but they should provide you with a solid starting point using the current best practices.

Set Up Your Environment

Clojure distribution is provided as a JAR (Java Archive file) that needs to be available on your project's classpath. Clojure requires the Java Virtual Machine (JVM) to run, and you will need a working Java Development Kit (JDK), version 1.7 or higher.[1] You'll also need to have Leiningen installed in order to create and build the projects.[2]

---

1. http://www.oracle.com/technetwork/java/javase/downloads/index.html
2. http://leiningen.org/

Managing Projects with Leiningen

Leiningen lets you create, build, test, package, and deploy your projects. In other words, it's your one-stop shop for all your project-management needs.

Leiningen is the Clojure counterpart of Maven,[3] a popular Java build tool. It uses a Maven-compatible dependency management system, and therefore it has access to large and well-maintained repositories of Java libraries. In addition, Clojure libraries are commonly found in the Clojars repository.[4] This repository is enabled by default in Leiningen.

With Leiningen, you don't need to worry about manually downloading all the libraries for your project. Specifying the top-level dependencies will cause any libraries that they depend on to be pulled in automatically.

Installing Leiningen is accomplished by downloading the installation script from the official project page and running it.[5] Let's test this. Create a new project by downloading the script and running the following commands:

```
wget https://raw.github.com/technomancy/leiningen/stable/bin/lein
chmod +x lein
mv lein ~/bin
lein new myapp
```

Note that the preceding code expects that ~/bin is available on the shell path. Since we're running lein for the first time, it needs to install itself. As long as the installation is successful, you should see the following output at the end:

```
Generating a project called myapp based on the 'default' template.
To see other templates (app, lein plugin, etc.), try `lein help new`.
```

Take a moment to look at what we have now.

A new folder called myapp has been created, containing a skeleton application. The code for the application can be found in the src folder. Here we have another folder called myapp containing a single source file named core.clj. This file has the following code inside:

```
(ns myapp.core)

(defn foo
  "I don't do a whole lot."
  [x]
  (println x "Hello, World!"))
```

---

3. http://maven.apache.org/
4. https://clojars.org/
5. http://leiningen.org/#install

Note that the namespace declaration matches the folder structure. Since the core namespace is inside the myapp folder, its name is myapp.core.

What's in the Leiningen Project File?

Inside the myapp project folder, we have a project.clj file. This file contains the description of our application. The project configuration is represented declaratively using regular Clojure data structures. It contains the application name, version, URL, license, and dependencies.

```
(defproject myapp "0.1.0-SNAPSHOT"
 :description "FIXME: write description"
 :url "http://example.com/FIXME"
 :license {:name "Eclipse Public License"
           :url "http://www.eclipse.org/legal/epl-v10.html"}
 :dependencies [[org.clojure/clojure "1.7.0"]])
```

The project.clj file allows us to manage many different aspects of our application. For example, we could set the foo function from the myapp.core namespace as the entry point for the application using the :main key:

```
(defproject myapp "0.1.0-SNAPSHOT"
 :description "FIXME: write description"
 :url "http://example.com/FIXME"
 :license {:name "Eclipse Public License"
           :url "http://www.eclipse.org/legal/epl-v10.html"}
 :dependencies [[org.clojure/clojure "1.7.0"]]
 ;;this will set foo as the main function
 :main myapp.core/foo)
```

The point of all this, though, is that you can now run the application from the command line using lein run. Since the foo function expects an argument, you have to pass one in:

```
lein run Obligatory
Obligatory Hello, World!
```

Build Your First Web App

In the preceding example we created a very simple application that has only a single dependency: the Clojure runtime. If you used this as the base for a web application, then you'd have to write a lot of boilerplate to get it up and running. Let's see how we can use a Leiningen template to create a web-application project with all the boilerplate already set up.

Our primary goal here is to get a high-level understanding of the project structure and get something done. I'll gloss over some of the finer details in order to maintain our momentum. Don't worry if you don't fully understand all the steps at this point. We'll get into the details in subsequent chapters.

Creating an Application from a Template

A template consists of a skeleton project that is instantiated with the desired parameters, such as the project name. A number of different templates exist to quickly initialize different kinds of projects. Later on we'll even see how we can create such templates ourselves. But the Luminus template provides a good base and we'll use it this time.[6]

By default, Leiningen will use the latest version of the template that has been published to the Clojars repository.[7] Therefore, the skeleton projects generated by the template may not be exactly the same as the ones discussed in the book. In order to ensure that you're able to follow the book exactly, I recommend adding the following plugin reference in the ~/.lein/profiles.clj file. This will ensure that the projects are generated using the same version of the template that was used in the book.

```
{:user {:plugins [[luminus/lein-template "2.9.10.74"]]}}
```

In order to tell Leiningen that we want to use a specific template for the project, we must specify it as the argument following the new parameter when running lein, followed by the name of the project. Any other parameters will be passed in as the arguments to the selected template.

Let's create a new application by specifying luminus as the template name and guestbook as the project name, and let's add the +h2 parameter to indicate that we want to have an instance of the H2 embedded database initialized for us.[8]

```
lein new luminus guestbook +h2
```

What's in a Web App

This type of application needs to start up a web server in order to run. The template project comes with an embedded Immutant server configured for us, and we can start it by running lein run as we did with the myapp project that we used to test the Leiningen setup.[9]

When you run the application, it may take a little while because Leiningen first has to retrieve all of its dependencies. Once downloaded, the dependencies

---

6. http://www.luminusweb.net/
7. https://clojars.org/luminus/lein-template
8. http://www.h2database.com/html/main.html
9. http://immutant.org/

are cached locally in the ~/.m2/repository folder and will be available on subsequent runs. After the dependencies are downloaded, you should see the following output in the console:

```
lein run
[2016-02-29][DEBUG][org.jboss.logging] Logging Provider: org.jboss.Log4jProvider
[2016-02-29][INFO][com.zaxxer.hikari.HikariDataSource] HikariPool-0 - is starting.
[2016-02-29][INFO][luminus.http-server] starting HTTP server on port 3000
[2016-02-29][INFO][org.xnio] XNIO version 3.4.0.Beta1
[2016-02-29][INFO][org.xnio.nio] XNIO NIO Implementation Version 3.4.0.Beta1
[2016-02-29][INFO][org.projectodd.wunderboss.web.Web] Registered web context /
[2016-02-29][INFO][luminus.repl-server] starting nREPL server on port 7000
[2016-02-29][INFO][guestbook.core] #'guestbook.config/env started
[2016-02-29][INFO][guestbook.core] #'guestbook.db.core/*db* started
[2016-02-29][INFO][guestbook.core] #'guestbook.core/http-server started
[2016-02-29][INFO][guestbook.core] #'guestbook.core/repl-server started
[2016-02-29][INFO][guestbook.env]
-=[guestbook started successfully using the development profile]=-
```

Should we want to start the application on a different port then we could pass it the -p flag followed by the port number, as follows.

```
lein run -p 8000
```

Once the application starts, we can open a new browser window and navigate to http://localhost:3000 to see the home page of our application.

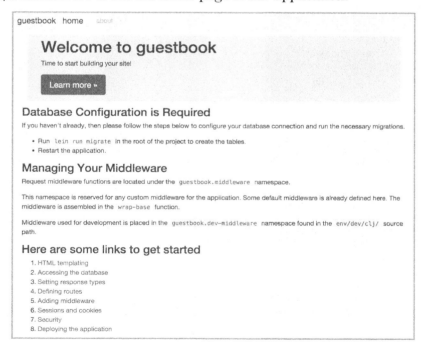

Now that we've created our applications and tested that it's working, let's take a brief tour of what's been generated for us. The following are the folders in the generated project, with the files omitted for brevity:

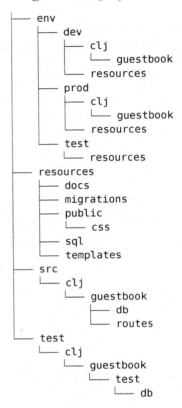

```
├── env
│   ├── dev
│   │   ├── clj
│   │   │   └── guestbook
│   │   └── resources
│   ├── prod
│   │   ├── clj
│   │   │   └── guestbook
│   │   └── resources
│   └── test
│       └── resources
├── resources
│   ├── docs
│   ├── migrations
│   ├── public
│   │   └── css
│   ├── sql
│   └── templates
├── src
│   └── clj
│       └── guestbook
│           ├── db
│           └── routes
└── test
    └── clj
        └── guestbook
            └── test
                └── db
```

The project structure is significantly more complex this time around than what we had in the myapp project. We'll learn what all the pieces are for as we build different applications throughout the book. For now, we'll just take a quick overview of how the project is structured and what files go where.

The majority of our code lives under the src folder. This folder contains a clj folder that's reserved for Clojure source files. Since our application is called *guestbook*, this is the root namespace for the project. The application is further broken down into different namespaces based on function. We'll explore each of these in detail in Chapter 3, *Luminus Architecture*, on page 49. The namespace that will be of immediate interest to us is the routes namespace.

The routes namespace is reserved for defining application routes. Each route is bound to a function that is responsible for processing the request and generating the response. This is where most of our application logic will live.

The db namespace houses the database-related logic and serves as the model layer for the application. The guestbook.db.core namespace contains the logic for defining queries and managing the database connection.

The other folder that will be relevant for our application is the resources folder that contains all the static assets associated with the application. These include HTML templates, CSS styles, and so on. Since we created a database for the app, it also contains a migrations folder with the SQL migration files.

Refine Your App

OK, enough with the overview. Let's write some code.

Managing Database Migrations

You'll notice that the home page of our application instructs us to run lein run migrate in order to initialize the database. This will use the resources/migrations/20150719215253-add-users-table.up.sql file to initialize the database for us. Note that the date on your file will be different since it's set to the date the application was instantiated.

Since we're writing a guestbook, let's delete the current files and add migrations that are appropriate for our application. We can create new migrations by running the following command:

```
lein migratus create guestbook
```

This creates two migration files, one for updating the database and another for rolling back the changes. The files are generated in the resources/migrations folder and should look something like the following:

```
resources/migrations/20150719215253-guestbook.up.sql
resources/migrations/20150719215253-guestbook.down.sql
```

The migration files are prefixed with the timestamp, followed by the name we provided and suffixed with the type of migration that they represent. Let's place the following SQL statement in the "up" migration file. We want to store the messages along with the name of the author and a timestamp indicating when the message was written. Let's also create an autogenerated ID column to keep track of the messages.

guestbook/resources/migrations/20150719215253-guestbook.up.sql

```
CREATE TABLE guestbook
(id INTEGER PRIMARY KEY AUTO_INCREMENT,
 name VARCHAR(30),
 message VARCHAR(200),
 timestamp TIMESTAMP);
```

Put this statement to delete the guestbook table in the "down" migration file.

`guestbook/resources/migrations/20150719215253-guestbook.down.sql`

```
DROP TABLE guestbook;
```

Try to run the migrations as instructed to create the guestbook database table.

```
lein run migrate
23:05:38 [main] DEBUG org.jboss.logging - Logging Provider: Slf4jLoggerProvider
23:05:39 INFO [migratus.core] (main) Starting migrations
23:05:39 INFO [migratus.database] (main) creating table 'schema_migrations'
23:05:39 INFO [migratus.core] (main) Running up for [20150719215253]
23:05:39 INFO [migratus.core] (main) Up 20150719215253-guestbook
23:05:39 INFO [migratus.core] (main) Ending migrations
```

Our database is now ready to use and we can start working with it. Our next step is to write the queries to create and list messages.

Querying to the Database

Luminus defaults to using SQL template files to interact with the database. The SQL template files are used by the HugSQL library to automatically create our database access functions.

Our project contains a file called resources/sql/queries.sql. This file is already populated with some sample query templates. The function names are specified using the -- :name comment followed by hints indicating the type of query, and the parameters are prefixed with the :. The -- :doc comment is used to generate the documentation metadata for the function. Otherwise, the queries are written using regular SQL syntax.[10]

The existing queries aren't very useful to us, so let's replace them with new queries that allow us to work with the tables we just created. We'd like to be able to save messages in our database, so let's create a query called save-message!. Note that the name ends with ! to indicate that it mutates data. The second query is used to retrieve stored messages. Let's call it get-messages.

`guestbook/resources/sql/queries.sql`

```
-- :name save-message! :! :n
-- :doc creates a new message using the name, message, and timestamp keys
INSERT INTO guestbook
(name, message, timestamp)
VALUES (:name, :message, :timestamp)
-- :name get-messages :? :*
-- :doc selects all available messages
SELECT * from guestbook
```

---

10. http://www.hugsql.org/

Notice that the save-message! query name is followed by :! and :n flags. The first flag indicates the query is destructive. The second flag indicates that the query returns the number of affected rows.

The get-messages query uses the :? flag to indicate that the query does a select, and the :* flag indicates that multiple rows are returned.

The guestbook.db.core namespace contains a call to the conman.core/bind-connection macro. This macro reads the SQL queries that we defined and creates Clojure functions that call them using the name specified using the -- :name comment.

guestbook/src/clj/guestbook/db/core.clj

```
(conman/bind-connection *db* "sql/queries.sql")
```

Now that we have our data layer set up, we can try querying it to make sure that everything works correctly. The entirety of the guestbook.db.core namespace looks as follows:

guestbook/src/clj/guestbook/db/core.clj

```
(ns guestbook.db.core
  (:require
    [conman.core :as conman]
    [mount.core :refer [defstate]]
    [guestbook.config :refer [env]]))

(defstate ^:dynamic *db*
          :start (conman/connect!
                   {:datasource
                    (doto (org.h2.jdbcx.JdbcDataSource.)
                          (.setURL (env :database-url))
                          (.setUser "")
                          (.setPassword ""))})
          :stop (conman/disconnect! *db*))

(conman/bind-connection *db* "sql/queries.sql")
```

The database connection is specified using a map that's passed to the conman/connect! function. It is populated with the database connection specification. The :database-url environment variable is used to provide the connection URL for the database. This variable is populated in the profiles.clj file found in the root of the project.

The profiles.clj file contains information about the local environment that's not meant to be checked into the shared code repository. Database connection parameters are an example of such environment variables. The contents of the file look as follows:

guestbook/profiles.clj

```
{:profiles/dev  {:env {:database-url "jdbc:h2:./guestbook_dev.db"}}
 :profiles/test {:env {:database-url "jdbc:h2:./guestbook_test.db"}}}
```

The :profiles/dev environment URL specifies that the database is stored in a file called guestbook_dev.db in the path where the application is run. In our case this will be the root folder of the project.

Back in the guestbook.db.core namespace, the state of the database is stored in the *db* variable. The state of the database is managed by the Mount library. We'll take a closer look at managing the life cycle of stateful resources in Chapter 3, *Luminus Architecture*, on page 49.[11]

The queries that we just wrote are bound to functions using the bind-connection macro when the namespace is loaded. The generated functions will automatically use the connection stored in the *db* variable.

The functions generated by the macro accept the parameter map representing the dynamic query variables as their arguments. Since the queries are parameterized, any variables we pass in are sanitized to prevent SQL injection.

Let's use the REPL to test that everything works correctly. When the application starts in development mode, it automatically runs the nREPL server on port 7000. We can connect to this REPL and inspect the running application as follows.

```
lein repl :connect 7000
```

The REPL starts in the user namespace that's found at the env/dev/clj/user.clj file. This namespace is reserved for any development code that we wouldn't want to package in our application. It also provides a scratch pad where we can try things out. This namespace provides start and stop helper functions that allow us to control the state of the application. We'll add a reference to the guestbook.db.core namespace:

```
(require '[guestbook.db.core :refer :all])
```

Next, we'll need to start the database connection. This would happen automatically if the connection were referenced in our application. However, since the connection isn't being used yet, we have to start it manually as follows:

```
(mount/start #'guestbook.db.core/*db*)
```

---

11. https://github.com/tolitius/mount

The database should now be ready to use, and we can try running the queries we just wrote:

```
;;check if we have any existing data
(get-messages)
;;output: ()

;;check the documentation
(doc save-message!)

;;create a test message
(save-message! {:name "Bob"
               :message "Hello, World"
               :timestamp (java.util.Date.)})
;;output 1

;;check that the message is saved correctly
(get-messages)
;;output
({:timestamp #inst "2015-01-18T16:22:10.010000000-00:00"
  :message "Hello, World"
  :name "Bob"
  :id 1})
```

As you can see, it's possible to do most tasks against the running instance of the application. While we used the REPL from the terminal in this instance, I highly recommended that you use a Clojure editor that allows you to connect to the REPL going forward. That way you'll be able to evaluate any code as you're writing it.

There are a few cases where you will need to restart the application. The most common reason is when you're adding new dependencies to the project, as those can't be loaded dynamically by the JVM. However, if you think your application has got in a bad state, then you may wish to restart it as well.

Creating Tests

Now that we've tested the database operations in the REPL, it's a good idea to create some tests based on them. The project already comes with some default test operations defined. These are found in the test folder of the application. The database tests are in the test/clj/guestbook/test/db/core.clj file.

The current tests are defined with the generated users table in mind. Since we've changed our table structure, let's replace it with the following test:

guestbook/test/clj/guestbook/test/db/core.clj

```clojure
(ns guestbook.test.db.core
  (:require [guestbook.db.core :refer [*db*] :as db]
            [luminus-migrations.core :as migrations]
            [clojure.test :refer :all]
            [clojure.java.jdbc :as jdbc]
            [guestbook.config :refer [env]]
            [mount.core :as mount]))

(use-fixtures
  :once
  (fn [f]
    (mount/start
      #'guestbook.config/env
      #'guestbook.db.core/*db*)
    (migrations/migrate ["migrate"] (select-keys env [:database-url]))
    (f)))

(deftest test-messages
  (jdbc/with-db-transaction [t-conn *db*]
    (jdbc/db-set-rollback-only! t-conn)
    (let [timestamp (java.util.Date.)]
      (is (= 1 (db/save-message!
                  t-conn
                  {:name "Bob"
                   :message   "Hello, World"
                   :timestamp timestamp}
                  {:connection t-conn})))
      (is (=
            {:name "Bob"
             :message "Hello, World"
             :timestamp timestamp}
            (-> (db/get-messages t-conn {})
                (first)
                (select-keys [:name :message :timestamp]))))))))
```

Run this command in the project folder to ensure our tests are passing:

```
lein test

Testing guestbook.test.db.core
23:30:39.404 [main] INFO  migratus.core - Starting migrations
23:30:39.786 [main] INFO  migratus.database - creating table 'schema_migrations'
23:30:39.806 [main] INFO  migratus.core - Running up for [20150719215253]
23:30:39.808 [main] INFO  migratus.core - Up 20150719215253-add-users-table
23:30:39.813 [main] DEBUG migratus.database - found 1 up migrations
23:30:39.822 [main] DEBUG migratus.database - marking 20150719215253 complete
23:30:39.827 [main] INFO  migratus.core - Ending migrations

Testing guestbook.test.handler

Ran 2 tests containing 4 assertions.
0 failures, 0 errors.
```

You might have noticed earlier that our profiles.clj file contained two database connections. One was defined under the :profiles/dev profile, while the other was defined under the :profiles/test profile. When Leiningen runs the tests, the program will use the :profiles/test environment and the development database will not be affected.

Now that we have some tests, we can use a Leiningen plugin called *lein-test-refresh* to run them automatically any time we update the code in the project.[12] This plugin is part of the Luminus template, so all we have to do is open a new terminal and run the following command there:

```
lein test-refresh
```

We can keep an eye on this terminal to make sure that all our tests are passing whenever we make changes to the code or add new tests. This provides us with an automated sanity check that everything is working as expected.

Developing the functionality using the REPL and then generating the tests is a common workflow in Clojure. This approach provides a faster feedback loop than Test Driven Development (TDD) since we don't have to constantly switch between tests and code while developing a feature. Instead, the development can be done interactively using the REPL. Once the feature works as desired, then we can take the code from the REPL session and turn it into unit tests for this feature.

Defining HTTP Routes

We've now confirmed that we're able to store and retrieve the messages from the database. Next we'll need to write a user interface and hook it up to these functions. We'll create HTTP end points and have these call the appropriate functions to facilitate the user workflows. The end points are commonly referred to as *routes*, and the route that renders the home page for our application is found in the guestbook.routes.home namespace.

```
(defn home-page []
  (layout/render
    "home.html" {:docs (-> "docs/docs.md" io/resource slurp)}))
(defn about-page []
  (layout/render "about.html"))
(defroutes home-routes
  (GET "/" [] (home-page))
  (GET "/about" [] (about-page)))
```

---

12. https://github.com/jakemcc/lein-test-refresh

You can see that the / route calls the home-page function that in turn renders the home.html template. You can also see that we're passing a map of parameters to the render function; currently the only parameter being passed is the :docs key. These parameters indicate dynamic content that is injected into our template before it's sent to the client. Let's take a quick look at the contents of the resources/templates/home.html file:

```
{% extends "base.html" %}
{% block content %}
  <div class="jumbotron">
    <h1>Welcome to guestbook</h1>
    <p>Time to start building your site!</p>
    <p><a class="btn btn-primary btn-lg" href="http://luminusweb.net">
       Learn more &raquo;
      </a>
    </p>
  </div>

  <div class="row">
    <div class="span12">
    {{docs|markdown}}
    </div>
  </div>
{% endblock %}
```

You can see that this file extends a template called base.html and renders a block called *content*. The parent template provides a common layout for the pages in our application, and each individual page can render the portion of the page relevant to it. If you're familiar with Rails or Django templates, then the preceding syntax should look very familiar. You'll also note that the templates are set up to use Twitter Bootstrap as the default scaffolding for the page layout.

The templates use a context map to populate the dynamic content. The keys in the map are used as template variables. For example, the {{docs|markdown}} statement corresponds to the :docs key in the map that was passed to the layout/render function by the home-page function.

Let's remove the existing content of the block and replace it with a div that displays the list of existing messages. The messages are supplied using a variable called messages. Each item in messages is a map containing keys called timestamp, message, and name. Then we iterate over the messages and create an li tag for each message inside a ul tag, like so:

guestbook/resources/templates/home.html

```
<div class="row">
    <div class="span12">
        <ul class="content">
            {% for item in messages %}
            <li>
                <time>{{item.timestamp|date:"yyyy-MM-dd HH:mm"}}</time>
                <p>{{item.message}}</p>
                <p> - {{item.name}}</p>
            </li>
            {% endfor %}
        </ul>
    </div>
</div>
```

OK, let's go back to the guestbook.routes.home namespace and add the code to render the existing messages. First we add a reference to the guestbook.db.core namespace.

guestbook/src/clj/guestbook/routes/home.clj

```
(ns guestbook.routes.home
  (:require [guestbook.layout :as layout]
            [compojure.core :refer [defroutes GET POST]]
            [ring.util.http-response :as response]
            [guestbook.db.core :as db]))
```

We can now update the home-page function to associate the messages with the :messages key when rendering the template.

guestbook/src/clj/guestbook/routes/home.clj

```
(defn home-page []
  (layout/render
    "home.html"
    {:messages (db/get-messages)}))
```

Since we've already populated a message in our database during earlier testing, we should see it when we reload the page. We can now take a look at adding a form to create new messages from the page.

Now we need to create another div that will contain a form for submitting new messages. Note that we need to provide a {% csrf-field %} in our form.[13] Luminus enables anti-forgery protection by default, and any POST requests that do not contain the anti-forgery token are rejected by the server.

---

13. http://en.wikipedia.org/wiki/Cross-site_request_forgery

guestbook/resources/templates/home.html

```
<div class="row">
    <div class="span12">
        <form method="POST" action="/message">
            <div class="form-group">
            {% csrf-field %}
            <p>
                Name:
                <input class="form-control"
                        type="text"
                        name="name"
                        value="" />
            </p>
            <p>
                Message:
                <textarea class="form-control"
                        rows="4"
                        cols="50"
                        name="message"></textarea>
            </p>
            <input type="submit" class="btn btn-primary" value="comment" />
            </div>
        </form>
    </div>
</div>
```

Our final template should look as follows:

guestbook/resources/templates/home.html

```
{% extends "base.html" %}
{% block content %}
<div class="row">
    <div class="span12">
        <ul class="content">
            {% for item in messages %}
            <li>
                <time>{{item.timestamp|date:"yyyy-MM-dd HH:mm"}}</time>
                <p>{{item.message}}</p>
                <p> - {{item.name}}</p>
            </li>
            {% endfor %}
        </ul>
    </div>
</div>
<div class="row">
    <div class="span12">
        <form method="POST" action="/message">
            <div class="form-group">
            {% csrf-field %}
            <p>
```

```
        Name:
        <input class="form-control"
                type="text"
                name="name"
                value="" />
    </p>
    <p>
        Message:
        <textarea class="form-control"
                    rows="4"
                    cols="50"
                    name="message"></textarea>
    </p>
    <input type="submit" class="btn btn-primary" value="comment" />
    </div>
    </form>
    </div>
</div>
{% endblock %}
```

We now need to create a new route on the server, called */message*, to respond to the HTTP POST method. The route calls the function save-message! with the request. In order to create a route that accepts a POST request method, we have to remember to reference the POST macro in our namespace definition.

```
(ns guestbook.routes.home
  (:require [guestbook.layout :as layout]
            [compojure.core :refer [defroutes GET POST]]
            ...))
```

guestbook/src/clj/guestbook/routes/home.clj

```
(POST "/message" request (save-message! request))
```

The route handler calls the save-message! function that follows. The function grabs the params key from the request. This key contains a map of parameters that were sent by the client when the form was submitted to the server.

guestbook/src/clj/guestbook/routes/home.clj

```
(defn save-message! [{:keys [params]}]
  (db/save-message!
   (assoc params :timestamp (java.util.Date.)))
  (response/found "/"))
```

Since we named our fields *name* and *message*, they match the fields we defined in our table: to create a new record all we have to do is add a timestamp field with the current date and call the save-message! function from the db namespace. Once the message is saved, we redirect back to the home page. The final code in the namespace should look as follows:

guestbook/src/clj/guestbook/routes/home.clj

```clojure
(ns guestbook.routes.home
  (:require [guestbook.layout :as layout]
            [compojure.core :refer [defroutes GET POST]]
            [ring.util.http-response :as response]
            [guestbook.db.core :as db]))
(defn home-page []
  (layout/render
    "home.html"
    {:messages (db/get-messages)}))
(defn save-message! [{:keys [params]}]
  (db/save-message!
    (assoc params :timestamp (java.util.Date.)))
  (response/found "/"))
(defn about-page []
  (layout/render "about.html"))
(defroutes home-routes
  (GET "/" [] (home-page))
  (POST "/message" request (save-message! request))
  (GET "/about" [] (about-page)))
```

At this point our guestbook should display existing messages as well as allow the users to post new messages. As a last touch, we'll add some CSS to style our app. Static assets such as CSS, images, and JavaScript are found in the resources/public folder and are served without the need to define routes for them. Let's add the following CSS in the resources/public/css/screen.css file:

guestbook/resources/public/css/screen.css

```css
.content {
        background: white;
        width: 520px;
}
form, .error {
        width: 520px;
        padding: 30px;
        margin-bottom: 50px;
        position: relative;
        background: white;
}
ul {
        list-style: none;
}
li {
        position: relative;
        font-size: 16px;
        padding: 5px;
```

```
        border-bottom: 1px dotted #ccc;
}
li:last-child {
        border-bottom: none;
}
li time {
        font-size: 12px;
        padding-bottom: 20px;
}
```

The guestbook page should now look like the following figure:

Validating Input

What else should we do? Currently, our guestbook doesn't do any validation of user input. That's weak. Let's see how we can ensure that user messages contain the necessary information before trying to store them in the database.

Luminus defaults to using the Bouncer library to handle input validation. The library provides a straightforward way to check that our parameter map contains the required values.[14]

Bouncer uses bouncer.core/validate and bouncer.core/valid? functions for handling validation. These functions each accept a map containing the parameters followed by the validators. The former will validate the input and return error messages for any invalid fields, while the latter returns a Boolean value indicating whether the input is valid.

---

14. https://github.com/leonardoborges/bouncer

Many common validators such as required, email, matches, and so on are provided by the library out of the box. These validators can be used individually or chained together to validate different aspects of the input value. We can easily create custom validators for situations where the default ones won't do.

Before we see how validation works, we want to include bouncer.core along with the bouncer.validators in our guestbook.routes.home namespace.

```
(ns guestbook.routes.home
  (:require
    [bouncer.core :as b]
    [bouncer.validators :as v]
    ...))
```

We can now use the b/validate function to check that the input values are valid and that we produce an error message when they are not. In our case, we need to ensure both that the username is not empty and that the message has at least ten characters before we persist them to the database. Our validation function looks as follows:

guestbook-validation/src/clj/guestbook/routes/home.clj

```
(defn validate-message [params]
  (first
   (b/validate
    params
    :name v/required
    :message [v/required [v/min-count 10]])))
```

We pass the params submitted from the form as the input and then create validators for the keys :name and :message. The :name key has a single validator, while the :message key has two. The second validator takes an additional parameter indicating the minimum length. Bouncer uses the vector notation for specifying additional parameters to the validator functions.

The result of the validate function is a vector where the first element is either nil when the validation passes or it is a map of errors. The keys in the map are the parameters that failed validation and the values are the error messages.

The next step is to hook up the validation function into our workflow. Currently, the save-message! function attempts to store the message and then redirects back to the home page. We need to add the ability to pass back the error message along with the original parameters when validation fails.

A common approach for this is to use a flash session variable to track the errors. Flash session variables have a lifespan of a single request, making them ideal storage for this purpose. The save-message! function validates the input and checks for errors. If it finds errors, it associates a :flash key with the response that contains the parameters along with the errors. If no errors are generated, it saves the message to the database and redirects as it did before.

guestbook-validation/src/clj/guestbook/routes/home.clj

```clojure
(defn save-message! [{:keys [params]}]
  (if-let [errors (validate-message params)]
    (-> (response/found "/")
        (assoc :flash (assoc params :errors errors)))
    (do
      (db/save-message!
       (assoc params :timestamp (java.util.Date.)))
      (response/found "/"))))
```

Let's now update the home route to pass the request to the home-page function that checks for the :flash key.

guestbook-validation/src/clj/guestbook/routes/home.clj

```clojure
(GET "/" request (home-page request))
```

guestbook-validation/src/clj/guestbook/routes/home.clj

```clojure
(defn home-page [{:keys [flash]}]
  (layout/render
   "home.html"
   (merge {:messages (db/get-messages)}
          (select-keys flash [:name :message :errors]))))
```

Let's select the name, message, and errors keys from the flash session and merge them with our parameter map. And finally, let's update our page to render the errors when they're present.

guestbook-validation/resources/templates/home.html

```html
<div class="row">
    <div class="span12">
        <form method="POST" action="/message">
            {% csrf-field %}
            <p>
                Name:
                <input class="form-control"
                       type="text"
                       name="name"
                       value="{{name}}" />
            </p>
            {% if errors.name %}
            <div class="alert alert-danger">{{errors.name|join}}</div>
            {% endif %}
            <p>
                Message:
```

```
            <textarea class="form-control"
                      rows="4"
                      cols="50"
                      name="message">{{message}}</textarea>
          </p>
          {% if errors.message %}
          <div class="alert alert-danger">{{errors.message|join}}</div>
          {% endif %}
          <input type="submit" class="btn btn-primary" value="comment" />
      </form>
    </div>
</div>
```

You should now be able to see error messages whenever bad parameters are
supplied in the form:

Running Standalone

Up to now, we've been running our app using the lein run command. This starts
an embedded server in development mode so that it watches files for changes
and reloads them as needed. In order to package our application for deployment, we can package it into a runnable JAR as follows:

```
lein uberjar
```

The archive will be created in the "target" folder of our application, and we
can run it using the java command.

Since we're using a database, we also have to make sure that the connection
is specified as an environment variable. When we ran our application in
development mode, the connection variable was provided in the profiles.clj file.

However, now that the application has been packaged for production, this variable is no longer available. Let's create a connection variable and then run our application as follows:

```
export DATABASE_URL="jdbc:h2:./guestbook_dev.db"
java -jar target/uberjar/guestbook.jar
```

What You've Learned

OK, that's the whirlwind tour. By this point you should be getting a feel for developing web applications with Clojure. And you should be comfortable with some of the Clojure basics. You saw how to use the Leiningen tool to create and manage an application. You learned about HTTP routing and some basic HTML templating. While we didn't explore many aspects of the skeleton application that was generated for us, you saw how the basic request life cycle is handled.

We'll be diving deeper and writing more code in upcoming chapters. If you aren't already, I encourage you to start using one of the popular Clojure-aware editors, such as Light Table, Emacs, Cursive, or Counterclockwise.

In the next chapter we'll delve into the details of the Clojure web stack to understand some of the details of how our application works.

CHAPTER 2

Luminus Web Stack

Now that we've gone through the process of building a web application using Clojure, let's take a step back and look at what we've been doing. And this means looking at the core components of the Luminus web stack.

Many popular platforms, such as Rails or Django, take the approach of providing a monolithic framework for building web applications. The Clojure community has traditionally shunned this approach in favor of using composable components that the user can assemble in a way that will best fit her particular application.

Of course, in order to do that the user has to know what libraries exist, what they are for, and how to put them together effectively. Even if you know the libraries that you wish to use, every project has a certain amount of boilerplate to be set up.

The Clojure community tackles this problem by using Leiningen templates that generate the necessary boilerplate for specific types of projects. In this book we're primarily using the Luminus template. Luminus removes the burden of having to find the libraries, configure middleware, and add the common boilerplate. The application generated by the template is ready for deployment out of the box. The only part that's missing is the domain logic for your application.

The core of the template consists of the Ring/Compojure stack that's well established and has been used to build many real-world apps. Ring provides the API for handling HTTP requests and responses, while Compojure provides routing, allowing us to bind request-handler functions to specific URIs.

Let's take a look at how to handle HTTP requests and responses using Ring, and how to structure routes using Compojure, by building a web app from scratch.

Route Requests with Ring

Ring aims to abstract the details of HTTP into a concise and modular API that can be used to build a large spectrum of applications. If you've developed web applications in Python or Ruby, then you'll find it similar to the WSGI and Rack libraries found in those languages.[1,2]

Since Ring has become the de facto standard for building web applications, a lot of tools and supporting libraries have been developed around it. While in most cases you won't need to use Ring directly, it's useful to have a high-level understanding of its design to help you develop and troubleshoot your applications.

Ring adapters for the Java HTTP servlet application programming interface (API) allow applications to be deployed on any servlet container, such as Tomcat.[3] However, the most common approach is to run Clojure applications standalone using an embedded HTTP server such as Immutant or Jetty.[4,5,6]

Ring applications consist of four basic components: the *handler*, the *request*, the *response*, and the *middleware*. Let's look at each one of these by creating a new Leiningen project.

Creating a Web Server

Let's create a new project called *ring-app* by running the following command:

```
lein new ring-app
```

Next let's open the project.clj file to add the dependency for Ring and specify the :main key that points to the namespace that has the -main function. This function is used as the entry point for starting the application.

```
(defproject ring-app "0.1.0-SNAPSHOT"
  :description "FIXME: write description"
  :url "http://example.com/FIXME"
  :license {:name "Eclipse Public License"
            :url "http://www.eclipse.org/legal/epl-v10.html"}
  :dependencies [[org.clojure/clojure "1.7.0"]
                 [ring "1.4.0"]]
  :main ring-app.core)
```

---

1. http://wsgi.readthedocs.org/en/latest/
2. http://rack.github.io/
3. http://www.oracle.com/technetwork/java/index-jsp-135475.html
4. http://tomcat.apache.org/
5. http://immutant.org/
6. http://www.eclipse.org/jetty/

We're now ready to update the ring-app.core namespace with the code to create a web server and handle HTTP requests.

Handling Requests

Ring uses standard Clojure maps to represent the client requests and the responses returned by the server. The handlers are functions that process the incoming requests and generate the responses. A very basic Ring handler might look like this:

```
(defn handler [request-map]
  {:status 200
   :headers {"Content-Type" "text/html"}
   :body (str "<html><body> your IP is: "
              (:remote-addr request-map)
              "</body></html>")})
```

As you can see, the handler function accepts a map representing an HTTP request and returns a map representing an HTTP response. Ring takes care of generating the request map from the incoming HTTP request, and converting the map returned by the function into the corresponding response. Let's open the ring-app.core and add the handler there.

The handler needs to be passed to an instance of the web server, so we reference it in the namespace declaration and then add the -main function to start it. Our namespace should look like this:

```
(ns ring-app.core
  (:require [ring.adapter.jetty :as jetty]))

(defn handler [request-map]
  {:status 200
   :headers {"Content-Type" "text/html"}
   :body (str "<html><body> your IP is: "
              (:remote-addr request-map)
              "</body></html>")})

(defn -main []
  (jetty/run-jetty
    handler
    {:port 3000
     :join? false}))
```

The run-jetty function accepts the handler function we just created, along with a map containing options such as the HTTP port. The :join? key indicates whether the server thread should block. Let's set it to false so that we're able to work in the REPL while it's running.

With the preceding changes to the namespace, we can open up the terminal and start our application using the lein run command.

```
lein run
2015-10-31:INFO:main: Logging initialized @1796ms
2015-10-31:INFO:main: jetty-9.2.10.v20150310
2015-10-31:INFO:main: Started ServerConnector{HTTP/1.1}{0.0.0.0:3000}
2015-10-31:INFO:main: Started @1902ms
```

At this point our server is ready to handle requests, and we can navigate to http://localhost:3000 to see our app in action. The page should be displaying the text "your IP is: 0:0:0:0:0:0:0:1" since we're accessing it from localhost and the server is listening on all of the available interfaces.

The handler that we wrote serves an HTML string with the client's IP address and sets the response status to 200. Since this is a common operation, the Ring API provides a helper function for generating such responses found in the ring.util.response namespace. Let's reference it and update our handler as follows.

```
(ns ring-app.core
  (:require [ring.adapter.jetty :as jetty]
            [ring.util.response :as response]))

(defn handler [request-map]
  (response/response
    (str "<html><body> your IP is: "
         (:remote-addr request-map)
         "</body></html>")))
```

We should now be able to restart the app in the terminal and see the same page displayed as before. If you want to create a custom response, you'll have to write a function that would accept a request map and return a response map representing your custom response. Let's look at the format for the request and response maps.

Request and Response Maps

The request and response maps will contain information such as the server port, URI, remote address, and content type, plus the body with the actual payload. The keys in these maps are based on the servlet API and the official HTTP RFC.[7]

---

7.   http://www.w3.org/Protocols/rfc2616/rfc2616.html

What's in the Request Map

The request defines the following standard keys. Note that not all of these keys, such as :ssl-client-cert, are guaranteed to be present in a request.

- :server-port—The port on which the server is handling the request
- :server-name—The server's IP address or the name it resolves to
- :remote-addr—The client's IP address
- :query-string —The request's query string
- :scheme—The specifier of the protocol, which can be either :http or :https
- :request-method—The HTTP request method, such as :get(), :head(), :options(), :put(), :post(), or :delete()
- :content-type—The request body's MIME type
- :content-length—The number of bytes in the request
- :character-encoding—The name of the request's character encoding
- :headers—A map containing the request headers
- :body—An input stream for the body of the request
- :context—The context in which the application can be found when not deployed as root
- :uri—The request URI path on the server; this string will have the :context prepended when available.
- :ssl-client-cert—The client's SSL certificate

In addition to the standard keys from the Ring specification, it is possible to use middleware functions to extend the request map with other application-specific keys. Later in this chapter we'll cover how to accomplish this.

What's in the Response Map

The response map contains three keys needed to describe the HTTP response:

- :status—The response's HTTP status
- :headers—Any HTTP headers to be returned to the client
- :body—The response's body

The status is a number representing one of the status codes specified in the HTTP RFC. The lowest allowed number is 100.

The header is a map containing the HTTP-header key/value pairs. Header values may either be strings or a sequences of strings. When the value will is a sequence, then a name/value header will be sent for each string in the sequence. You can see examples of setting each type of header here:

```
{:headers {"content-type" "text/html"}
 :body "<html><body>hi</body></html>"}

{:headers {"content-type" ["text/plain" "text/html"]}
 :body "<html><body>hi</body></html>"}
```

The response body can contain a string, a sequence, a file, or an input stream. The body must correspond appropriately with the response's status code.

When the response body is a string, it will be sent back to the client as is. If it is a sequence, then a string representing each element is sent to the client. Finally, if the response is a file or an input stream, then the server sends its contents to the client.

Adding Functionality with Middleware

Middleware allows wrapping the handlers in functions that can modify the way the request is processed. Middleware functions are often used to extend the base functionality of Ring handlers to match your application's needs.

A middleware handler is a function that accepts an existing handler with some optional parameters and then returns a new handler with some added behavior. The following is an example of such a function:

```
(defn handler [request]
  (response/response
    (str "<html><body> your IP is: "
         (:remote-addr request)
         "</body></html>")))

(defn wrap-nocache [handler]
  (fn [request]
    (-> request
        handler
        (assoc-in [:headers "Pragma"] "no-cache"))))

(defn -main []
  (jetty/run-jetty
    (wrap-nocache handler)
    {:port 3000
     :join? false}))
```

The wrapper in our example accepts the handler and returns a function that in turn acts as a handler. Since the returned function was defined in the local scope, it can reference the handler internally. When invoked, it will call the handler with the request and add Pragma: no-cache to the headers of the response map. The wrapper function is called a *closure* because it closes over the handler parameter and makes it accessible to the function it returns.

The technique you've just seen allows us to create small functions, each dealing with a particular aspect of the application. We can then easily chain them together to provide complex behaviors needed for real-world applications.

Many libraries provide middleware functions for modifying request and response maps. Ring itself comes with a number of such middleware helpers. For example, you may have noticed that we didn't have to keep restarting the guestbook app to see the changes. Instead, the code on the server was automatically reloaded by the wrap-reload middleware function found in the ring.middleware.reload namespace. Let's add this piece of middleware to our app.

```
(ns ring-app.core
  (:require [ring.adapter.jetty :as jetty]
            [ring.util.response :as response]
            [ring.middleware.reload :refer [wrap-reload]]))
(defn handler [request]
  (response/response
    (str "<html><body> your IP is: "
         (:remote-addr request)
         "</body></html>")))
(defn wrap-nocache [handler]
  (fn [request]
    (-> request
        handler
        (assoc-in [:headers "Pragma"] "no-cache"))))
(defn -main []
  (jetty/run-jetty
    (-> handler var wrap-nocache wrap-reload)
    {:port 3000
     :join? false}))
```

Note that we have to create a var from the handler in order for this middleware to work. This is necessary to ensure that the var object containing the current handler function is returned. If we used the handler instead, then the app would only see the original value of the function and changes would not be reflected. A more common way to create a var would be to use the #' prefix as follows: (-> #'handler wrap-nocache wrap-reload).

With the wrap-reload middleware in place, you'll have to restart the server one more time for it to take effect. After the server is restarted, you should be able to modify the handler function, save the file, and reload the page to see the changes.

What Are the Adapters?

Adapters sit between the handlers and the underlying HTTP protocol. They provide any necessary configuration, such as port mappings, and they parse HTTP requests into request maps and construct HTTP responses from the handler response maps. The adapters allow Ring to run on a number of different containers, such as Jetty and HTTP Kit.[8] You will generally not need to interact with adapters directly in your application.

Extend Ring

Ring provides a simple base for handling the HTTP request and response cycle. We'll now look at several libraries that provide many additional utility functions that extend the functionality of Ring.

As we saw earlier, the Ring stack consists of a chain of middleware functions. Each function accepts the request map, modifies it in some way, and then passes it on to the next function in the chain. The middleware functions have to be wrapped in order of dependency. For example, session-based authentication relies on the presence of a session, and the session middleware must run before it to make the session available.

A library called *ring-defaults* provides a standard set of middleware that's useful for typical web applications. The middleware is split into API middleware and site middleware. The configuration *api-defaults* is meant to be used for web service APIs, and its counterpart, *secure-api-defaults*, extends it with SSL redirects and enables HSTS. Conversely, *site-defaults* provide the middleware stack for a typical website, while *secure-site-defaults* provide security extensions such as SSL and secure cookies. Luminus defaults to using the site-defaults middleware.

Ideally, the responses returned by the server should follow the HTTP status codes whenever appropriate. When an operation is successful, we return a status of 200, when we have an internal error we return a status of 500, and so on. The ring-http-response library provides a set of handler functions that map to HTTP codes.[9]

Using this library we can return meaningful responses that map to specific HTTP status codes, such as *ok*, *found*, *internal-server-error*, and so on.

---

8.   http://www.http-kit.org//
9.   https://github.com/metosin/ring-http-response

Let's add the library to the dependencies in project.clj and update the handler function in the project.

```
(defproject ring-app "0.1.0-SNAPSHOT"
  :description "FIXME: write description"
  :url "http://example.com/FIXME"
  :license {:name "Eclipse Public License"
            :url "http://www.eclipse.org/legal/epl-v10.html"}
  :dependencies [[org.clojure/clojure "1.7.0"]
                 [ring "1.4.0"]
                 [metosin/ring-http-response "0.6.5"]]
  :main ring-app.core)
```

Note that if the project is currently running, then we'll have to restart it for the changes to take effect. While Clojure namespaces can be reloaded dynamically, any changes on the classpath require the JVM to be restarted to take effect. Since adding a new libraries updates the classpath, the project needs to be reloaded for it to be found.

We can now replace the ring.util.response reference with a reference to ring.util.http-response and update the handler as follows.

```
(ns ring-app.core
  (:require [ring.adapter.jetty :as jetty]
            [ring.util.http-response :as response]
            [ring.middleware.reload :refer [wrap-reload]]))

(defn handler [request]
  (response/ok
    (str "<html><body> your IP is: "
         (:remote-addr request)
         "</body></html>")))
```

Try using different types of responses, as seen in the following examples:

```
(response/continue)
=> {:status 100, :headers {}, :body ""}

(response/ok "<html><body><h1>hello, world</h1></body></html>")
=> {:status 200
    :headers {}
    :body "<html><body><h1>hello, world</h1></body></html>"}

(response/found "/messages")
=> {:status 302, :headers {"Location" "/messages"}, :body ""}

(response/internal-server-error "failed to complete request")
=> {:status 500, :headers {}, :body "failed to complete request"}
```

When exposing a service API, it's often necessary to communicate with external clients that use different encoding formats. The ring-middleware-format library provides middleware for automatically serializing and deserializing different data formats based on the Accept and Content-Type request headers. The library handles common formats, such as JSON and YAML, as well as Clojure-specific formats such as EDN and transit. Let's add this library.

```
(defproject ring-app "0.1.0-SNAPSHOT"
  :description "FIXME: write description"
  :url "http://example.com/FIXME"
  :license {:name "Eclipse Public License"
            :url "http://www.eclipse.org/legal/epl-v10.html"}
  :dependencies [[org.clojure/clojure "1.7.0"]
                 [ring "1.4.0"]
                 [metosin/ring-http-response "0.6.5"]
                 [ring-middleware-format "0.7.0"]]
  :main ring-app.core)
```

The library provides a middleware wrapper function called *ring.middleware.format/wrap-restful-format*. This function accepts the handler and an optional map of parameters. Let's reference the wrap-restful-format middleware and change the handler to accept a request containing a JSON-encoded request. The request contains a parameter called id and returns a response where the :result key is set to the value of this parameter.

```
(ns ring-app.core
  (:require [ring.adapter.jetty :as jetty]
            [ring.util.http-response :as response]
            [ring.middleware.reload :refer [wrap-reload]]
            [ring.middleware.format :refer [wrap-restful-format]]))

(defn handler [request]
  (response/ok
    {:result (-> request :params :id)}))

(defn wrap-nocache [handler]
  (fn [request]
    (-> request
        handler
        (assoc-in [:headers "Pragma"] "no-cache"))))

(defn wrap-formats [handler]
  (wrap-restful-format
    handler
    {:formats [:json-kw :transit-json :transit-msgpack]}))

(defn -main []
  (jetty/run-jetty
    (-> #'handler wrap-nocache wrap-reload wrap-formats)
    {:port 3000
     :join? false}))
```

We can test the functionality from the command line using the program *curl*:

```
curl -H "Content-Type: application/json" -X POST -d '{"id":1}' localhost:3000/json
```

The result of running the cURL command should look as follows:

```
{"result":1}
```

Using middleware such as ring-middleware-format is a common pattern for capturing ordinary tasks, such as a data encoding, in a centralized fashion. The alternative would be to have each handler function handle its own serialization and deserialization logic. The latter approach is both error-prone and repetitive; thus it should be avoided whenever possible. As a rule, general patterns that are not specific to a particular request are good candidates for middleware functions.

It's also worth noting that different sets of handlers can be wrapped with their own middleware. For example, CSRF protection makes sense for routes that are called by the pages generated within the same session, as you saw with the guestbook application. However, if you were creating a public service API, then you would not wish the routes to require a CSRF token.

If you look at the app-routes in the guestbook.handler namespace, you can see that the home-routes are wrapped with middleware/wrap-csrf by calling the compojure.core/wrap-routes macro.

guestbook/src/clj/guestbook/handler.clj

```
(def app-routes
  (routes
    (-> #'home-routes
        (wrap-routes middleware/wrap-csrf)
        (wrap-routes middleware/wrap-formats))
    (route/not-found
      (:body
        (error-page {:status 404
                     :title "page not found"})))))

(defn app [] (middleware/wrap-base #'app-routes))
```

The macro makes sure that the route is resolved before the middleware is applied. This ensures that middleware is only applied to specific routes, instead of being run globally for all routes. Another example we'll see later in the book will be to selectively apply authentication middleware for the routes that require that the user is logged in in order for the route to be accessed.

We already saw some examples of routing using Compojure when we built our first application in Chapter 1, *Getting Your Feet Wet*, on page 1. Now let's take a closer look at the functionality it provides.

Define the Routes with Compojure

Compojure is a routing library built on top of Ring. It provides a way to associate handler functions with a URL and an HTTP method. Let's add it as a dependency in the ring-app project and see how it works.

ring-app/project.clj

```
(defproject ring-app "0.1.0-SNAPSHOT"
  :description "FIXME: write description"
  :url "http://example.com/FIXME"
  :license {:name "Eclipse Public License"
            :url "http://www.eclipse.org/legal/epl-v10.html"}
  :dependencies [[org.clojure/clojure "1.7.0"]
                 [ring "1.4.0"]
                 [metosin/ring-http-response "0.6.5"]
                 [ring-middleware-format "0.7.0"]
                 [compojure "1.4.0"]]
  :main ring-app.core)
```

With the dependency in place, let's update the namespace to reference compojure.core and add a route for the / URI.

```
(ns ring-app.core
  (:require [ring.adapter.jetty :as jetty]
            [compojure.core :as compojure]
            [ring.util.http-response :as response]
            [ring.middleware.reload :refer [wrap-reload]]))

(defn response-handler [request]
  (response/ok
    (str "<html><body> your IP is: "
         (:remote-addr request)
         "</body></html>")))

(def handler
  (compojure/routes
    (compojure/GET "/" request response-handler)))
```

The function that generates the response is now called response-handler, and it's being called by the compojure/GET macro when the client requests the / URI. The GET() route is wrapped using the routes function that aggregates a set of routes into a Ring handler.

The route name maps to an HTTP method name, such as GET, POST, PUT, DELETE, or HEAD. There's also a route called ANY that matches any method the client supplies. The URI can contain keys denoted by using a colon, and their values can be used as parameters to the route. This feature was inspired by a similar mechanism used in Rails and Sinatra.[10,11] The route's response is automatically wrapped in the Ring response described earlier.

The route URI can contain dynamic segments that are specified using the :. Let's add another route to our handler that accepts an :id URI segment and displays its value on the page.

```
(def handler
  (compojure/routes
    (compojure/GET "/" request response-handler)
    (compojure/GET "/:id" [id] (str "<p>the id is: " id "</p>" ))))
```

We can now navigate to a URI such as http://localhost:3000/foo and see the text "the id is: foo" displayed on the page.

Compojure also lets us extract JavaScript Object Notation (JSON) parameters using the same destructuring syntax. For example, we can now rewrite the route for handling JSON-encoded POST requests as follows:

```
(def handler
  (compojure/routes
    (compojure/GET "/" request response-handler)
    (compojure/GET "/:id" [id] (str "<p>the id is: " id "</p>" ))
    (compojure/POST "/json" [id] (response/ok {:result id}))))
```

Since defining routes is a very common operation, Compojure also provides the defroutes macro that generates a Ring handler from the supplied routes:

ring-app/src/ring_app/core.clj

```
(compojure/defroutes handler
  (compojure/GET "/" request response-handler)
  (compojure/GET "/:id" [id] (str "<p>the id is: " id "</p>" ))
  (compojure/POST "/json" [id] (response/ok {:result id})))
```

Using Compojure routes, we can easily map functionality to each URL of our site to provide much of the core functionality needed in a web application. We can then group these routes together using the defroutes macro as we did previously. Compojure, in turn, creates the Ring handlers for us.

Compojure also provides a powerful mechanism for filtering out common routes in the application based on the shared path elements. Let's say we have several routes that handle operations for a specific user:

---

10. http://rubyonrails.org/
11. http://www.sinatrarb.com/

```clojure
(defn display-profile [id]
  ;;TODO: display user profile
  )

(defn display-settings [id]
  ;;TODO: display user account settings
  )

(defn change-password [id]
  ;;TODO: display the page for setting a new password
  )

(defroutes user-routes
  (GET "/user/:id/profile" [id] (display-profile id))
  (GET "/user/:id/settings" [id] (display-settings id))
  (GET "/user/:id/change-password" [id] (change-password-page id)))
```

That code has a lot of repetition, since each route starts with the /user/:id segment. We can use the context macro to factor out the common portion of these routes:

```clojure
(def user-routes
    (context "/user/:id" [id]
        (GET "/profile" [] (display-profile id))
        (GET "/settings" [] (display-settings id))
        (GET "/change-password" [] (change-password-page id))))
```

In that code the routes defined in the context of /user/:id will behave exactly the same as the previous version and have access to the id parameter. The context macro exploits the fact that handlers are closures. When the outer context handler closes over the common parameters, they are also available to handlers defined inside it.

Accessing Request Parameters

For some routes, we'll need to access the request map to access the request parameters. We do this by declaring the map as the second argument to the route.

```clojure
(GET "/foo" request (clojure.string/join ", " (keys request)))
```

That route reads out all the keys from the request map and displays them. The output looks like this:

```
:ssl-client-cert, :remote-addr, :scheme, :query-params, :session, :form-params,
:multipart-params, :request-method, :query-string, :route-params, :content-type,
:cookies, :uri, :server-name, :params, :headers, :content-length, :server-port,
:character-encoding, :body, :flash
```

Compojure also provides some useful functionality for handling the request maps and the form parameters. For example, in the guestbook application, which we created in Chapter 1, *Getting Your Feet Wet*, on page 1, we saw the following route defined:

```
(POST "/" request (save-message! request))
```

The route takes the request and passes it as a parameter to the save-message! function. If you recall, the request contains the name and message parameters that are entered by the user in the form. We could extract these parameters from the request like this:

```
(POST "/" [name message] (println name message) "ok")
```

This route extracts the :name and :message keys found in the request map under the :params key and then binds them to variables of the same name. We can now use them as any other declared variable within the route's scope. Note that the route is expected to return a response. A route that returns nil will be treated as "not found" (404) by Ring.

It's also possible to use the regular Clojure destructuring inside the route. Given a request map containing the following parameters...

```
{:params {"name" "some value"}}
```

...we can extract the parameter with the key "name" as follows:

```
(GET "/:foo" {{value :name} :params}
  (str "The value of name is " value))
```

Furthermore, Compojure lets you destructure a subset of form parameters and create a map from the rest:

```
[x y & z]
x -> "foo"
y -> "bar"
z -> {:v "baz", :w "qux"}
```

In the preceding code, parameters x and y have been bound to variables, while parameters v and w remain in a map called z. Finally, if we need to get at the complete request along with the parameters, we can do the following:

```
(GET "/" [x y :as request] (str x y request))
```

Here we bind the form parameters x and y and bind the complete request map to the request variable.

Armed with the functionality that Ring and Compojure provide, we can easily create pages and routes for our site. However, any nontrivial application requires many other features, such as HTML templating. We'll take a look at that in the next section.

HTML Templating Using Selmer

Selmer is a general-purpose templating engine that's content-agnostic. While it's primarily geared toward working with HTML, it can be used to transform any kind of text. If you're already familiar with Django or similar templating languages, you should feel right at home using Selmer.

When applied to generating HTML templates, Selmer encourages a clean separation between the presentation and the business logic. On top of that, the templates can be maintained by someone who has no knowledge of Clojure. Let's create a new project where we'll learn to use different features of Selmer. Let's use the default Leiningen template for this purpose.

```
lein new html-templating
```

Once the project is created, add the Selmer dependency in the project.clj file.

```
[selmer "1.0.2"]
```

We're now ready to take a look at what Selmer has to offer using the REPL. Open up the html-templating.core namespace and add a reference to Selmer there.

```
(ns html-templating.core
  (:require [selmer.parser :as selmer]))
```

Once we've added the reference we should be able to load the namespace and test that everything is working by evaluating this command in the REPL:

```
(selmer/render "Hello, {{name}}" {:name "World"})
```

When the code runs we should see the "Hello, World" text printed. The render function accepts the template string followed by a context map containing the dynamic content. This map contains any variables that we'd like to render in our template. In our case we're populating the name tag using the :name key in the map.

In most real-world applications we'll want to keep the templates as separate files instead of using strings directly in code. Selmer is optimized for this use case and will memoize the file templates when it parses them. Let's take a look at how Selmer works with files.

Creating Templates

The templates are expected to be found on the resource path. Let's create a new template called hello.html and place it in the resources folder in our project. The template consists of HTML with additional template tags.

```html
<html>
  <head>
    <meta http-equiv="Content-Type" content="text/html; charset=UTF-8"/>
    <title>My First Template</title>
  </head>
  <body>
    <h2>Hello {{name}}</h2>
  </body>
</html>
```

With the file created, we can run the render-file function to render it.

```clojure
(selmer/render-file "hello.html" {:name "World"})
```

The result once again has the {{name}} tag replaced with the string World.

The render-file function accepts a string pointing to a resource that's expected to be found relative to the resource path of the application. Since we placed our template file in the resources folder, the path consists of its name.

Selmer also provides us with the ability to set a custom resource path using the selmer.parser/set-resource-path! function. For example, we could run the following code to specify that the templates should be found in the /var/html/templates folder.

```clojure
(selmer.parser/set-resource-path! "/var/html/templates/")
```

In the preceding code we passed in a string as the value for the variable name. However, we're not restricted to strings and can pass in any type we like. For example, if we pass in a collection we can iterate over it using the for tag. Let's add the following content to our hello.html template.

```html
<ul>
{% for item in items %}
<li> {{item}} </li>
{% endfor %}
</ul>
```

When we run the render-file function, we pass it a range of numbers keyed on the :items key.

```clojure
(selmer/render-file "hello.html" {:items (range 10)})
```

Note that since we passed no value for the {{name}} tag, its content is left blank. If an item happens to be a map, we can access the keys by name, as follows.

```clojure
(selmer/render "<p>Hello {{user.first}} {{user.last}}</p>"
        {:user {:first "John" :last "Doe"}})
```

When no special processing is specified in the template, the parameter's default str representation will be used.

Using Filters

Filters allow for postprocessing the variables before they are rendered. For example, you can use a filter to convert the variable to uppercase, compute a hash, or count its length. Filters are specified by using a pipe symbol (|) after the variable name, as seen here:

```
{{name|upper}}
```

Selmer comes with a number of handy filters, such as upper, date, and pluralize, out of the box. On top of that we can easily define our own filters using the selmer.filters/add-filter! function. Try this in the REPL by adding a reference to selmer.filters and creating a custom filter to check if a collection is empty.

```
    (ns html-templating.core
  (:require [selmer.parser :as selmer]
            [selmer.filters :as filters]))

(filters/add-filter! :empty? empty?)

(selmer/render "{% if files|empty? %}no files{% else %}files{% endif %}"
  {:files []})
```

By default the content of the filters is escaped; we can override this behavior as follows:

```
(filters/add-filter! :foo
  (fn [x] [:safe (.toUpperCase x)]))

(selmer/render "{{x|foo}}" {:x "<div>I'm safe</div>"})
```

You should only unescape content that's generated by the server and known to be safe. You should always escape any user input because it can contain malicious content.

Using Template Tags

Selmer provides two types of tags. The first is inline tags such as extends and include. These tags are self-contained statements and do not require an end tag. The other type is the block tags. These tags have a start and an end tag, with the tag content inbetween. An example of this is the if ... endif block.

Defining Custom Tags

In addition to tags already provided, you can also define custom tags using the selmer.parser/add-tag! macro. Let's look at an example to see how it works:

```
(selmer/add-tag!
 :image
 (fn [args context-map]
    (str "<img src=" (first args) "/>")))

(selmer/render "{% image \"http://foo.com/logo.jpg\" %}" {})
```

We can also define a block tag by using the overloaded add-tag! definition. In this case we provide the opening tag, followed by the handler function and any closing tags. The handler accepts an addition parameter that holds the content of each block. The content is keyed on the name of the block, as in the following example:

```
(selmer/add-tag!
 :uppercase
 (fn [args context-map content]
   (.toUpperCase (get-in content [:uppercase :content])))
 :enduppercase)

(selmer/render "{% uppercase %}foo {{bar}} baz{% enduppercase %}" {:bar "injected"})
```

Inheriting Templates

Selmer templates can refer to other templates. We have two ways to refer to a template. We can either extend templates using the extends tag or include templates with the include tag.

Extending Templates

When we use the extends tag, the current template will use the template it's extending as the base. Any block tags in the base template with the names matching the current template will be overwritten.

Let's look at a concrete example. First, we define our base template, called base.html, and place it in the resources folder alongside the hello.html template we already have.

```
<!DOCTYPE html>
<html>
  <head>
      <link rel="stylesheet" href="style.css" />
      <title>{% block title %}My amazing site{% endblock %}</title>
  </head>
  <body>
      <div id="content">
          {% block content %}default content{% endblock %}
      </div>
  </body>
</html>
```

We then update the hello.html to extend base.html as follows:

```
{% extends "base.html" %}

{% block content %}
  <h2>Hello {{name}}</h2>

  <ul>
  {% for item in items %}
  <li> {{item}} </li>
  {% endfor %}
  </ul>
{% endblock %}
```

When the hello.html is rendered, the content block displays the entries defined there. However, since we did not define a block for the title, the base template (base.html) is used.

Optionally, we can include the parent content in the child block by using the {{block.super}} tag. It is replaced by the content of the parent when the template is rendered.

```
{% extends "base.html" %}

{% block content %}
  {{block.super}}
  <h2>Hello {{name}}</h2>

  <ul>
  {% for item in items %}
  <li> {{item}} </li>
  {% endfor %}
  </ul>
{% endblock %}
```

Note that you can chain extended templates together. In this case the latest occurrence of a block tag will be the one that's rendered.

One caveat to be aware of is that the templates are memoized by default. This means that a final version of the template will be compiled once and kept in memory. This can be toggled with the selmer.parser/cache-on! and selmer.parser/cache-off! functions. You'd likely want to turn caching off during development.

Including Templates

The include tag allows us to include content from other templates in the current template. Let's look at an example. Say we want to include some additional content in our hello.html template. Let's create another template called register.html with the following content:

```
<form action="/register" method="POST">
    <label for="id">user id</label>
    <input id="id" name="id" type="text">
    <input pass="pass" name="pass" type="text">
    <input type="submit" value="register">
</form>
```

Then we update the hello.html template to include register.html.

```
{% extends "base.html" %}

{% block content %}
  {% include "register.html" %}
  <h2>Hello {{name}}</h2>

  <ul>
  {% for item in items %}
  <li> {{item}} </li>
  {% endfor %}
  </ul>
{% endblock %}
```

Note that the hello.html template extends the base.html template. Any content in the template must be placed inside the block tags. When the template is compiled, the parser looks for the matching blocks in the parent and injects the content from the child. Any content outside the blocks is therefore ignored.

When hello.html is rendered, it replaces the include tags with the content from the included template.

Error Handling

Selmer attempts to provide meaningful errors when the templates contain syntax errors. For example, if we try to run the following code, we get an exception informing us that "safea" is not a valid tag.

```
(selmer/render "{{content|safea}}" {})
```

Selmer also provides a middleware function called selmer.middleware/wrap-error-page. This function captures errors and generates a page that can be rendered in the browser to notify you that a template compilation error has occurred.

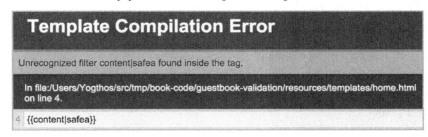

You can try out this middleware in the REPL yourself. Let's create a template file called error.html with the following content:

```
{{content|safea}}
```

Middleware functions accept a handler function as a parameter and return a function that accepts the request map. Let's create a renderer function that returns a handler that accepts the template name as its input and returns a 200 status response.

We start by adding a reference for the selmer.middleware/wrap-error-page function.

```
(ns html-templating.core
  (:require [selmer.parser :as selmer]
            [selmer.filters :as filters]
            [selmer.middleware :refer [wrap-error-page]]))
```

Then we proceed to write a renderer function that looks like this:

```
(defn renderer []
  (wrap-error-page
    (fn [template]
      {:status 200
       :body (selmer/render-file template {})})))
```

We can now call it with different template files to see the result. First let's call it with a proper template, such as hello.html. The result is the response from calling the handler.

```
((renderer) "hello.html")
```

However, if we call it with the error.html template, then we get a response of 500 with the body containing the error page.

```
((renderer) "error.html")
```

This middleware for development is set up by default in Luminus, providing feedback right in the browser when a template fails to compile.

Revisiting Guestbook Templates

Now that we're familiar with the basics of HTML templating using Selmer, let's see how it's used in our guestbook application. As we saw, Luminus places HTML templates in the resources/templates folder. Here we have three files, base.html, home.html, and about.html. As we saw earlier, home.html and about.html files are used to render the home and about pages, respectively. The base template is extended by both these templates and provides all the common elements for each page.

The base template is where we declare common assets, such as JavaScript, CSS, or ClojureScript, as well as common UI elements, such as navbars, headers, and footers. Both home and about page templates extend the base and override its content block.

When the browser requests a particular page, the route calls the handler for the page. It in turn handles any business logic and then calls guestbook.layout/render to generate the page. The render function accepts the name of the template along with an optional context map containing dynamic content to be rendered. This is then passed to Selmer and the rendered page is returned.

What You've Learned

In this chapter we saw how to handle requests using Ring, how to structure routes using Compojure, and how to template HTML using Selmer. In the following chapter we'll take a deeper look at overall application structure and how all the pieces fit together.

CHAPTER 3

Luminus Architecture

At the start of the book we jumped right into building a simple application. This let us get comfortable with the development environment and provided a glimpse of what to expect in terms of project structure. We looked at the directory layout, as well as at the purpose of some of the files found in the project. However, we didn't focus very closely on the code in these files. In this chapter, you'll learn the background necessary to fully understand our guestbook application.

Manage the Project

As we already saw working on the guestbook application, the project is managed using the project.clj and the profiles.clj files. The former contains the common configuration for the project, while the latter is used for any local configuration that's not meant to be checked into source control.

Leiningen uses the concept of profiles to identify different build scenarios for the project. The dev and the test profiles are used for development and testing, respectively. The :dev profile is composed of the :project/dev and the :profiles/dev subprofiles, while the :test profile is composed using :project/test and :profiles/test. This allows us to merge the local and global configuration parameters.

The UberJar profile is used for packaging the application for production. When the production build happens, the compiled bytecode is emitted into the resulting *JAR*. This results in a self-contained application that can be run using the standard Java Runtime Environment (JRE).

Profile-Specific Resources

The profiles can specify any configuration options that can be specified in the global scope. For example, we can add specific dependencies or plugins that are only necessary for development. Since we wouldn't want to package those for production, we don't specify them at the top level.

Each profile also specifies its own paths for source files and resources. The :dev profile has the :resource-paths ["env/dev/resources"] resource path. This path will be used in addition to the global resources. This allows us to provide environment-specific settings for the app. Such settings include the environment variables, such as the HTTP port, that would be expected to be found in the system environment variables when running in production.

The environment variables are specified using EDN configuration files. These files are found in the env folder. This folder contains separate environments called dev, test, and prod. Each one has a resources folder containing the config.edn file. In the case of the guestbook project, the local configuration consists of the HTTP and nREPL ports.

The profiles are also responsible for deciding what additional source paths should be used the same way as the resources. The :uberjar profile sets the :source-paths key to point to ["env/prod/clj"], while the :dev profile points to ["env/dev/clj"]. These paths become available in addition to the default src path, where the compiler looks for the application code.

Running Code Selectively

Some code in the application may behave differently between development and production modes. For example, we may wish to disable HTML template caching while developing the application. However, once we put it in production, we'd like to default to settings optimized for performance.

One approach is to use an environment variable to indicate the mode that the application runs in and use conditional logic to select what code should be executed at runtime. This approach has a number of drawbacks. The conditional logic is error prone, it can add runtime overhead, and we end up having to package all the libraries used for development in our production build.

A better approach is to decide what code should be included at build time. This way only the code that's necessary ends up being packaged for production, and we don't have to worry about checking what mode the application is in at runtime. This is the approach that Luminus defaults to.

The development code includes a guestbook.env namespace with the configuration optimized for development use.

guestbook/env/dev/clj/guestbook/env.clj

```
(ns guestbook.env
  (:require [selmer.parser :as parser]
            [clojure.tools.logging :as log]
            [guestbook.dev-middleware :refer [wrap-dev]]))
(def defaults
  {:init
   (fn []
     (parser/cache-off!)
     (log/info "\n-=[guestbook started successfully using the development profile]=-"))
   :stop
   (fn []
     (log/info "\n-=[guestbook has shut down successfully]=-"))
   :middleware wrap-dev})
```

The namespace consists of the defaults map that contains keys called :init, :stop, and :middleware. The first key points to a function that should be run during startup. The second points to a function that's called when the application shuts down. Meanwhile, the last one specifies some additional development middleware for live code reloading and error reporting. The middleware itself is found in the guestbook.dev-middleware namespace.

Meanwhile, the production version of guestbook.env contains the following code.

guestbook/env/prod/clj/guestbook/env.clj

```
(ns guestbook.env
  (:require [clojure.tools.logging :as log]))
(def defaults
  {:init
   (fn []
     (log/info "\n-=[guestbook started successfully]=-"))
   :stop
   (fn []
     (log/info "\n-=[guestbook has shut down successfully]=-"))
   :middleware identity})
```

As you can see the version found in the prod source path doesn't disable the HTML template caching or wrap any development middleware.

Think in Terms of Application Components

The approach that a typical Clojure web application takes is probably different from what you're used to. Most frameworks favor using the model-view-controller (MVC) pattern for partitioning the application logic, with strong separation between the view, the controller, and the model.

Luminus does not enforce any strict separation between the view and the controller portion of the application. Instead, Luminus encourages organizing the application to keep any related code in the same namespace. The route handler functions are typically responsible for processing HTTP requests from the client and dispatching actions based on them. This approach provides a clean separation between the domain logic and the presentation layer of your application without introducing any unnecessary indirection.

However, since the Clojure web stack is designed to be flexible, it will let you design the site any way you like. If you do feel strongly about having a traditional-style MVC in your application, nothing will stop you from doing that.

A typical application would be broken up into several logical components. Let's look at these in some more detail. A Luminus application is typically composed of the following core namespaces:

- core—The core manages the life cycle of the HTTP server.

- config—The config manages the map containing the configuration variables used by the application.

- handler—The handler namespace is the root handler for the requests and responses that aggregates all the routes.

- routes—The routes namespace contains the namespaces that are responsible for handling different types of client requests.

- db—The db namespace is reserved for the data model of the application and the persistence layer.

- layout—The layout namespace contains common logic for generating the application layout.

- middleware—The middleware namespace contains any custom middleware we want to use in our application.

Application Core

The core namespace is used to start the application. This is where the -main function is found. The -main function is the entry point for the application; the - in front of the function name indicates that it should be compiled to a Java method. This is necessary in order for the JVM to be able to invoke it. The namespace compilation is triggered by the :gen-class hint in its declaration.

The two functions that control the life cycle of the application are start-app and stop-app.

The start-app function is called by the -main function when the application is run, and it's responsible for running any initialization tasks.

guestbook/src/clj/guestbook/core.clj

```
(defn start-app [args]
  (doseq [component (-> args
                        (parse-opts cli-options)
                        mount/start-with-args
                        :started)]
    (log/info component "started"))
  (.addShutdownHook (Runtime/getRuntime) (Thread. stop-app)))
```

The life cycle of these resources is managed by the Mount library. It provides a defstate macro that allows us to declare a resource. We're further able to provide the :start and :stop keys that specify the code that should run when the resource is started and stopped, respectively. We can see an example of this by looking at how the HTTP and the nREPL servers are defined.[1]

guestbook/src/clj/guestbook/core.clj

```
(mount/defstate ^{:on-reload :noop}
                http-server
                :start
                (http/start
                  (-> env
                      (assoc :handler (handler/app))
                      (update :port #(or (-> env :options :port) %))))
                :stop
                (http/stop http-server))
(mount/defstate ^{:on-reload :noop}
                repl-server
                :start
                (when-let [nrepl-port (env :nrepl-port)]
                  (repl/start {:port nrepl-port}))
                :stop
                (when repl-server
                  (repl/stop repl-server)))
```

The template defaults to using the Immutant HTTP server unless otherwise specified.[2] The server is passed the guestbook.handler/app function to handle the incoming client requests. The initialization logic is associated with the :start key.

The start-app function calls the mount/start-with-args function. This function is responsible for starting stateful components defined using the defstate macro.

---

1. https://github.com/tolitius/mount
2. http://immutant.org/

The stop-app function is set as the shutdown hook in the start-app function. It will be called when the JVM runtime is shutting down. This function is responsible for handling any cleanup that needs to be done when the app stops, such as shutting down the HTTP server.

guestbook/src/clj/guestbook/core.clj

```
(defn stop-app []
  (doseq [component (:stopped (mount/stop))]
    (log/info component "stopped"))
  (shutdown-agents))
```

That's all there is to bootstrapping the application. Now let's see how we can add some routes to provide the functionality specific to our application.

Application Configuration

The configuration is managed by the guestbook.config namespace. This namespace contains a defstate definition for the env variable. This variable contains the configuration aggregated from the config.edn file found on the resources path, the optional EDN config file pointed to by the conf Java parameter, the Java parameters, and the environment variables. The entirety of the namespace looks like this:

guestbook/src/clj/guestbook/config.clj

```
(ns guestbook.config
  (:require [cprop.core :refer [load-config]]
            [cprop.source :as source]
            [mount.core :refer [args defstate]]))

(defstate env :start (load-config
                       :merge
                       [(args)
                        (source/from-system-props)
                        (source/from-env)]))
```

The configuration management is handled by a library called *cprop*. This library provides intelligence for massaging the environment variables into a Clojure-friendly format.[3]

The guestbook.config namespace calls the load-config function to create the configuration. Different configuration sources are merged explicitly to produce the final configuration using the :merge flag. Note that the cprop library does a deep merge of the configurations that it finds. This merge allows us to specify a base configuration and then overwrite specific parts of it later on.

---

3. https://github.com/tolitius/cprop

Application Handler

The guestbook.handler namespace is responsible for aggregating all the routes and wrapping them with any necessary middleware in the app-routes definition.

The routes function aggregates the routes for handling all the requests to our application. In addition to the user-defined routes, it provides a default not-found route that will serve the 404 page if none of the routes match the URI specified in the request. The routes are then wrapped with the wrap-base function in the app definition to apply the common middleware.

guestbook/src/clj/guestbook/handler.clj

```clojure
(ns guestbook.handler
  (:require [compojure.core :refer [routes wrap-routes]]
            [guestbook.layout :refer [error-page]]
            [guestbook.routes.home :refer [home-routes]]
            [compojure.route :as route]
            [guestbook.env :refer [defaults]]
            [mount.core :as mount]
            [guestbook.middleware :as middleware]))

(mount/defstate init-app
                :start ((or (:init defaults) identity))
                :stop  ((or (:stop defaults) identity)))
(def app-routes
  (routes
    (-> #'home-routes
        (wrap-routes middleware/wrap-csrf)
        (wrap-routes middleware/wrap-formats))
    (route/not-found
      (:body
        (error-page {:status 404
                     :title "page not found"})))))

(defn app [] (middleware/wrap-base #'app-routes))
```

Notice that the home-routes are additionally wrapped with the wrap-csrf middleware. But, instead of the routes being wrapped directly with the middleware, the wrap-routes function is used instead.

Recall that Compojure routes are simply Ring handlers and that handlers are chained together in order to handle requests. Therefore, when we wrap routes directly with (middleware/wrap-csrf home-routes), the wrap-csrf middleware becomes part of the request-processing chain.

However, in our case, we'd like to ensure that the wrap-csrf middleware is only applied to the routes defined by the home-routes. The wrap-routes function ensures that the middleware is applied after the route is matched, allowing us to restrict it to the routes defined by the home-routes.

Application Middleware

The guestbook.middleware namespace is reserved for any wrapper functions that are used to modify the requests and responses. The main purpose of the middleware is to provide a central place for handling common tasks such as CSRF protection.

If you recall, we had to specify an anti-forgery token when submitting forms in our guestbook application. This token is checked by the wrap-csrf middleware function. It checks each request to see if it contains a valid token and returns an error page if it doesn't. This way we don't have to remember to check for a CSRF token in each handler function, which eliminates potential errors.

The wrap-base function is used to tie all the common middleware together in the order of dependency. It also adds the ring-defaults middleware that we discussed earlier, along with wrap-webjars for serving static assets from the WebJars repository.[4]

Routing Requests

As we discussed earlier, application routes represent URIs that the client can call to cause the server to perform an action. Each route is mapped to a particular function that will be executed when the client requests the URI associated with it.

Any real-world applications will require more than a single route. In our guestbook application, we have three separate routes, each performing a distinct action:

`guestbook/src/clj/guestbook/routes/home.clj`

```
(defroutes home-routes
  (GET "/" [] (home-page))
  (POST "/message" request (save-message! request))
  (GET "/about" [] (about-page)))
```

When an incoming request matches the URI and the HTTP method, then the associated handler function will be invoked. For example, when the server receives an HTTP GET request for the / URI, then the home-page function will be called. This retrieves the messages from the database and renders a page displaying them alongside a form for creating a new message.

---

4.   http://www.webjars.org/

Even a trivial workflow requires more than a single route. One such workflow can be seen in the *guestbook* application. The / route is responsible for displaying the page that renders the messages, along with the form to write new messages. The corresponding /message() route is responsible for handling the creation of new messages.

When we identify a specific workflow in our application, it makes sense to group all the logic relating to this workflow in a single place. The routes namespace in our application is reserved for housing the namespaces that describe these workflows.

Since our guestbook application is very small, we define a single set of routes, along with some helper functions, right in the guestbook.routes.home namespace.

In an application that has more pages, we would want to create additional namespaces to keep the code manageable. We would then create separate routes under each namespace and group them together in the handler namespace using the routes macro provided by Compojure.

Creating separate route groups also allows us to selectively apply middleware using wrap-routes, as we've already seen with the wrap-csrf middleware being applied specifically to home-routes.

The routes function combines all the routes into a single set that is used to create the final handler. Be aware that the handler for the first route that matches will be called. The app-routes function contains the catch-all route/not-found route; any routes placed following it are masked by the not-found route.

Application Model

All but the most trivial applications need some sort of a model. The model describes the data stored by the application and the relationships between individual data elements.

When we use a relational database, it can often become the model for our application. Unlike object-oriented languages, Clojure does not require us to define a separate model in code and map it to the one defined in the database. Instead, the query results are represented by sequences of maps, where the keys correspond to the column names in the tables being queried.

All namespaces dealing with the model and the persistence layer traditionally live under the application's db package. This is a topic that warrants further discussion, and we'll revisit it in Chapter 7, *Database Access*, on page 117.

The guestbook database connection resides in the *db* variable. Note that the connection URI is populated using an environment variable called :database-url.

This ensures that we're not hardcoding our connection in the application or checking it into the code repository.

In development mode, the connection variable is populated in the profiles.clj file that's used to keep the local configuration.

guestbook/profiles.clj

```
{:profiles/dev  {:env {:database-url "jdbc:h2:./guestbook_dev.db"}}
 :profiles/test {:env {:database-url "jdbc:h2:./guestbook_test.db"}}}
```

When you run the application in production, the database connection URL should instead be provided via an environment variable, as shown here:

```
export DATABASE_URL="jdbc:h2:./guestbook.db"
```

The application reads the environment variable when it starts up and uses it to connect to the database. This approach ensures that the application is environment-agnostic.

Application Layout

The layout namespace is reserved for providing the visual layout as well as other common elements for our pages.

guestbook/src/clj/guestbook/layout.clj

```
(ns guestbook.layout
  (:require [selmer.parser :as parser]
            [selmer.filters :as filters]
            [markdown.core :refer [md-to-html-string]]
            [ring.util.http-response :refer [content-type ok]]
            [ring.util.anti-forgery :refer [anti-forgery-field]]
            [ring.middleware.anti-forgery :refer [*anti-forgery-token*]]]))

(declare ^:dynamic *app-context*)
(parser/set-resource-path! (clojure.java.io/resource "templates"))
(parser/add-tag! :csrf-field (fn [_ _] (anti-forgery-field)))
(filters/add-filter! :markdown (fn [content] [:safe (md-to-html-string content)]))

(defn render
  "renders the HTML template located relative to resources/templates"
  [template & [params]]
  (content-type
    (ok
      (parser/render-file
        template
        (assoc params
          :page template
          :csrf-token *anti-forgery-token*
          :servlet-context *app-context*)))
    "text/html; charset=utf-8"))
```

```
(defn error-page
  "error-details should be a map containing the following keys:
   :status - error status
   :title - error title (optional)
   :message - detailed error message (optional)

   returns a response map with the error page as the body
   and the status specified by the status key"
  [error-details]
  {:status  (:status error-details)
   :headers {"Content-Type" "text/html; charset=utf-8"}
   :body    (parser/render-file "error.html" error-details)})
```

The namespace declares the *app-context* variable. This variable is dynamically bound by the guestbook.middleware/wrap-context middleware either to the value of the :servlet-context key in the request map or the :app-context environment variable.

JVM servlet containers allow us to run multiple web applications on the same server. When that is the case, each application is assigned its own context as its unique identifier.[5] The context is then used by the server to route requests and responses to the appropriate applications.

Alternatively, we may wish to front multiple applications using a server such as Apache or Nginx. In this case each application could have its own context, and any requests from the browser will be required to include that context as part of the URL. This allows you to run multiple applications without having to set up subdomains for each one.

Next, the resource path is set to the resources/templates folder. This sets the base template directory for the Selmer HTML templating library. Without setting the variable, we'd have to prefix all template names with templates/.

Following the parser/set-resource-path! call, a custom tag is defined for the CSRF field. We already saw this tag in action when we submitted the form in the last chapter.

Next, a filter is added for processing Markdown content in the HTML templates. We'll take a closer look at how tags and filters work shortly.

The render function sets some default keys on the context map used to generate the HTML from the template. Since these keys are common to all pages, it makes sense to keep them centralized in one place. The result of the function is a regular response map with the rendered template string set as the body.

---

5.   http://docs.oracle.com/javaee/7/api/javax/servlet/ServletContext.html

We call it when we render our page in the guestbook.routes.home/home-page function. It accepts the name of the template file located under resources/templates and an optional map of context variables that will be used to inject dynamic content in the template.

Finally, we have the error-page function that provides a common layout for rendering error pages in our application. This function is used to generate the 404 page in the handler, the 500 page for server errors, and the 403 page by the anti-forgery middleware.

The function accepts a map that contains the :status, the :title, and the :message keys. These are passed to the resources/templates/error.html template in order to generate the error page.

Defining Pages

The pages are defined by creating routes that accept the request parameters and generate the appropriate response. A route can return HTML markup, perform a server-side operation, redirect to a different page, or return a specific type of data, such as a JSON string or a file.

In many cases a page will have multiple route components. One route responds to GET requests and returns HTML to be rendered by the browser. The rest handle events such as form submissions generated by the client when the user interacts with the page.

The page body can be generated by any means we choose, and Compojure is agnostic about the method we use. This leaves us with the option of using any templating library we like; we have several to choose from. Some popular choices are Hiccup, Enlive, and Selmer.[6,7,8]

Hiccup uses Clojure data structures to define the markup and generates the corresponding HTML from it. Enlive takes the opposite approach of defining pages using pure HTML, without the use of any special processing tags. The HTML templates are then transformed by adapters specific to your models and domains. Selmer is modeled on the Django template system from Python and uses template tags to inject dynamic content into the page.[9]

In this book we'll primarily focus on using Selmer for server-side templates. Later on we'll also see how to write single-page applications (SPAs) where

---

6. https://github.com/weavejester/hiccup
7. https://github.com/cgrand/enlive
8. https://github.com/yogthos/Selmer
9. https://docs.djangoproject.com/en/dev/ref/templates/

most of the templating is done on the client.[10] The SPA approach nicely separates your application's client and server components. Keeping the UI logic in the browser also facilitates using other clients, such as native mobile applications, with the server.

Regardless of your favorite templating strategy, it's good practice not to mix domain logic with views. In a properly designed application, it should be relatively easy to swap out one templating engine for another.

Managing Stateful Components

Most applications will rely on stateful external resources such as database connections and queues. These resources often have a life cycle associated with them. Typically, we would like to start such resources when the application initializes and stop them when it shuts down.

One popular approach for managing stateful resources in object-oriented languages is to use a dependency injection framework. This approach can also be used in Clojure using the Component library. It's a solid approach. One major downside is that it requires us to structure our app around it.[11]

Another problem with Component is that stateful resources are described using protocols. This doesn't play well with the REPL workflow, because changes to defrecord declarations do not affect the instances that have already been created. The app needs to be reloaded in order to make sure that the REPL is in a good state. I find that the reloaded workflow used with Component is much closer to TDD than the traditional Lisp-style, REPL-driven workflow.

One of the advantages of working with a language like Clojure is that we have an interactive development environment available to us. REPL-driven development provides a much tighter feedback loop than TDD. Using this approach, we can develop the features interactively and then create the tests based on the REPL session once the code is doing what's needed.

In order to facilitate a REPL-driven workflow, Luminus uses the Mount library to manage the life cycle of stateful resources in the application. This library treats resources as variables bound to namespaces. Naturally, this means that we should be careful regarding how we access these variables.

Conceptually, Mount takes the approach of encapsulating stateful resources using namespaces. This leads to a natural separation between the code that deals with state from the pure core of the application business logic.

---

10. http://en.wikipedia.org/wiki/Single-page_application
11. https://github.com/stuartsierra/component

I think it helps to treat the core business logic as you would a library. It should be completely agnostic regarding where the data is coming from and where it's going. We should never pass resources directly to our business logic when writing a non-trivial apps. Instead, we should create a thin layer that deals with external resources and calls the business logic to process the data.

Separating the business logic from the code that interacts with state also helps ensure that the majority of the code in the application is reusable outside the application as well.

Keeping the logic that deals with IO at the edges of our application allows us to keep most of the code pure. This makes it possible to test most code without needing to access the external resources or create mocks in their place.

Luminus encourages keeping related logic close together. Therefore, in cases where we have functions that rely on an external resource, the management of the state for that resource should ideally be handled in the same namespace where the functions using it are defined. A namespace that contains a stateful resource with the functions that operate on it is analogous to an instance of a class in object-oriented languages.

Mount uses the defstate declarations to identify stateful resources. It then leverages the Clojure compiler to infer the order for starting and stopping the resources based on the namespace hierarchy. This approach allows us to use the Clojure compiler itself as the dependency injection mechanism.

For example, if namespace A contains a resource and depends on namespace B, which contains another resource, then state B will be started before state A. Conversely, the resources are stopped in the reverse order of the one they're started in. Let's take a closer look at how the state of the HTTP server in the guestbook.core namespace is managed.

guestbook/src/clj/guestbook/core.clj

```
(mount/defstate ^{:on-reload :noop}
            http-server
            :start
            (http/start
              (-> env
                  (assoc :handler (handler/app))
                  (update :port #(or (-> env :options :port) %))))
            :stop
            (http/stop http-server))
```

The server instance is defined as the http-server var that's declared using the defstate macro. The :start key calls the http/start function. This function returns an instance of the running server. The :stop key calls the http/stop function and passes it the http-server. These two functions are called by Mount when the mount.core/start and mount.core/stop functions are called, respectively.

Finally, note that the ^{:on-reload :noop} annotation is used to indicate that the component should not be restarted on reload. This allows the server to retain its state when namespaces are reloaded during development.

As you can see, the defstate macro provides an elegant way to manage resource life cycle. It doesn't require us to manage the dependencies manually or to pass a dependency graph around by hand. However, it can be useful to see the generated graph visually. This can be accomplished by running the states-with-deps function found in the mount.tools.graph namespace.

```
(require '[mount.tools.graph :as graph])
(graph/states-with-deps)
({:name "#'guestbook.config/env",
  :order 1,
  :status #{:started},
  :deps #{}}
 {:name "#'guestbook.db.core/*db*",
  :order 2,
  :status #{:started},
  :deps #{"#'guestbook.config/env"}}
 {:name "#'guestbook.core/http-server",
  :order 3,
  :status #{:started},
  :deps #{"#'guestbook.config/env"}}
 {:name "#'guestbook.core/repl-server",
  :order 4,
  :status #{:started},
  :deps #{"#'guestbook.config/env"}})
```

We can see that the env state is started first and has no dependencies, *db* is started second since it depends on env, and so on.

Mount lets us start only the specified states, as seen in the guestbook.test.db.core namespace. Since we only need the env and the *db* resources for testing the database, we omit starting other resources, such as the HTTP server.

guestbook/test/clj/guestbook/test/db/core.clj

```
(use-fixtures
  :once
  (fn [f]
    (mount/start
      #'guestbook.config/env
      #'guestbook.db.core/*db*)
    (migrations/migrate ["migrate"] (select-keys env [:database-url]))
    (f)))
```

Conversely, we can choose to start and stop Mount with specific states omitted, as seen in the user namespace.

guestbook/env/dev/clj/user.clj

```
(ns user
  (:require [mount.core :as mount]
            guestbook.core))
(defn start []
  (mount/start-without #'guestbook.core/repl-server))
(defn stop []
  (mount/stop-except #'guestbook.core/repl-server))
(defn restart []
  (stop)
  (start))
```

This covers all the basics of how Mount is used in Luminus, but I encourage you to explore its other features at a later time.

What You've Learned

In this chapter you learned about the general layout of a Luminus application and how different pieces interact with one another. Hopefully, you're now comfortable reading and understanding the code in the guestbook project we created in Chapter 1, *Getting Your Feet Wet*, on page 1. If this isn't the case, I urge you to reread this chapter and try the examples yourself using the REPL environment.

So far we've focused on building a traditional application, where all the logic lives on the server and the client simply renders the HTML generated by the back end. In the next chapter we'll revisit our guestbook project and see how it could be implemented as a single-page application (SPA) using ClojureScript for client-side scripting.[12]

---

12. https://en.wikipedia.org/wiki/Single-page_application

CHAPTER 4

Add ClojureScript

In the preceding chapters you wrote a typical web application and learned how its components interact with one another. For example, you now know how to manage the routes, write HTML templates, and use sessions to manage user state. In this chapter we'll look at ClojureScript and see how to use it to improve the way we write web applications.

As you've probably noticed, the separation between the client and the server portions of the application is not enforced. If we're not careful, we could easily end up with tightly coupled client and server components. This could become a problem if we want to add a different client later on—for example, if we decided to create a native mobile version of our application.

Up to now, we've been using Clojure exclusively on the back end. In this chapter we'll look at ClojureScript, a dialect of Clojure that compiles to JavaScript, bringing Clojure to the browser. Let's look at some specifics of why you might want to use ClojureScript for front-end development.

Understand ClojureScript

If you've worked with JavaScript, you've probably concluded that it has a few shortcomings. On the other hand, JavaScript does have the advantage of being a standard programmable environment for all of the modern browsers. JavaScript engines have been improving their performance dramatically as the demand for rich client-side applications continues to grow.

It would be nice to leverage this platform with a robust programming language like Clojure, wouldn't it? This is precisely where ClojureScript comes into play. Much like its cousin Clojure, ClojureScript embraces its hosting platform and allows seamless interoperability with JavaScript. We can continue leveraging mature JavaScript libraries while enjoying the benefits of Clojure language semantics.

Finally, if you're using Clojure on the server, then it's possible to share code between the server and the client. One example where this is useful is validation logic that can now be written in a single place.

You should be aware of a few issues when using ClojureScript. Since Clojure-Script runs in the browser, you can't leverage any code that relies on interfacing with Java. The syntax for interop with JavaScript is also slightly different from that for interacting with Java. Keep those facts in mind, though, and you'll be fine.

JavaScript Interop

Interacting with JavaScript turns out to be remarkably straightforward. You can access any standard JavaScript functions using the js namespace. For example, if you want to make a logger that logs in to the console, you can write something like the following:

```
(defn log [& items]
  (.log js/console (apply str items)))
```

One thing that's not obvious is the interaction with JavaScript object properties. To access these, we use (.-property obj) notation, where the hyphen (-) indicates that we're referencing a property and not a function. We update properties by calling the set! function. Here's an example:

```
(defn init []
  (let [canvas (.getElementById js/document "canvas")
        ctx    (.getContext canvas "2d")
        width  (.-width canvas)
        height (.-height canvas)]
    (.log js/console (str "width: " width " height: " height))
    ;;set a property
    (set! (.-fillStyle ctx) "black")
    (.fillRect ctx 0 0 width height)))
```

In the preceding example we call the getElementById and the getContext methods the same way we would call Java methods in Clojure. However, we access the width and height properties using the ClojureScript-specific .- interop syntax. We set the .-fillStyle property to the "black" string by calling the set! helper.

Macros

Another way ClojureScript differs from Clojure is that you have to reference macros with the :require-macros keyword in your namespace declaration:

```
(ns my.app
  (:require-macros [app.macros :refer [fancy-macro]]))
```

Furthermore, you can't mix macros with regular ClojureScript source inside .cljs files. You have to place them inside .clj files in order for them to be compiled by the Clojure compiler instead.

Concurrency

While ClojureScript supports atoms, it has no software transactional memory and therefore no refs or agents. The binding semantics are slightly different as well, because there are no vars or runtime reification. Aside from these differences, development in ClojureScript is very similar to that in regular Clojure.

Aside from these differences, development in ClojureScript is very similar to that in regular Clojure. However, if you're new to Clojure and ClojureScript, then I recommend exploring the official ClojureScript documentation before moving on.[1]

Configure ClojureScript

ClojureScript leverages the Google Closure compiler.[2] The compiler can perform a number of optimizations, such as dead code pruning, to produce lean JavaScript output.

You leverage the Google Closure library to provide a rich API for common tasks, such as handling AJAX requests, managing cookies, currency formatting, and so on.[3] This means that you don't need to include any additional JavaScript libraries such as jQuery in order to do most tasks.

The easiest way to add ClojureScript support to the project is by using the lein-cljsbuild plugin.[4] The plugin will compile the ClojureScript sources and output the resulting JavaScript in the specified location.

Add ClojureScript Support

Currently, our guestbook application uses server-side rendering and the browser simply displays a static page. We'll now see how to rewrite it as a single-page application (SPA) using ClojureScript.

---

1. https://github.com/clojure/clojurescript/wiki
2. https://github.com/google/closure-compiler
3. https://github.com/google/closure-library
4. https://github.com/emezeske/lein-cljsbuild

You can compile ClojureScript in development mode using a few different approaches. The simplest approach is to use the incremental compilation feature. Using this approach, the compiler will watch for changes in the source and recompile JavaScript as needed.

The downside of this approach is that you have to reload the page to see the changes. A slightly more sophisticated approach that we'll see later allows you to push the changes to the browser live without reloading the page.

The first thing we have to do is to add the ClojureScript runtime dependency to our project. Note that it's scoped as "provided." Since we are outputting compiled JavaScript, it only needs to be present for development.

```clojure
:dependencies
[...
 [org.clojure/clojurescript "1.7.228" :scope "provided"]]
```

Next, we have to update our project.clj to add the plugin and provide a default configuration for it.

guestbook-cljs/project.clj

```clojure
:plugins [[lein-cprop "1.0.1"]
          [migratus-lein "0.2.6"]
          [lein-cljsbuild "1.1.1"]]
:resource-paths ["resources" "target/cljsbuild"]
:target-path "target/%s/"
:cljsbuild
{:builds {:app {:source-paths ["src/cljs"]
               :compiler {:output-to      "target/cljsbuild/public/js/app.js"
                          :output-dir     "target/cljsbuild/public/js/out"
                          :main "guestbook.core"
                          :asset-path "/js/out"
                          :optimizations :none
                          :source-map true
                          :pretty-print  true}}}}
:clean-targets
^{:protect false}
[:target-path
 [:cljsbuild :builds :app :compiler :output-dir]
 [:cljsbuild :builds :app :compiler :output-to]]
```

The compiler configuration has the following options and compiler hints:

- :source-paths—Specifies where to find ClojureScript source files

- :resource-paths—Specifies the paths to static assets, such as the generated JavaScript files produced by the ClojureScript build

- :main—Used by the compiler to find the entry point for the compiled app

- :asset-path—Used to specify where to look for supporting JavaScript assets

- :output-to—Outputs the name of the resulting JavaScript file

- :output-dir—Specifies where the temporary JavaScript files will be generated

- :source-map—Used to map from the compiled JavaScript to the original ClojureScript source

Finally, we also added a :clean-targets key below the :cljsbuild key. This tells Leiningen that we would like to delete any JavaScript that is generated in the target/cljsbuild folder when lein clean is run.

We're now ready to create a new source folder and a ClojureScript namespace called guestbook.core in src/cljs/guestbook/core.cljs. Note that the ClojureScript extension is .cljs, as opposed to the .clj extension for Clojure files. If the file ends with .clj it will still compile, but it will not have access to the JavaScript runtime.

We start by putting the obligatory "Hello, World!" on the page to make sure everything is working correctly. To do that we update the namespace with the following code:

```
(ns guestbook.core)
(-> (.getElementById js/document "content")
    (.-innerHTML)
    (set! "Hello, World!"))
```

When the script runs it will find the tag with the ID content on the page and set its inner HTML to "Hello, World!" Next, let's replace the contents of the resources/templates/home.html template with a div with the ID content.

```
{% extends "base.html" %}
{% block content %}
<div id="content"></div>
{% endblock %}
```

Finally, we update the resources/templates/base.html template to load the compiled ClojureScript. Let's replace all the JavaScript libraries that are currently included with the app.js script that contains our compiled applications.

guestbook-cljs/resources/templates/base.html

```
<script type="text/javascript">
  var context = "{{servlet-context}}";
</script>
{% script "/js/app.js" %}
{% block page-scripts %}
{% endblock %}
```

We're now ready to see if our setup works. To do that we have to run the server as we've been doing up to now, and in addition we run the ClojureScript compiler to generate the app.js file we're referencing in the template. The following commands compile ClojureScript and start the server, respectively.

```
lein cljsbuild once
lein run
```

If everything went well, you should now see the "Hello, World!" text displayed when the page loads.

Build the UI with Reagent

Reagent is a ClojureScript UI component library built on top of the popular Facebook React library.[5] Reagent provides a way to define UI elements using Hiccup-style syntax for DOM representation.[6,7] Each UI component is a data structure that represents a particular DOM element. By taking a DOM-centric view of the UI, Reagent provides a way to write composable components.

To build our UI, we first add the Reagent dependency to our project:

```
:dependencies
[...
 [reagent "0.5.1"]]
```

Let's start the lein-cljsbuild plugin using the auto mode so that it watches for changes in the source and automatically recompiles it as we go. Nothing to it. Just open a new terminal and run the following command:

```
lein cljsbuild auto
```

The plugin now waits for you to make changes and recompile the relevant source files. Note that the compiler uses incremental compilation. Once the compiler finishes the initial compilation, any further changes are recompiled nearly instantly. Now that we have the compiler running, let's create some Reagent components and see how we can use them to replicate our existing UI being rendered by the server.

In order to use Reagent, you first have to include it in your namespace. Let's open up the guestbook.core ClojureScript namespace. Recall that it is found in the src/cljs source folder and not the src folder that contains the Clojure source files. Update the namespace declaration to include the following reference:

---

5.   https://facebook.github.io/react/blog/2015/12/18/react-components-elements-and-instances.html

6.   https://github.com/weavejester/hiccup

7.   http://facebook.github.io/react/

```
(ns guestbook.core
  (:require [reagent.core :as reagent :refer [atom]]))
```

You'll note that we're referencing the atom from Reagent instead of using the regular ClojureScript atom. Reagent atoms behave the same way as regular atoms, with one important difference: any UI components that reference Reagent atoms will be repainted whenever the value of the atom is changed. When we want to create a local or a global state we create an atom to hold it.

This approach automates the process of keeping the UI in sync with the model. With Reagent we're able to write our UI in a declarative fashion and have it automatically render the current state of our model. That's the idea; now let's see it in practice. We can begin to see exactly how all this works by implementing the form in our guestbook application using Reagent.

Reagent Components

Reagent uses plain Clojure vectors to define UI elements, so you don't have to learn a separate domain-specific language. Let's create a simple component that displays the contents of our page.

```
(defn home []
  [:h2 "Hello, Reagent"])
```

We now have to tell Reagent to render this component on the page. We do that by calling the render function, providing it the component and the target DOM node.

```
(reagent/render
  [home]
  (.getElementById js/document "content"))
```

At this point our namespace should look like this:

```
(ns guestbook.core
  (:require [reagent.core :as reagent :refer [atom]]))

(defn home []
  [:h2 "Hello, Reagent"])

(reagent/render
  [home]
  (.getElementById js/document "content"))
```

We can take a look at the terminal where the ClojureScript compiler is running and see a message that looks like the following:

```
Compiling "target/cljsbuild/public/js/app.js" from ["src/cljs"]...
Successfully compiled "target/cljsbuild/public/js/app.js" in 0.057 seconds.
```

This indicates that a recompilation of ClojureScript was triggered, and when we reload the page we should see the "Hello Reagent" text rendered.

The HTML nodes are represented using a vector with the structure corresponding to that of the resulting HTML tag, as shown in the following example:

```
[:tag-name {:attribute-key "attribute value"} tag body]
```

```
<tag-name attribute-key="attribute value">tag body</tag-name>
```

If you wanted to create a div with a paragraph in it, you could create a vector, where the first element is a keyword :div, followed by the map containing the ID and the div's class. The rest of the content consists of a vector representing the paragraph.

```
[:div {:id "hello", :class "content"} [:p "Hello, World!"]]
```

```
<div id="hello" class="content"><p>Hello, World!</p></div>
```

Since it's easy to set element attributes via the attribute map, you could style elements inline if you wanted. However, you should resist this temptation and instead use a CSS to style elements. Using a CSS ensures that the structure is kept separate from the presentation.

Setting the id and the class attributes for elements is a very common operation. Reagent provides CSS-style shortcuts for these actions. Instead of what we wrote earlier, we could simply write our div as follows:

```
[:div#hello.content [:p "Hello, World!"]]
```

Reagent also provides syntactic sugar for collapsing nested tags into a single tag. The preceding code could be rewritten this way:

```
[:div#hello.content>p "Hello, World!"]
```

The > indicates that the p tag is nested inside the div tag. This syntax sugar is very helpful with CSS frameworks, such as Bootstrap, that rely on deeply nested tags to style elements.

As you can see, creating Reagent components takes very little code and produces output markup that's easy to correlate back to the template definitions.

Reimplementing the Form

By this point you should have an understanding of how you can create different kinds of HTML elements using Reagent. Now let's take a look at how you can hook them up with some data. The form that allows users to input their names and a message will be bound to an atom that will contain the entered values.

So far we've only looked at components that directly represent HTML. However, Reagent allows you to treat any function as a component. The function simply has to return either a Reagent vector or a component that can be rendered by React directly. The latter becomes useful when you want to use React libraries or create your own custom components. Let's not worry about that just yet, though.

In our case, let's create a function called message-form. The function uses a let statement to create a binding for the atom that contains the form data. It then returns a function that generates the form and references the previously defined atom in the input fields of the following component:

```
(defn message-form []
  (let [fields (atom {})]
    (fn []
      [:div.content
       [:div.form-group
        [:p "Name:"
         [:input.form-control
          {:type :text
           :name :name
           :on-change #(swap! fields assoc :name (-> % .-target .-value))
           :value (:name @fields)}]]
        [:p "Message:"
        [:textarea.form-control
         {:rows 4
          :cols 50
          :name :message
          :value (:message @fields)
          :on-change #(swap! fields assoc :message (-> % .-target .-value))}]]
        [:input.btn.btn-primary {:type :submit :value "comment"}]]]])))
```

Note that we're using a closure to create a local state for the fields binding and then return a function that references it. Reagent calls the returned function on subsequent re-renders of the component, and the local state is preserved.

Aside from that, the content of the form should look very familiar, since it closely mimics the HTML we used previously. The changes to note are that we've changed the form element to a div, and in addition we've added the :on-change key to bind the input and the textarea elements to functions that are responsible for updating the fields atom with the current values entered by the user. These functions accept the DOM event object as their input and grab the value from its target. Since we're now using a div as the container, we also have to update our CSS accordingly.

```
.content {
    background: white;
    width: 520px;
    padding: 30px;
}
.error {
    width: 520px;
    padding: 30px;
    margin-bottom: 50px;
    position: relative;
    background: white;
}
```

This component can now be used in our home function, as shown here:

```
(defn home []
 [:div.row
  [:div.span12
   [message-form]]])
```

Note that we're placing the message-form in a vector instead of calling it as a function, as we normally would. This allows Reagent to decide when the function needs to be evaluated in case the component has to be repainted. The components can now be reevaluated as the state of their corresponding atoms changes. We'll see how this becomes important shortly.

We should now be able to reload the page and see the form rendered there looking very much like the form we had previously. We can even type text in the fields, but we obviously can't see that it's being stored anywhere. Let's modify the form to convince ourselves that the inputs are actually writing the data to our fields atom by adding the following element to it:

```
(defn message-form []
 (let [fields (atom {})]
   (fn []
     [:div.content
      [:div.form-group
      [:p "name:" (:name @fields)]
      [:p "message:" (:message @fields)]
      [:p "Name:"
      ...
```

Now we can clearly see that whenever the value of the name or the message field changes, it is immediately reflected in the atom. Once the value of the atom changes, then the component will be repainted and we'll see the new values displayed on the screen.

Talking to the Server

At this point we'd like to take the values of the fields and send them to the server when we click the comment button. We'll use the cljs-ajax library to communicate with the server. The first thing we need to do is to add a dependency for it in our project.clj file.[8]

guestbook-cljs/project.clj

```
[cljs-ajax "0.5.2"]
[reagent "0.5.1"]
[org.clojure/clojurescript "1.7.228" :scope "provided"]
```

Once the library is added we have to clean out the existing generated Java-Script and restart the ClojureScript compiler by rerunning these commands:

```
lein clean
lein cljsbuild auto
```

We can now add the following reference in our namespace declaration [ajax.core :refer [GET POST]]:

```
(ns guestbook.core
  (:require [reagent.core :as reagent :refer [atom]]
            [ajax.core :refer [GET POST]]))
```

This allows us to call GET and POST functions in order to talk to our server. We can now write a function that attempts to submit the information in our form.

```
(defn send-message! [fields]
  (POST "/message"
        {:params @fields
         :handler #(.log js/console (str "response:" %))
         :error-handler #(.error js/console (str "error:" %))}))
```

The preceding function will attempt to POST to the /message route using the value of the fields atom as the params and print the response to the console. The function uses the :handler and the :error-handler keys to handle the success and the error responses, respectively. For now, let's just print a message to the console in both cases. We can now hook this function up to our Submit button by using the :on-click key, as seen in the following example:

```
[:input.btn.btn-primary
  {:type :submit
   :on-click #(send-message! fields)
   :value "comment"}]
```

---

8. https://github.com/JulianBirch/cljs-ajax

Let's check the terminal to see that our ClojureScript recompiled successfully and then reload the browser window. When the page reloads, open up the browser console and click on the comment button. You should see the following error in the console as a result:

```
error:{:status 403,
       :status-text "Forbidden",
       :failure :error,
       :response "<h1>Invalid anti-forgery token</h1>"}
```

The error indicates that we did not supply the anti-forgery token in our request. If you recall, the server has anti-forgery protection enabled and requires the client to submit the token generated on the page to be submitted in the POST request. Previously, we used the {% csrf-field %} tag in our template to supply the token. Since we're now using an Ajax call, we have to provide this field manually.

In order to do that, we first have to update our home.html template to create a hidden field with the value of the token:

guestbook-cljs/resources/templates/home.html

```
{% extends "base.html" %}
{% block content %}
<input id="token" type="hidden" value="{{csrf-token}}">
<div id="content"></div>
{% endblock %}
```

We set this token as a header on our request using the x-csrf-token key, as seen in the following version of the send-message! function.

```
(defn send-message! [fields]
  (POST "/message"
        {:format :json
         :headers
         {"Accept" "application/transit+json"
          "x-csrf-token" (.-value (.getElementById js/document "token"))}
         :params @fields
         :handler #(.log js/console (str "response:" %))
         :error-handler #(.log js/console (str "error:" %))}))
```

We also set the Accept header to application/transit+json to tell the server we'd like to get the response encoded using Transit.[9] This allows encoding the data using the native EDN format.[10] The advantage of this is it encodes data using Clojure data structures, thus preserving types such as keywords and dates.

---

9.   https://github.com/cognitect/transit-format
10.   https://github.com/edn-format/edn

We're not quite done yet, however. Previously, we've sent our parameters to the server using a form POST. The parameters were sent in the request body and looked something like the following:

```
x-csrf-token=%2F4wIVStDj9Fl...4PsKx&name=Bob&message=Hello
```

The ring-anti-forgery middleware would then have checked the value of the x-csrf-token header to determine whether the request was valid.[11]

Our original code for the /message route used the redirect function to display the page after attempting to add the message. This time around we want to return a JSON response indicating success or failure. We need to add the following references in order to generate the appropriate responses.

```
[ring.util.response :refer [response status]]
```

With that in place, we can update our save-message! functions as follows:

guestbook-cljs/src/clj/guestbook/routes/home.clj

```
(defn save-message! [{:keys [params]}]
  (if-let [errors (validate-message params)]
    (response/bad-request {:errors errors})
    (try
      (db/save-message!
        (assoc params :timestamp (java.util.Date.)))
      (response/ok {:status :ok})
      (catch Exception e
        (response/internal-server-error
          {:errors {:server-error ["Failed to save message!"]}})))))
```

The updated function will return a 400 response when validation fails, a 200 response when it's saved successfully, and a 500 response in case of errors.

We can now replace the route that handles the POST request with the new URI and we should be able to test our new functionality.

```
(POST "/message" req (save-message! req))
```

Note that we do not have to manually deserialize the request nor serialize the response in our route. This is handled by the ring-middleware-format library.[12] The library checks the Content-Type header in the request and deserializes the content based on that. The response is serialized to the format specified in the Accept header. The cljs-ajax library defaults to using the transit format. If you recall, we explicitly set the Accept header to transit as well. No additional work is needed on your part.

---

11. https://github.com/ring-clojure/ring-anti-forgery
12. https://github.com/metosin/ring-middleware-format

When we try to POST invalid parameters, we should see a response in the console that looks similar to the following:

```
error:{:status 400,
       :status-text "Bad Request",
       :failure :error,
       :response {:errors {:message ("message is less than the minimum")}}}
```

When we submit a valid request, we should see the following printed instead:

```
response:{:status :ok}
```

Notice that in the first case our error-handler was triggered, while in the second case our success handler function is triggered. The cljs-ajax library uses the status code in the response to select the appropriate handler.

Now that we're communicating with the server, let's update our code to display the errors on the page:

```
(defn message-form []
  (let [fields (atom {})
        errors (atom nil)]
    (fn []
      [:div.content
       [errors-component errors :server-error]
       [:div.form-group
        [errors-component errors :name]
        [:p "Name:"
         [:input.form-control
          {:type :text
           :name :name
           :on-change #(swap! fields assoc :name (-> % .-target .-value))
           :value (:name @fields)}]]
        [errors-component errors :message]
        [:p "Message:"
        [:textarea.form-control
         {:rows 4
          :cols 50
          :name :message
          :value (:message @fields)
          :on-change #(swap! fields assoc :message (-> % .-target .-value))}]]
        [:input.btn.btn-primary
         {:type :submit
          :on-click #(send-message! fields errors)
          :value "comment"}]]])))
```

The updated code uses a second atom called errors to store any errors received from the server. We pass the errors to the send-message! function. The function now either clears the errors on success or sets the errors from the response.

```
(defn send-message! [fields errors]
  (POST "/add-message"
        {:format :json
         :headers
         {"Accept" "application/transit+json"
          "x-csrf-token" (.-value (.getElementById js/document "token"))}
         :params @fields
         :handler #(do
                     (.log js/console (str "response:" %))
                     (reset! errors nil))
         :error-handler #(do
                           (.log js/console (str %))
                           (reset! errors (get-in % [:response :errors])))}))
```

We also create a new component called errors-component. The component accepts the errors and the field ID. It checks if any errors are associated with the ID and returns an alert with the message if that's the case.

guestbook-cljs/src/cljs/guestbook/core.cljs

```
(defn errors-component [errors id]
  (when-let [error (id @errors)]
    [:div.alert.alert-danger (clojure.string/join error)]))
```

If the component sees no errors, we simply return a nil. Reagent will handle this intelligently and omit the component in that case. You can see that with the new approach the errors are showing up just as they did in the previous version.

Reimplementing the List

Now that our form is working as expected, let's turn our attention to displaying the messages on the page. In order to do that, we'll have to add a route on the server to return the list of messages, create a component to display the messages, and add a function on the client to fetch them.

Since we're no longer baking the messages in our page, we can update our home-page function to render the HTML on load without any parameters.

guestbook-cljs/src/clj/guestbook/routes/home.clj

```
(defn home-page []
  (layout/render "home.html"))
```

Next we update the home-routes to call our home-page function without passing it the request, and we add a new route to serve messages.

guestbook-cljs/src/clj/guestbook/routes/home.clj

```
(defroutes home-routes
  (GET "/" [] (home-page))
  (GET "/messages" [] (response/ok (db/get-messages)))
  (POST "/message" req (save-message! req))
  (GET "/about" [] (about-page)))
```

We can now update the client-side code to call this route when the page loads and retrieve the messages from the server.

Let's write a function called get-messages that calls our route and retrieves the messages. The function accepts an atom as a parameter and populates it with the retrieved messages in the handler.

guestbook-cljs/src/cljs/guestbook/core.cljs

```
(defn get-messages [messages]
  (GET "/messages"
       {:headers {"Accept" "application/transit+json"}
        :handler #(reset! messages (vec %))}))
```

Note that we are not required to pass the anti-forgery header for the GET requests, and we can safely omit it when retrieving messages from the server.

We can now write a component that uses the messages atom to render the messages in the same format as we had in our server-side template:

guestbook-cljs/src/cljs/guestbook/core.cljs

```
(defn message-list [messages]
  [:ul.content
   (for [{:keys [timestamp message name]} @messages]
     ^{:key timestamp}
     [:li
      [:time (.toLocaleString timestamp)]
      [:p message]
      [:p " - " name]])])
```

The only thing to note in this function is that we're using the ^{:key timestamp} annotation for each element in the ul. This allows Reagent to efficiently check if a particular element needs to be re-rendered. We could safely omit the annotation in this case, but it could result in loss of performance for big lists.

The ^{} notation is used to supply metadata in Clojure. The metadata is a map that can contain annotations for a symbol or a collection. In our case the metadata is used to provide a unique identifier key for each item in the collection.[13]

---

13. http://clojure.org/reference/metadata

Finally, let's update our home component function to use an atom called messages to store the state of the message list. The function calls the get-messages function we wrote earlier and passes it the atom.

```
(defn home []
  (let [messages (atom nil)]
    (get-messages messages)
    (fn []
      [:div
       [:div.row
        [:div.span12
         [message-list messages]]]
       [:div.row
        [:div.span12
         [message-form]]]])))
```

The component then returns a function that renders the message-list and the message-form components. It passes the messages atom to the message-list components. The component in turn renders the current state of the atom. When the get-messages function finishes, the atom is reset with the messages and the component is repainted.

This provides us with an extremely powerful mechanism for connecting producers and consumers in our application. The get-messages and the message-list functions have no direct coupling between them and are not aware of each other. The Reagent atoms provide a way for any component to observe the current value in the model without having the knowledge of how and when it's populated.

One last thing we need to do is to add the message we submit to the server to the list of messages on the page. We can do that in the handler of the send-message! function. The function currently accepts the fields and the errors as its parameters. Let's update it to also accept the messages atom and append our message to it if the server returns a success:

guestbook-cljs/src/cljs/guestbook/core.cljs

```
(defn send-message! [fields errors messages]
  (POST "/message"
      {:headers {"Accept"       "application/transit+json"
                 "x-csrf-token" (.-value (.getElementById js/document "token"))}
       :params @fields
       :handler #(do
                   (reset! errors nil)
                   (swap! messages conj (assoc @fields :timestamp (js/Date.))))
       :error-handler #(do
                         (.log js/console (str %))
                         (reset! errors (get-in % [:response :errors])))}))
```

Our handler now can swap! the messages atom and append the fields the user entered and the timestamp set to the current date.

Now we have to update the form function to accept the messages, and the home function to pass the messages to it as a parameter:

guestbook-cljs/src/cljs/guestbook/core.cljs

```
(defn errors-component [errors id]
  (when-let [error (id @errors)]
    [:div.alert.alert-danger (clojure.string/join error)]))

(defn message-form [messages]
  (let [fields (atom {})
        errors (atom nil)]
    (fn []
      [:div.content
       [errors-component errors :server-error]
       [:div.form-group
        [errors-component errors :name]
        [:p "Name:"
         [:input.form-control
          {:type      :text
           :name      :name
           :on-change #(swap! fields assoc :name (-> % .-target .-value))
           :value     (:name @fields)}]]
        [errors-component errors :message]
        [:p "Message:"
         [:textarea.form-control
          {:rows      4
           :cols      50
           :name      :message
           :value     (:message @fields)
           :on-change #(swap! fields assoc :message (-> % .-target .-value))}]]
        [:input.btn.btn-primary
         {:type      :submit
          :on-click #(send-message! fields errors messages)
          :value     "comment"}]]])))
```

guestbook-cljs/src/cljs/guestbook/core.cljs

```
(defn home []
  (let [messages (atom nil)]
    (get-messages messages)
    (fn []
      [:div
       [:div.row
        [:div.span12
         [message-list messages]]]
       [:div.row
        [:div.span12
         [message-form messages]]]])))
```

The message will be appended to the list of displayed messages when the server acknowledges that it was saved successfully. Unlike with the previous version of the app, we do not have to reload the entire page or even the list of messages. We simply add the new message to the list, and Reagent takes care of repainting the component for us.

Using atoms to coordinate different components is a common pattern in Reagent. Since the atoms can either be created as global variables or within individual components, we have a lot of flexibility in how we manage the state of the application.

A good rule of thumb is to keep the application state in a global atom and to use local atoms to manage the local states of the components. Such states might include the currently selected item in a list to indicate the state of a button or to handle local notifications, as we did earlier with errors. Ideally, the components should not directly reference the application state and it should be passed in as a parameter instead. This approach maximizes the reusability of components since you can instantiate them with different data in different parts of the application.

Let's take a look at the components we created for some concrete examples. The message-list component accepts the messages as a parameter. This makes it possible to use it in different parts of the UI to display different sets of messages. For example, you might want to display messages for a specific user later on and you wouldn't have to create a new component to do that.

The message-form component also accepts the messages as its parameter; however, it creates local atoms called the fields and the errors. These represent the local concerns of the message-form that are not part of the overall workflow in our application. Therefore it makes sense to keep these local to the component.

The home component is the root of our UI that manages the messages atom and passes it to its children as a parameter. Once again, it's important to note that it doesn't call the components; it places them in vectors. This allows Reagent to decide when these components should be reevaluated based on the state of the messages atom.

What You've Learned

In this chapter you've learned how using ClojureScript can make your app cleaner. In the next chapter, we'll look at using WebSockets to facilitate asynchronous communication between the client and the server. With Web-Sockets, the server is able to send push notifications to the client when server-side events occur.

CHAPTER 5

Real-Time Messaging with WebSockets

In this chapter we'll take a look at using WebSockets for client-server communication. In the traditional Ajax approach, the client first sends a message to the server and then handles the reply using an asynchronous callback. WebSockets provide the ability for the web server to initiate the message exchange with the client.

Currently, our guestbook application does not provide a way to display messages generated by other users without reloading the page. If we wanted to solve this problem using Ajax, our only option would be to poll the server and check if any new messages are available since the last poll. This is inefficient since the clients end up continuously polling the server regardless of whether any new messages are actually available.

Instead, we'll have the clients open a WebSocket connection when the page loads, and then the server will notify all the active clients any time a new message is created. This way the clients are notified in real time and the messages are only sent as needed.

Set Up WebSockets on the Server

WebSockets require support on both the server and the client side. While the browser API is standard, each server provides its own way of handling WebSocket connections. In this section we'll take a look at using the API for the Immutant web server that Luminus defaults to.

Let's start by updating the server-side code in the project to provide a WebSocket connection. Once the server is updated we'll look at the updates required for the client.

Add WebSocket Routes

The first thing we'll do is create a new namespace for handling WebSocket connections. Let's call this namespace guestbook.routes.ws and put the following references in its declaration.

guestbook-websockets/src/clj/guestbook/routes/ws.clj

```
(ns guestbook.routes.ws
  (:require [compojure.core :refer [GET defroutes]]
            [clojure.tools.logging :as log]
            [immutant.web.async :as async]
            [cognitect.transit :as transit]
            [bouncer.core :as b]
            [bouncer.validators :as v]
            [guestbook.db.core :as db]))
```

The immutant.web.async reference is the namespace that provides the functions necessary to manage the life cycle of the WebSocket connection.

The cognitect.transit namespace provides the functions to encode and decode messages using the transit format. When we used Ajax, the middleware was able to serialize and deserialize the messages automatically based on the content type; however, we'll have to do that manually for messages sent over the WebSocket.

Since we'll be saving messages, we need to reference the bouncer and the database namespaces so that we can move over the validate-message and the save-message! functions that we originally used in the guestbook.routes.home namespace.

The server needs to keep track of all the channels for the clients that are currently connected in order to push notifications. Let's use an atom containing a set for this purpose.

guestbook-websockets/src/clj/guestbook/routes/ws.clj

```
(defonce channels (atom #{}))
```

Next, we need to implement a callback function to handle the different states that the WebSocket can be in, such as when the connection is opened and closed. We want to add the channel to the set of open connections when a client connects, and we want to remove the associated channel when the client disconnects.

guestbook-websockets/src/clj/guestbook/routes/ws.clj

```
(defn connect! [channel]
  (log/info "channel open")
  (swap! channels conj channel))
```

```clojure
(defn disconnect! [channel {:keys [code reason]}]
  (log/info "close code:" code "reason:" reason)
  (swap! channels clojure.set/difference #{channel}))
```

As mentioned earlier, the messages have to be encoded and decoded manually. Let's create a couple of helper functions for that purpose.

guestbook-websockets/src/clj/guestbook/routes/ws.clj

```clojure
(defn encode-transit [message]
  (let [out    (java.io.ByteArrayOutputStream. 4096)
        writer (transit/writer out :json)]
    (transit/write writer message)
    (.toString out)))

(defn decode-transit [message]
  (let [in (java.io.ByteArrayInputStream. (.getBytes message))
        reader (transit/reader in :json)]
    (transit/read reader)))
```

When the client sends a message, we'll want to validate it and attempt to save the message, as we did earlier. Let's take the save-message! and the validate-message function from the guestbook.routes.home and move them over to the new namespace. The save-message! function no longer needs to generate a Ring response, so we have it return the result directly instead.

guestbook-websockets/src/clj/guestbook/routes/ws.clj

```clojure
(defn validate-message [params]
  (first
    (b/validate
      params
      :name v/required
      :message [v/required [v/min-count 10]])))

(defn save-message! [message]
  (if-let [errors (validate-message message)]
    {:errors errors}
    (do
      (db/save-message! message)
      message)))
```

Finally, we create the handle-message! function that will be called when the client sends a message to the server. When the message is saved successfully, we notify all the connected clients; when any errors occur we notify only the client that sent the original message.

guestbook-websockets/src/clj/guestbook/routes/ws.clj

```clojure
(defn handle-message! [channel message]
  (let [response (-> message
                     decode-transit
```

```
                    (assoc :timestamp (java.util.Date.))
                    save-message!)]
      (if (:errors response)
        (async/send! channel (encode-transit response))
        (doseq [channel @channels]
          (async/send! channel (encode-transit response)))))))
```

The function accepts the channel of the client that sent the message along with the message payload. The message has to be decoded using the decode-transit function that we wrote earlier. The result should be a map with the same keys as before. Let's associate the timestamp and attempt to save the message to the database using the save-message! function.

When the response map contains the :error key, we notify the client on the channel that was passed in; otherwise we notify all clients in the channels atom. The response is sent using the async/send! call that accepts the channel and the message as a string, so we have to call encode-transit on the response before it's passed to async/send!.

Now that we've implemented all the callbacks, let's put these in a map and pass it to the async/as-channel function that will create the actual WebSocket channel. This is done in the ws-handler function that follows.

guestbook-websockets/src/clj/guestbook/routes/ws.clj

```
(defn ws-handler [request]
  (async/as-channel
    request
    {:on-open    connect!
     :on-close   disconnect!
     :on-message handle-message!}))
```

All that's left to do is create the route definition using the defroutes macro, just as we would with any other Compojure routes.

guestbook-websockets/src/clj/guestbook/routes/ws.clj

```
(defroutes websocket-routes
          (GET "/ws" [] ws-handler))
```

Note that we could define multiple WebSockets and assign them to different routes. In our case we have just a single /ws route for our socket.

Now that we've migrated the code for saving messages to the guestbook.routes.ws namespace, we can clean up the guestbook.routes.home namespace as follows.

guestbook-websockets/src/clj/guestbook/routes/home.clj

```
(ns guestbook.routes.home
  (:require [guestbook.layout :as layout]
            [guestbook.db.core :as db]
```

```
              [bouncer.core :as b]
              [bouncer.validators :as v]
              [compojure.core :refer [defroutes GET POST]]
              [ring.util.response :refer [response status]]]))
(defn home-page []
  (layout/render "home.html"))

(defn about-page []
  (layout/render "about.html"))

(defroutes home-routes
  (GET "/" [] (home-page))
  (GET "/messages" [] (response (db/get-messages)))
  (GET "/about" [] (about-page)))
```

Update the Handler

Now that we've added the new routes, we need to navigate to the guestbook.handler namespace, reference the new namespace, and add the routes to the app-routes definition.

```
(ns guestbook.handler
  (:require ...
            [guestbook.routes.ws :refer [websocket-routes]]))
```

guestbook-websockets/src/clj/guestbook/handler.clj

```
(def app-routes
  (routes
    #'websocket-routes
    (wrap-routes #'home-routes middleware/wrap-csrf)
    (route/not-found
      (:body
        (error-page {:status 404
                     :title "page not found"})))))
(def app (middleware/wrap-base #'app-routes))
```

We're now done with all the necessary server-side changes to facilitate Web-Socket connections. Let's turn our attention to the client.

Make WebSockets from ClojureScript

Now that we've created a WebSocket route on the server, we need to write the client-side portion of the socket. Once that's done we'll have full-duplex communication between the server and the client.

Create the WebSocket

Let's start by creating a namespace called guestbook.ws for the WebSocket client. This namespace will be responsible for creating a socket as well as for sending and receiving messages over it. In the namespace declaration, let's add a reference to cognitect.transit.

guestbook-websockets/src/cljs/guestbook/ws.cljs

```
(ns guestbook.ws
  (:require [cognitect.transit :as t]))
```

Next, let's create an atom to house the channel for the socket and add helpers for reading and writing transit-encoded messages.

guestbook-websockets/src/cljs/guestbook/ws.cljs

```
(defonce ws-chan (atom nil))
(def json-reader (t/reader :json))
(def json-writer (t/writer :json))
```

We can now add functions to receive and send transit-encoded messages using the channel. The receive-message! function is a closure that accepts a handler function and returns a function that deserializes the message before passing it to the handler.

guestbook-websockets/src/cljs/guestbook/ws.cljs

```
(defn receive-message! [handler]
  (fn [msg]
    (->> msg .-data (t/read json-reader) handler)))
```

The send-message! function checks if there's a channel available and then encodes the message to transit and sends it over the channel.

guestbook-websockets/src/cljs/guestbook/ws.cljs

```
(defn send-message! [msg]
  (if @ws-chan
    (->> msg (t/write json-writer) (.send @ws-chan))
    (throw (js/Error. "WebSocket is not available!"))))
```

Finally, let's write a function to initialize the WebSocket. The function calls js/WebSocket with the supplied URL to create the channel. Once the channel is created, it sets the onmessage callback to the supplied handler function and puts the channel in the ws-chan atom.

guestbook-websockets/src/cljs/guestbook/ws.cljs

```
(defn connect! [url receive-handler]
  (if-let [chan (js/WebSocket. url)]
    (do
      (set! (.-onmessage chan) (receive-message! receive-handler))
      (reset! ws-chan chan))
    (throw (js/Error. "WebSocket connection failed!"))))
```

As you can see, setting up a basic WebSocket connection is no more difficult than using Ajax. The main differences are that we have to manually handle serialization and that the messages received by the receive-message! function are not directly associated with the ones sent by the send-message! function.

Let's navigate back to the guestbook.core to use a WebSocket connection to communicate with the server instead of Ajax for saving and receiving messages. Noting that WebSockets and Ajax are not mutually exclusive, and we can continue using the existing Ajax call to retrieve the initial list of messages.

First, let's update the namespace declaration to remove the unused POST reference and add the guestbook.ws that we just wrote.

guestbook-websockets/src/cljs/guestbook/core.cljs

```
(ns guestbook.core
  (:require [reagent.core :as reagent :refer [atom]]
            [ajax.core :refer [GET]]
            [guestbook.ws :as ws]))
```

The functions message-list, get-messages, and errors-component remain unchanged. However, we no longer need the old send-message! function, because the messages are sent using the send-message! function from the guestbook.ws namespace.

guestbook-websockets/src/cljs/guestbook/core.cljs

```
(defn message-list [messages]
  [:ul.content
   (for [{:keys [timestamp message name]} @messages]
     ^{:key timestamp}
     [:li
      [:time (.toLocaleString timestamp)]
      [:p message]
      [:p " - " name]])])

(defn get-messages [messages]
  (GET "/messages"
       {:headers {"Accept" "application/transit+json"}
        :handler #(reset! messages (vec %))}))

(defn errors-component [errors id]
  (when-let [error (id @errors)]
    [:div.alert.alert-danger (clojure.string/join error)]))
```

The message-form function no longer needs to update the message list; it gets updated by the callback that we use to initialize the WebSocket. Conversely, we can no longer set the values of the fields and the errors, so the atoms that hold these values are passed in instead.

The form sets the values in the fields atom and displays the currently populated values in the errors atom. The comment button now sends the current value of the fields atom to the server by calling ws/send-message!.

guestbook-websockets/src/cljs/guestbook/core.cljs

```clojure
(defn message-form [fields errors]
  [:div.content
   [:div.form-group
    [errors-component errors :name]
    [:p "Name:"
     [:input.form-control
      {:type       :text
       :on-change #(swap! fields assoc :name (-> % .-target .-value))
       :value      (:name @fields)}]]
    [errors-component errors :message]
    [:p "Message:"
     [:textarea.form-control
      {:rows       4
       :cols       50
       :value      (:message @fields)
       :on-change #(swap! fields assoc :message (-> % .-target .-value))}]]
    [:input.btn.btn-primary
     {:type       :submit
      :on-click #(ws/send-message! @fields)
      :value      "comment"}]]])
```

Now let's add the response-handler function that receives the messages from the server and sets the values of the messages, the fields, and the errors atoms accordingly. Specifically, if the :errors key is present in the response, then the errors atom is set with its value. Otherwise, the errors and fields are cleared and the response is added to the list of messages.

guestbook-websockets/src/cljs/guestbook/core.cljs

```clojure
(defn response-handler [messages fields errors]
  (fn [message]
    (if-let [response-errors (:errors message)]
      (reset! errors response-errors)
      (do
        (reset! errors nil)
        (reset! fields nil)
        (swap! messages conj message)))))
```

The home function now initializes all the atoms and then passes these to the response-handler, which in turn is passed to the ws/connect! function and used to handle responses. The URL for the WebSocket is composed of the ws:// protocol definition, the host of origin, and the /ws route that we defined earlier.

Next, the function calls get-messages to load the messages currently available on the server and return a component that is used to render the page. This function remains largely unchanged aside from the fact that it passes the updated arguments to the message-form component.

guestbook-websockets/src/cljs/guestbook/core.cljs

```
(defn home []
  (let [messages (atom nil)
        errors   (atom nil)
        fields   (atom nil)]
    (ws/connect! (str "ws://" (.-host js/location) "/ws")
                 (response-handler messages fields errors))
    (get-messages messages)
    (fn []
      [:div
       [:div.row
        [:div.span12
         [message-list messages]]]
       [:div.row
        [:div.span12
         [message-form fields errors]]]])))
```

With these changes implemented we should be able to test that our app behaves as expected by running it as we did previously:

```
lein cljsbuild once
lein run
```

Everything should look exactly the same as it did before; however, we're not done yet. Now that we're using WebSockets, we should be able to open a second browser and add a message from there. The message will now show up in both browsers as soon as it's processed by the server!

WebSockets Using Sente

Now that we have some familiarity with how WebSockets work, let's take a look at using the Sente library,[1] which provides a number of useful features, as seen in the following list.

- Ajax fallback support—Automatically falls back to using Ajax polling when WebSockets are not available

- keep-alives—Ensures the connection is not dropped

- buffering—Provides internal buffering for messages

---

1. https://github.com/ptaoussanis/sente

- data encoding—Takes care of serializing and deserializing the message data

- Ring security—Is compatible with Ring anti-forgery middleware

Update the Server

Let's start by adding the Sente dependencies in the project.clj file.

```
:dependencies [...
               [com.taoensso/sente "1.8.0"]]
```

We can now update the guestbook.routes.ws namespace to use Sente to manage the server-side WebSocket connection. Let's update the dependencies to add taoensso.sente and taoensso.sente.server-adapters.immutant references.

guestbook-sente/src/clj/guestbook/routes/ws.clj

```
(ns guestbook.routes.ws
  (:require [compojure.core :refer [GET POST defroutes]]
            [bouncer.core :as b]
            [bouncer.validators :as v]
            [guestbook.db.core :as db]
            [mount.core :refer [defstate]]
            [taoensso.sente :as sente]
            [taoensso.sente.server-adapters.immutant
             :refer [sente-web-server-adapter]]]))
```

With Sente we don't have to worry about manually serializing the data, so we won't need the transit helpers we used previously, nor will we have to worry about managing the set of connected clients.

Sente is initialized by calling the sente/make-channel-socket! function. The function accepts the server adapter and a map of initialization options. We pass in the Immutant server adapter, since that's the server we're using, and we set the :user-id-fn option to use the :client-id key in the request parameters. This is needed in order to provide a unique identifier for each client. The reason we have to specify this option is that Sente defaults to using a :uid key from the session, and we won't be creating Ring sessions for the clients. The :client-id key is a UUID that's automatically generated for each client connection and provides a perfect way to identify each anonymous client.

The sente/make-channel-socket! function returns a map that contains a number of variables that were initialized.

- :ajax-post-fn—The function that handles Ajax POST requests

- :ajax-get-or-ws-handshake-fn—The function that negotiates the initial connection

- :ch-recv—The receive channel for the socket

- :send-fn—The function that's used to send push notifications to the client

- :connected-uids—An atom containing the IDs of the connected clients

We assign each of these keys to local variables using def statements.

guestbook-sente/src/clj/guestbook/routes/ws.clj

```
(let [connection (sente/make-channel-socket!
                    sente-web-server-adapter
                    {:user-id-fn
                      (fn [ring-req] (get-in ring-req [:params :client-id]))})]
  (def ring-ajax-post (:ajax-post-fn connection))
  (def ring-ajax-get-or-ws-handshake (:ajax-get-or-ws-handshake-fn connection))
  (def ch-chsk (:ch-recv connection))
  (def chsk-send! (:send-fn connection))
  (def connected-uids (:connected-uids connection)))
```

The functions for validating and saving the message remain unchanged. However, the handle-message! function will be replaced by a version that has to be updated to act as the event handler.

guestbook-sente/src/clj/guestbook/routes/ws.clj

```
(defn validate-message [params]
  (first
    (b/validate
      params
      :name v/required
      :message [v/required [v/min-count 10]])))
(defn save-message! [message]
  (if-let [errors (validate-message message)]
    {:errors errors}
    (do
      (db/save-message! message)
      message)))
(defn handle-message! [{:keys [id client-id ?data]}]
  (when (= id :guestbook/add-message)
    (let [response (-> ?data
                       (assoc :timestamp (java.util.Date.))
                       save-message!)]
      (if (:errors response)
        (chsk-send! client-id [:guestbook/error response])
        (doseq [uid (:any @connected-uids)]
          (chsk-send! uid [:guestbook/add-message response]))))))
```

Sente calls the event handler function whenever an event, such as receiving a new message from the client, occurs. The function is passed a map containing the keys that describe the event.

Sente uses the :id key to identify messages of different types and handle them accordingly. The :client-id is the unique UUID for each client that matches the ID used by the :user-id-fn that we specify when we create the socket. The :?data key contains the request payload.

The handle-message! function checks the request ID to see if it matches the :guestbook/add-message key. This key allows us to identify messages for creating new guestbook entries. When we receive such a message, we can take the value of the :?data key and process it as we did previously.

If the save-message! result contains errors, we use the chsk-send! function to send the :guestbook/error-type message back to the client that made the request. Otherwise, we broadcast the response to all the connected clients listed by the connected-uuids variable.

Sente uses a core.async go-loop to manage the message routing between clients. This router is initialized by calling the sente/start-chsk-router! function and passing it handle-message! as the event handler. Once the router is started, a function that stops routing is returned. Let's store this function in the router atom.

guestbook-sente/src/clj/guestbook/routes/ws.clj

```
(defn stop-router! [stop-fn]
  (when stop-fn (stop-fn)))

(defn start-router! []
  (sente/start-chsk-router! ch-chsk handle-message!))

(defstate router
  :start (start-router!)
  :stop (stop-router! router))
```

Finally, we have to update the routes to use the ring-ajax-get-or-ws-handshake and the ring-ajax-post functions to handle client requests. These are all the changes that are needed for us to start using Sente on the server.

guestbook-sente/src/clj/guestbook/routes/ws.clj

```
(defroutes websocket-routes
           (GET "/ws" req (ring-ajax-get-or-ws-handshake req))
           (POST "/ws" req (ring-ajax-post req)))
```

Update the Client

Now that we've switched the server implementation to use Sente, we need to update our client to match it. Let's start by updating the guestbook.ws namespace. First let's update the namespace declaration by replacing the current references with taoensso.sente.

```clojure
(ns guestbook.ws
  (:require [taoensso.sente :as sente]))
```

Once again, we won't need to manually serialize our messages to the transit protocol, since the library will handle that for us. Likewise, we won't need the send-message and the receive-message functions any longer.

Instead, let's initialize the connection using the sente/make-channel-socket! function that matches the one we used on the server. The difference is that we have to specify the route /ws where the connection is made. In the options, let's specify the :type key set as :auto to indicate that we want the client to automatically decide whether to use WebSockets or Ajax based on availability.

The function returns a map with the initialized variables. Use it to define the ch-chsk channel for receiving and the chsk-send! function for sending messages.

```clojure
(let [connection (sente/make-channel-socket! "/ws" {:type :auto})]
  (def ch-chsk (:ch-recv connection))     ; ChannelSocket's receive channel
  (def send-message! (:send-fn connection)))
```

The event handling is done on the client, analogous to what we did for the server. We use a message router to handle incoming messages. The router uses the event-msg-handler function to process them. This function checks the :id key on the message and routes it accordingly. We initialize it with a map containing functions for handling the events for handshake, state change, and incoming message. We also define some default event-handling functions.

```clojure
(defn state-handler [{:keys [?data]}]
  (.log js/console (str "state changed: " ?data)))

(defn handshake-handler [{:keys [?data]}]
  (.log js/console (str "connection established: " ?data)))

(defn default-event-handler [ev-msg]
  (.log js/console (str "Unhandled event: " (:event ev-msg))))

(defn event-msg-handler [& [{:keys [message state handshake]
                             :or {state state-handler
                                  handshake handshake-handler}}]]
  (fn [ev-msg]
    (case (:id ev-msg)
      :chsk/handshake (handshake ev-msg)
      :chsk/state (state ev-msg)
      :chsk/recv (message ev-msg)
      (default-event-handler ev-msg))))
```

Next we add the router code, which looks similar to the code we added on the server. We set the event-msg-handler function as the event handler and initialize it with the functions to handle different socket events. The function for handling the incoming messages is passed in when start-router! is called.

guestbook-sente/src/cljs/guestbook/ws.cljs

```clojure
(def router (atom nil))

(defn stop-router! []
  (when-let [stop-f @router] (stop-f)))

(defn start-router! [message-handler]
  (stop-router!)
  (reset! router (sente/start-chsk-router!
                   ch-chsk
                   (event-msg-handler
                     {:message    message-handler
                      :state      state-handler
                      :handshake  handshake-handler}))))
```

All that's left is to modify the guestbook.core namespace to reflect the changes in the guestbook.ws namespace. We need to update the comment button in the message-form component to call the updated version of the send-message! function that's now defined by calling sente/make-channel-socket!. The function accepts a vector containing the message ID and the data followed by the timeout value. The message ID :guestbook/add-message is the same one we defined on the server in the last section.

guestbook-sente/src/cljs/guestbook/core.cljs

```clojure
(defn message-form [fields errors]
  [:div.content
   [:div.form-group
    [errors-component errors :name]
    [:p "Name:"
     [:input.form-control
      {:type       :text
       :on-change #(swap! fields assoc :name (-> % .-target .-value))
       :value      (:name @fields)}]]
    [errors-component errors :message]
    [:p "Message:"
     [:textarea.form-control
      {:rows       4
       :cols       50
       :value      (:message @fields)
       :on-change #(swap! fields assoc :message (-> % .-target .-value))}]]
    [:input.btn.btn-primary
     {:type       :submit
      :on-click #(ws/send-message! [:guestbook/add-message @fields] 8000)
      :value      "comment"}]]])
```

The response-handling function returned by the response-handler also has to be updated to match the data that is passed to it by Sente when a message is received. The function has to accept a map representing the message. This map contains a key called ?data that contains the actual message payload.

The payload format matches the one we use in the comment button, where it's a vector with the ID of the message followed by the value. All we need to do is to destructure this map to access the message data.

guestbook-sente/src/cljs/guestbook/core.cljs

```clojure
(defn response-handler [messages fields errors]
  (fn [{[_ message] :?data}]
    (if-let [response-errors (:errors message)]
      (reset! errors response-errors)
      (do
        (reset! errors nil)
        (reset! fields nil)
        (swap! messages conj message)))))
```

Finally, we have to replace the ws/connect! call with the call to start the router.

guestbook-sente/src/cljs/guestbook/core.cljs

```clojure
(defn home []
  (let [messages (atom nil)
        errors   (atom nil)
        fields   (atom nil)]
    (ws/start-router! (response-handler messages fields errors))
    (get-messages messages)
    (fn []
      [:div
       [:div.row
        [:div.span12
         [message-list messages]]]
       [:div.row
        [:div.span12
         [message-form fields errors]]]])))
```

At this point our app should work just as it did before, while having Sente handle many of the underlying details, such as keep-alives and data encoding. This is the recommended method for building any nontrivial applications using WebSockets.

What You've Learned

You've now learned some basics about writing Clojure web applications. Next we'll take a look at adding a bit of structure for our service end points. The guestbook application has a very simple service API, and using undecorated

Compojure routes is not a problem here. However, a more complex application may have a large number of service end points. Each of these will take its own set of parameters and return different kinds of data.

In the next chapter, we'll see how to use the Compojure-api library to define service end points in our application.[2] This library will allow us to annotate each route using a schema. This schema will provide documentation and validation for each service operation, ensuring that the API is well documented.

---

2.   https://github.com/metosin/compojure-api

CHAPTER 6

Writing RESTful Web Services

In the last chapter, we saw how we can leverage ClojureScript on the client to handle the UI state. This allowed us to refactor our server-side code into stateless service operations. However, our services were declared in ad-hoc fashion using an arbitrary convention. While this approach works fine for small applications, it doesn't scale well for situations where we have many service operations and many common concerns, such as authentication, that are shared between them. In this chapter we'll cover how to use a library called compojure-api to provide some structure for our service end points.[1]

Use Compojure-api

Having a well-documented and discoverable service API is key to building a stable and maintainable application. Let's see how Compojure-api allows us to achieve this goal. The Schema library is used to define the Swagger-style RESTful service end points.[2,3] Schema provides us with a number of benefits, such as documentation for the structure of the data, input validation, and optional data coercion. Couple this with the Ring-Swagger library and we can automatically generate an interactive documentation page for our API.[4]

Let's see how this all works in practice by working through a new project. The goal of our project will be to entertain the users with an endless stream of cat pictures. Luckily for us, a public API exists for just such an occasion —the Cat API site.[5] Our app will fetch the cat picture links from there and use these links to display the pictures on the page using ClojureScript.

---

1.   https://github.com/metosin/compojure-api
2.   https://github.com/plumatic/schema
3.   http://swagger.io/
4.   https://github.com/metosin/ring-swagger
5.   http://thecatapi.com/docs.html

Let's create the project with the +swagger and the +cljs profiles. The first flag adds the boilerplate for using Compojure-api, and the second enables Clojure-Script support out of the box.

```
lein new luminus swagger-service +swagger +cljs
```

The project has a couple of sample routes already set up for us. Let's take a look at these to get a taste for how Compojure-api works. The generated routes can be found in the swagger-service.routes.services namespace. We can see that routes are declared using Compojure-api helpers such as compojure.api.sweet/GET, as opposed to the compojure.core/GET that we used previously. The syntax for these end points is similar to the standard Compojure syntax except that it also requires us to annotate each service operation, as seen here:

```
(GET "/plus" []
    :return      Long
    :query-params [x :- Long, {y :- Long 1}]
    :summary     "x+y with query-parameters. y defaults to 1."
    (ok (+ x y)))
```

The service routes are wrapped using the context macro that sets the base path as /api for all the routes inside it. The macro also specifies a :tags key that contains the metadata for grouping the routes in the generated documentation.

Each service route must declare its return type and the types of its parameters, and it must provide a description of its functionality. We can further see that we must specify where the parameters are found in the request. We specify :query-params for the URL query parameters, :body-params when the parameters are part of the request body, and :path-params when the parameters are part of the request path. Alternatively, we can specify the :body key that points to the description of the request body.

This is seen in the last two /echo routes:

```
(PUT "/echo" []
        :return   [{:hot Boolean}]
        :body     [body [{:hot Boolean}]]
        :summary  "echoes a vector of anonymous hotties"
        (ok body))
(POST "/echo" []
        :return   Thingie
        :body     [thingie Thingie]
        :summary  "echoes a Thingie from json-body"
        (ok thingie))
```

The :body key points to a vector that has the symbol name on the left and the type on the right. The request body is checked against the type specified and bound to the supplied name. The first route creates an anonymous inline schema definition, while the second uses the schema element that's defined at the top of the namespace.

The :return key specifies the type returned by the function. This can be a simple type, such as Long, or a complex schema, such as the Thingie in the example.

We can also see that the first argument to service-routes is a configuration map. This map specifies the routes for the JSON API, a Swagger UI test page, and the description metadata for the services.

```
{:swagger {:ui "/swagger-ui"
           :spec "/swagger.json"
           :data {:info {:version "1.0.0"
                         :title "Sample API"
                         :description "Sample Services"}}}}
```

Let's start the application and see what the generated documentation looks like by executing lein run in the terminal. Navigate to http://local-host:3000/swagger-ui/index.html, where you should see a page listing the API end points defined in our services namespace.

We can try out the services directly from the page and see how they behave. Note that we're able to call services that use the HTTP POST method without getting the anti-forgery errors we saw in the last chapter. Since anti-forgery protection only makes sense for pages generated by the server, it's not applicable to public API end points. Therefore, the generated service-routes are not wrapped using the wrap-csrf middleware and are exempt from CSRF checks.

swagger-service/src/clj/swagger_service/handler.clj

```
(def app-routes
  (routes
    #'service-routes
    (wrap-routes #'home-routes middleware/wrap-csrf)
    (route/not-found
      (:body
        (error-page {:status 404
                     :title "page not found"})))))
```

Now that we've seen a few examples of how Compojure-api works, let's go ahead and write a service end point using it.

Creating the API

As the first step, let's see how we can connect to the REST API provided by the Cat API site and extract the content that we need.

Parsing Cat Picture Links

In order to fetch our links, we need to create an HTTP client. Let's use the excellent clj-http library for this task.[6] As always, we start by adding the dependency to our project.clj file.

```
:dependencies [... [clj-http "2.0.0"]]
```

Note that if your application is running, you need to restart it in order for the library to become available.

With the library in place, we can navigate to the swagger-service.routes.services namespace and add the code for reading the links. Let's first reference it in our namespace as client.

```
(:require ...
          [clj-http.client :as client])
```

Let's test getting some data back from the service by writing this function:

```
(defn get-links [link-count]
  (client/get
    (str
      "http://thecatapi.com/api/images/get?format=xml&results_per_page="
      link-count)))
```

The function calls the HTTP GET method on the remote server and requests the results packaged using the XML format. We pass in the number of results to fetch as a parameter. When we call the function in the REPL, we should see something like the following as the result:

```
(get-links 3)
=>
{:status 200
 :headers {"Date" "Sun, 15 Nov 2015 07:00:35 GMT"
           "Server" "Apache"
           "X-Powered-By" "PHP/5.4.45"
           "Connection" "close"
           "Transfer-Encoding" "chunked"
           "Content-Type" "text/xml"}
 :body
 "<?xml version=\"1.0\"?>
  <response>
    <data>
      <images>
        <image>
          <url>http://24.media.tumblr.com/tumblr_m4ikzs7XtT1r6jd7fo1_500.jpg</url>
          <id>egs</id>
```

---

6.   https://github.com/dakrone/clj-http

```
          <source_url>http://thecatapi.com/?id=egs</source_url>
        </image>
        <image>
          <url>http://25.media.tumblr.com/tumblr_m4ilk0nsyd1r3ikrmo1_1280.jpg</url>
          <id>a1c</id>
          <source_url>http://thecatapi.com/?id=a1c</source_url>
        </image>
        <image>
          <url>http://24.media.tumblr.com/tumblr_liqpn3aOHC1qfv1wpo1_500.jpg</url>
          <id>d60</id>
          <source_url>http://thecatapi.com/?id=d60</source_url>
        </image>
      </images>
   </data>
</response>\n"
 :request-time 681
 :trace-redirects
 ["http://thecatapi.com/api/images/get?format=xml&results_per_page=3"]
 :orig-content-encoding nil}
```

As you can see, the result consists of a map representing the HTTP response
from the server. The :body key of this map contains the XML describing the
links to the cat pictures that we want. Now that we're getting the data from
the remote server, we need a way to parse out the links from it.

Clojure provides the clojure.xml namespace for working with XML data. This
namespace contains the parse function that can be used to turn an XML input
stream into a Clojure data structure. We need to reference the clojure.xml and
the clojure.java.io namespaces to create an input stream from the response string
and then parse it.

```
(:require ...
          [clojure.java.io :as io]
          [clojure.xml :as xml])
```

With the namespaces referenced, write the parse-xml function that takes the
XML string as the input, gets the byte array from the string, wraps it with an
input stream, and passes it to the clojure.xml/parse function to extract the data.

swagger-service/src/clj/swagger_service/routes/services.clj

```
(defn parse-xml [xml]
  (-> xml .getBytes io/input-stream xml/parse))
```

We can now update the get-links function to parse the XML result as follows:

```clojure
(defn get-links [link-count]
  (-> "http://thecatapi.com/api/images/get?format=xml&results_per_page="
      (str link-count)
      client/get
      :body
      parse-xml))
```

When we call the function again, we see a Clojure data structure as the result.

```clojure
(get-links 1)
=>
{:tag :response,
 :attrs nil,
 :content
 [{:tag :data,
   :attrs nil,
   :content
   [{:tag :images,
     :attrs nil,
     :content
     [{:tag :image,
       :attrs nil,
       :content
       [{:tag :url,
         :attrs nil,
         :content
         ["http://25.media.tumblr.com/tumblr_m4371fTcUo1qb4lb6o1_500.jpg"]}
        {:tag :id, :attrs nil, :content ["ddk"]}
        {:tag :source_url,
         :attrs nil,
         :content ["http://thecatapi.com/?id=ddk"]}]}]}]}]}
```

All we have to do now is parse out the :url tags from the :image tags in the data. We can accomplish that by writing a few helper functions.

swagger-service/src/clj/swagger_service/routes/services.clj

```clojure
(defn get-first-child [tag xml-node]
  (->> xml-node :content (filter #(= (:tag %) tag)) first))

(defn parse-link [link]
  (->> link (get-first-child :url) :content first))

(defn parse-links [links]
  (->> links
       (get-first-child :data)
       (get-first-child :images)
       :content
       (map parse-link)))
```

While XML format allows for multiple tags in the :content, most of the tags in the structure we're working with only have a single child node. The get-first-child function is used to extract these tags by their name. Once we parse out the collection of links, we can map the parse-link function across them to get the actual URL strings.

We can now update the get-links function to call parse-links to extract the links from the XML structure.

swagger-service/src/clj/swagger_service/routes/services.clj

```clojure
(defn get-links [link-count]
  (-> "http://thecatapi.com/api/images/get?format=xml&results_per_page="
      (str link-count)
      client/get
      :body
      parse-xml
      parse-links))
```

Finally, you might have noticed that the app produces a very noisy log in the console each time we call the client/get function. The log should look something like the following:

```
[2016-02-02 19:12:17,802][DEBUG][org.apache.http.wire]
>> "GET /api/images/get?format=xml&results_per_page=50 HTTP/1.1[\r][\n]"
[2016-02-02 19:12:17,803][DEBUG][org.apache.http.wire]
>> "Connection: close[\r][\n]"
[2016-02-02 19:12:17,804][DEBUG][org.apache.http.wire]
>> "accept-encoding: gzip, deflate[\r][\n]"
[2016-02-02 19:12:17,804][DEBUG][org.apache.http.wire]
>> "Host: thecatapi.com[\r][\n]"
[2016-02-02 19:12:17,804][DEBUG][org.apache.http.wire
 >> "User-Agent: Apache-HttpClient/4.5 (Java/1.8.0_25)[\r][\n]"
[2016-02-02 19:12:17,804][DEBUG][org.apache.http.wire]
>> "[\r][\n]"
```

The reason is that the global logging configuration is set to debug level in the development mode. This causes any libraries we use to log at this level as well. However, we can easily fix this problem by adding an exclusion for org.apache.http in the log configuration. Let's open the env/dev/resources/log4j.properties file and add the following line there:

```
log4j.logger.org.apache.http=INFO
```

When we restart the app, the noisy logs should now be gone. The line says that we would like to configure the logger for the org.apache.http package to use info level rather than debug level. Any time you see the logs get noisy, you can use this method to suppress the logs for the particular package.

Creating the API

All that's left to do is to create a compojure-api route for this operation. At this point we can safely remove the existing sample end points from the namespace. Let's replace these with an end point that accepts the number of links to fetch as the argument and return a collection of link strings as its result. The response will be of type [s/Str].

swagger-service/src/clj/swagger_service/routes/services.clj

```clojure
(defapi service-routes
  {:swagger
   {:ui "/swagger-ui"
    :spec "/swagger.json"
    :data {:info {:title "cat link api"
                  :version "1.0.0"
                  :description "cats api"}
           :tags [{:name "thecatapi", :description "cat's api"}]}}}
  (context "/api" []
    :tags ["thecatapi"]
    (GET "/cat-links" []
      :query-params [link-count :- Long]
      :summary "returns a collection of image links"
      :return [s/Str]
      (ok (get-links link-count)))))
```

Since we're using a GET operation, the input parameter is parsed as a string by default. However, compojure-api provides autocoercion for many common data types, such as UUIDs, integers, longs, and Booleans. Therefore, the argument is coerced automatically to the expected type.

Finally, we can test that our service works as expected by visiting the localhost:3000/swagger-ui/index.html#!/thecatapi/get_api_cat_links page and testing the GET method that we created. We should see something like the figure on page 109.

Next let's take a look at using a ClojureScript client with the Compojure-api service we've just created.

Adding the UI

Now that we have all these exciting links to amazing cat pictures, it would be nice for us to actually see them. Let's navigate to the src/cljs/swagger_service/core.cljs file and add the code to fetch them from the server and display them there. Let's partition the list of URLs that we get from the server and then create pages, each displaying a subset of images.

The lein-cljsbuild plugin we used previously requires us to reload the page each time the sources are recompiled.

When we created our current project, we used the +cljs flag that added Clo-jureScript support for us. This profile adds a more sophisticated way to compile ClojureScript using the lein-figwheel plugin.[7] This plugin not only compiles the code but also reloads it in the browser as it changes.

Compiling ClojureScript with Figwheel

With lein-figwheel, the changes are pushed to the browser using a WebSocket and are reflected live without the need to reload the page. Start the server and navigate to http://localhost:3000 once it's ready.

```
lein run
```

---

7. https://github.com/bhauman/lein-figwheel

Now you should see the following page, stating that you need to run lein figwheel to compile our ClojureScript sources:

```
Loading...
If you're seeing this message, that means you haven't yet compiled your ClojureScript!

Please run  lein figwheel  to start the ClojureScript compiler and reload the page.

See ClojureScript documentation for further details.
```

When you run the command you should see the following output in the console. The last line in the output tells us that Figwheel is waiting to connect to the application in the browser.

```
lein figwheel
Figwheel: Starting server at http://localhost:3449
Focusing on build ids: app
Compiling "target/cljsbuild/public/js/app.js" from ["src/cljs" "env/dev/cljs"]...
Successfully compiled "target/cljsbuild/public/js/app.js" in 8.719 seconds.
Started Figwheel autobuilder

Launching ClojureScript REPL for build: app
Figwheel Controls:
(stop-autobuild)                   ;; stops Figwheel autobuilder
(start-autobuild [id ...])         ;; starts autobuilder focused on optional ids
(switch-to-build id ...)           ;; switches autobuilder to different build
(reset-autobuild)                  ;; stops, cleans, and starts autobuilder
(build-once [id ...])              ;; builds source one time
(clean-builds [id ..])             ;; deletes compiled cljs target files
(fig-status)                       ;; displays current state of system
(add-dep [org.om/om "0.8.1"]) ;; add a dependency. very experimental
Switch REPL build focus:
:cljs/quit                         ;; allows you to switch REPL to another build
Docs: (doc function-name-here)
Exit: Control+C or :cljs/quit
Results: Stored in vars *1, *2, *3, *e holds last exception object
Prompt will show when figwheel connects to your application
```

Once you reload the page you should see a navbar and a "Welcome to Clojure-Script" message on the page. These elements were generated by the compiled ClojureScript, as seen in the figure on page 111.

We can now navigate to the src/cljs/swagger_service/core.cljs file that contains our swagger-service.core ClojureScript namespace and start editing it. Any changes we make will be reflected live in the browser. For example, let's change the content of the home-page function as follows:

```
(defn home-page []
  [:div
   [:h2 "Welcome to ClojureScript"]
   [:p "live code reloading is fun!"]]])
```

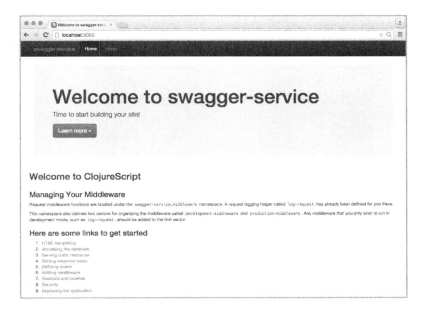

Note that any compilation errors or warnings are displayed directly on the page, as seen in the figure on page 112.

At mentioned earlier, Figwheel uses a WebSocket to push the code to the browser. The socket requires additional code to be run when the ClojureScript application starts. This code should only be run in development mode, not in production mode.

In order to automate loading different environments for development and production, the template sets up env/dev and env/prod source paths. The dev path is then included in the :dev profile and the prod path is included in the :uberjar profile in the project.clj file.

The env/dev/cljs/dev.cljs file contains the namespace that's the entry point for our ClojureScript application and has the following contents.

swagger-service/env/dev/cljs/swagger_service/dev.cljs

```
(ns ^:figwheel-no-load swagger-service.app
  (:require [swagger-service.core :as core]
            [figwheel.client :as figwheel :include-macros true]))

(enable-console-print!)

(figwheel/watch-and-reload
  :websocket-url "ws://localhost:3449/figwheel-ws"
  :on-jsload core/mount-components)

(core/init!)
```

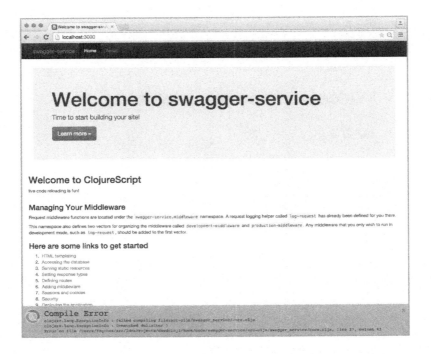

It enables console printing, creates a Figwheel WebSocket, and connects the Weasel REPL library to the Clojure nREPL started by the server.[8] Finally, the swagger-service.core/init! function is called. The "prod" entry point disables the console printing functionality and then calls the core/init! function to bootstrap the application.

swagger-service/env/prod/cljs/swagger_service/prod.cljs

```
(ns swagger-service.app
  (:require [swagger-service.core :as core]))

;;ignore println statements in prod
(set! *print-fn* (fn [& _]))

(core/init!)
```

Since the source path is selected based on the profile, no application-specific code needs to be aware of the environment. This approach avoids the need to manually track what parts of the application need to be loaded for development and deployment.

8.　https://github.com/tomjakubowski/weasel

Using Figwheel

With Figwheel running, any changes we make in our ClojureScript sources should be automatically updated in the page. Let's replace the existing code from the namespace with the following code:

```
(ns swagger-service.core
  (:require [reagent.core :as reagent :refer [atom]]
            [ajax.core :refer [GET]])
  (:require-macros [secretary.core :refer [defroute]]))
(defn home-page []
  [:div
   [:h1 "TODO: show some cats..."]])
(defn mount-components []
  (reagent/render-component [home-page] (.getElementById js/document "app")))
(defn init! []
  (mount-components))
```

When we check the browser, it should now display the new content without our having to refresh the page. The Figwheel compiler is able to reflect most changes seamlessly. However, we still have to reload the page for certain changes to take effect. For example, when we remove a mounted element such as the navbar, we need to refresh the page for that to take effect.

We're now ready to think about what our UI should look like. We're planning on querying the server for a list of links. We then partition these into groups and show them on the page. Next we need to create an atom to hold the results. Let's create one in our home-page component and populate it with some sample links from our API test page and display them using the img tag.

```
(defn home-page []
  (let [links
        (atom
         ["http://25.media.tumblr.com/Jjkybd3nSafemf3rYocB7QcC_500.jpg"
          "http://25.media.tumblr.com/tumblr_ln4zdhp4Uj1qcnzavo1_500.gif"
          "http://24.media.tumblr.com/tumblr_m2kmg2VK2a1qhwmnpo1_1280.jpg"
          "http://24.media.tumblr.com/tumblr_m30w1mNl1w1qgjltdo1_1280.jpg"
          "http://25.media.tumblr.com/tumblr_m3gm5oqm9e1r73wdao1_500.jpg"])]
    (fn []
      [:div
       (for [link @links]
         [:img {:src link}])])))
```

As you may recall, we create a local state using the let binding and return a function that is called on each subsequent update of this component.

Next, we add a fetch-links! function that grabs the list of images from the server. This function accepts an atom along with the number of links to fetch as its parameters and resets the atom with the links from the server. We can now update our home-page component to fetch the links when it's first called. Then we can see all the links start appearing on the page.

```
(defn fetch-links! [links link-count]
  (GET "/api/cat-links"
       {:params {:link-count link-count}
        :handler #(reset! links %)}))

(defn home-page []
  (let [links
        (atom nil)]
    (fetch-links! links 20)
    (fn []
      [:div
       (for [link @links]
         [:img {:src link}])])))
```

As you can see, that's a lot of links to load all at once. A better user experience would be to partition these into groups and allow the user to navigate these. First, change the fetch-links! function to partition the links into groups of six.

swagger-service/src/cljs/swagger_service/core.cljs

```
(defn fetch-links! [links link-count]
  (GET "/api/cat-links"
       {:params {:link-count link-count}
        :handler #(reset! links (vec (partition-all 6 %)))}))
```

Now write a component that renders a group of links as two rows of images:

swagger-service/src/cljs/swagger_service/core.cljs

```
(defn images [links]
  [:div.text-xs-center
   (for [row (partition-all 3 links)]
     ^{:key row}
     [:div.row
      (for [link row]
        ^{:key link}
        [:div.col-sm-4 [:img {:width 400 :src link}]])])])
```

Let's update the home-page function to track the partition and display it using the component we just wrote:

```
(defn home-page []
  (let [links (atom nil)
        page (atom 0)]
    (fetch-links! links 20)
    (fn []
      [:div
       (when @links
```

```
      [images (@links @page)])]])))
```

All that's left is to create a pager component to allow us to navigate the partitions. The pager creates buttons based on the count of partitions and hooks up the logic to navigate back and forth within them. Any time the value of the page atom is changed, it causes the home-page component to be repainted to show the selected partition.

swagger-service/src/cljs/swagger_service/core.cljs

```
(defn forward [i pages]
  (if (< i (dec pages)) (inc i) i))
(defn back [i]
  (if (pos? i) (dec i) i))
(defn nav-link [page i]
  [:li.page-item>a.page-link.btn.btn-primary
   {:on-click #(reset! page i)
    :class     (when (= i @page) "active")}
   [:span i]])
(defn pager [pages page]
  (when (> pages 1)
    (into
      [:div.text-xs-center>ul.pagination.pagination-lg]
      (concat
        [[:li.page-item>a.page-link.btn
          {:on-click #(swap! page back pages)
           :class     (when (= @page 0) "disabled")}
          [:span "«"]]]
        (map (partial nav-link page) (range pages))
        [[:li.page-item>a.page-link.btn
          {:on-click #(swap! page forward pages)
           :class     (when (= @page (dec pages)) "disabled")}
          [:span "»"]]]))))
```

Note that the pager function uses unicode characters for the forward and backward arrows. Alternatively, we could use HTML codes, as follows:

```
(ns swagger-service.core
  (:require ...
            [goog.string :as gs]))

...

(defn pager [pages page]
  (when (> pages 1)
    (into
      [:div.text-xs-center>ul.pagination.pagination-lg]
      (concat
        [[:li.page-item>a.page-link.btn
          {:on-click #(swap! page back pages)
```

```
        :class    (when (= @page 0) "disabled")}
      [:span (gs/unescapeEntities "&laquo;")]]]
   (map (partial nav-link page) (range pages))
   [[:li.page-item>a.page-link.btn
     {:on-click #(swap! page forward pages)
      :class    (when (= @page (dec pages)) "disabled")}
      [:span (gs/unescapeEntities "&raquo;")]]]]))))
```

Finally, let's update the home-page component to add the pager:

swagger-service/src/cljs/swagger_service/core.cljs

```
(defn home-page []
  (let [page  (atom 0)
        links (atom nil)]
    (fetch-links! links 50)
    (fn []
      (if (not-empty @links)
        [:div.container>div.row>div.col-md-12
         [pager (count @links) page]
         [images (@links @page)]]
        [:div "Standby for cats!"]))))
```

That's all there is to it. We're now fetching data from the server, partitioning it into groups, and providing a way to navigate these partitions, all in under a hundred lines of code.

What You've Learned

We now have a way to organize our service end points in a structured way, and we have a much better development story when it comes to ClojureScript compilation. In the next chapter we'll take a deeper look at connecting to and working with databases.

CHAPTER 7

Database Access

In the previous chapters we've primarily focused on handling the interaction between the client and the server and only skimmed over the topic of persisting our data. In this chapter, we'll cover how to work with relational databases using the clojure.java.jdbc library. We'll then discuss how to write a simple application to generate a PDF report from database records that will teach you about serving binary content in your web application.

Work with Relational Databases

By virtue of running on the Java Virtual Machine, Clojure works with any database that can be accessed via Java Database Connectivity (JDBC).[1] With it, we can easily access a large number of RDBMS databases, such as MySQL, SQL Server, PostgreSQL, and Oracle. The core library for dealing with relational databases is clojure.java.jdbc. When using this library we have to write custom SQL for each type of database we intend to use.

Most Clojure database libraries are based on clojure.java.jdbc. One such library that we'll cover in this chapter is called *HugSQL*.[2] This library takes the approach of keeping the SQL separate from the Clojure source files.

Another popular library is called *Honey SQL*.[3] This library represents SQL queries using Clojure data structures. This is the same approach we saw when we generated HTML in Reagent. The advantage of this approach is that we can manipulate and compose the queries directly in Clojure.

Finally, SQL Korma lets us write our queries using a Clojure domain-specific language (DSL) and generate the SQL statements targeting the specified back

1. http://en.wikipedia.org/wiki/Java_Database_Connectivity
2. http://www.hugsql.org/
3. https://github.com/jkk/honeysql

end.[4] However, we have to learn the DSL and will be limited to accessing only the databases it supports.

We'll start by seeing how to use the clojure.java.jdbc library, since it provides all the functionality we need without any additional complexity. We'll use PostgreSQL as our database engine throughout the rest of the book. If you choose to use a different database engine, be aware that there might be slight syntactic differences in our SQL queries.

Before we start working through the examples in this chapter, make sure you have an instance of the PostgreSQL database available in order to follow along.

Setting Up the PostgreSQL Database

Installing PostgreSQL is quite straightforward. If you're using OS X, then you can simply run Postgres.app.[5] On Linux, you can install PostgreSQL from your package manager. For example, if you're using Ubuntu, you can run sudo apt-get install postgresql. You may also need to modify the pg_hba.conf file to enable password-based authentication.[6]

Once PostgreSQL is installed, we set the password for the user postgres using the psql shell. The shell can be invoked by running the psql command from the console.

```
sudo -u postgres psql postgres
\password postgres
```

With the default user set up, let's create an admin user with the password set to admin.

```
CREATE USER admin WITH PASSWORD 'admin';
```

Then we can create a schema called REPORTING to store our reports by running the following command:

```
CREATE DATABASE REPORTING OWNER admin;
```

Note that we're using the admin user here to save time. You should always create a dedicated user and grant only the necessary privileges for any database you wish to run in production.

Accessing the Database

We'll start by creating a new project called *db-examples* by running Leiningen.

---

4. http://sqlkorma.com/
5. http://postgresapp.com/
6. https://fedoraproject.org/wiki/PostgreSQL#pg_hba.conf

```
lein new db-examples
```

To access the database, we need to include the necessary libraries in our project.clj file. We need to reference the org.clojure/java.jdbc library as well as the driver for the database we're accessing. Because we are using PostgreSQL, we require the following dependencies:

db-examples/project.clj

```
(defproject db-examples "0.1.0-SNAPSHOT"
  :description "FIXME: write description"
  :url "http://example.com/FIXME"
  :license {:name "Eclipse Public License"
            :url "http://www.eclipse.org/legal/epl-v10.html"}
  :dependencies [[org.clojure/clojure "1.8.0"]
                 [com.layerware/hugsql "0.4.7"]
                 [org.clojure/java.jdbc "0.6.1"]
                 [org.postgresql/postgresql "9.4-1201-jdbc41"]])
```

With that in place, we'll navigate to the db-examples.core namespace and reference the clojure.data.jdbc library the same way we did in the examples in Chapter 1, *Getting Your Feet Wet*, on page 1.

```
(:require [clojure.java.jdbc :as sql])
```

Next we need to define our database connection. We can do this in several ways. Let's look at the pros and cons of the different options.

Defining a Parameter Map

The simplest way to define a connection is to provide a map of connection parameters.

db-examples/src/db_examples/core.clj

```
(def db {:subprotocol "postgresql"
         :subname "//localhost/reporting"
         :user "admin"
         :password "admin"})
```

In the preceding example, we've defined a connection for an instance of the PostgreSQL database located on localhost using a schema called reporting along with the username and password. This is the schema that we'll be using for the following examples, so go ahead and create it locally before proceeding.

This method is the most common approach for declaring the connection information. In a real-world application, the values should be read from the environment instead of being baked directly into our application.

Extracting the configuration variables into the environment allows us to separate the configuration concerns from the code. For example, we might have separate development, staging, and production servers. We can configure each server environment to specify its respective database, and when we deploy the application it will pick up the connection details from there. Later on we'll see how we can use the Environ library to extract this information.[7]

Specifying the Driver Directly

Another option is to provide a JDBC data source and configure it manually. This option is useful if we wish to specify any driver-specific parameters not accessible through the idiomatic parameter map configuration.

```
(def db
  {:datasource
    (doto (PGPoolingDataSource.)
      (.setServerName   "localhost")
      (.setDatabaseName "my_website")
      (.setUser         "admin")
      (.setPassword     "admin")
      (.setMaxConnections 10))})
```

Defining a JNDI String

Finally, we can define the connection by specifying the Java Naming and Directory Interface (JNDI) name for a connection managed by the application server.

```
(def db {:name "jdbc/myDatasource"})
```

Here we've provided the JNDI name as a string. The actual connection is configured on the application server we're using and must be given the same name as the one defined in the application. When the application runs, it queries the server for the connection details using the name supplied. Now that we have a database connection, let's look at how to accomplish some common tasks with it.

Creating Tables

We can create tables programmatically by calling the create-table-ddl function and providing it the table name, followed by the columns and their types. Let's write a function to create a table to store user records, where each record has an ID and a password.

db-examples/src/db_examples/core.clj

```
(defn create-users-table! []
  (sql/db-do-commands db
```

---

7.   https://github.com/weavejester/environ

```
(sql/create-table-ddl
  :users
  [[:id "varchar(32) PRIMARY KEY"]
   [:pass "varchar(100)"]]))
```

Here, create-table-ddl is called to create a users table. The macro takes a keyword specifying the table name, followed by vectors representing the columns. Each column has the format of [:name type], where *name* is the name of the column and the type can either be a SQL string or a keyword such as :int, :boolean, or :timestamp. Note: The name of the column can't have dashes because that isn't valid SQL syntax.

Note that the DDL statement is wrapped inside the db-do-commands function that accepts the connection parameters we defined earlier and executes the statement within the context of that connection.

Selecting Records

To select records from our database, we use the query function. It accepts the connection and a vector containing the SQL string followed by its arguments, and it returns a result as a lazy sequence. This function allows us to work with the returned data without having to load the entire result set into memory.

db-examples/src/db_examples/core.clj

```
(defn get-user [id]
  (first (sql/query db ["select * from users where id = ?" id])))

(get-user "foo")
```

In the preceding code, we've created a function that accepts the user ID as its argument and returns the first item from the result set. Note that we're using a parameterized query by specifying a vector containing the prepared statement string followed by its parameters. This approach should always be used in order to prevent SQL injection attacks.

Inserting Records

A number of options are available for inserting records into the database. If we have a map whose keys match the names of the columns in the table, then we can simply use the insert! function.

db-examples/src/db_examples/core.clj

```
(defn add-user! [user]
  (sql/insert! db :users user))

(add-user! {:id "foo" :pass "bar"})
```

If we wish to insert multiple records simultaneously, we can pass a vector of maps to the insert-multi! function instead.

db-examples/src/db_examples/core.clj

```
(defn add-users! [& users]
  (sql/insert-multi! db :users users))

(add-users!
 {:id "foo1" :pass "bar"}
 {:id "foo2" :pass "bar"}
 {:id "foo3" :pass "bar"})
```

Alternatively, we can supply a vector containing the column IDs that we wish to insert, followed by vectors containing the column values.

```
(sql/insert! db :users [:id] ["bar"])
```

Conversely, we can use similar syntax to insert multiple rows using the insert-multi! function. This time around, each row is represented by a vector containing column values.

```
(sql/insert-multi! db :users [:id] [["bar"] ["baz"]])
```

Updating Existing Records

To update an existing record, use the update! function. The function expects to be passed the connection, followed by the table name, the map representing the updated rows, and the WHERE clause represented by a vector.

db-examples/src/db_examples/core.clj

```
(defn set-pass! [id pass]
  (sql/update!
    db
    :users
    {:pass pass}
    ["id=?" id]))

(set-pass! "foo" "bar")
```

Deleting Records

Records can be deleted from the database using the delete! function.

db-examples/src/db_examples/core.clj

```
(defn remove-user! [id]
  (sql/delete! db :users ["id=?" id]))

(remove-user! "foo")
```

Transactions

We use transactions when we want to run multiple statements and ensure that the statements are executed only if all of them can be run successfully. If any statement fails, then the transaction is rolled back to the state prior to running any of the statements.

```
(sql/with-db-transaction [t-conn db]
  (sql/update!
      t-conn
      :users
      {:pass "bar"}
      ["id=?" "foo"])
    (sql/update!
      t-conn
      :users
      {:pass "baz"}
      ["id=?" "bar"]))
```

As can be seen in the preceding code, we use the with-db-transaction macro to create a transactional connection that is used inside the transaction. The [t-conn db] part of the macro creates a binding the same way a let statement does. All the statements wrapped by with-db-transaction must use the t-conn connection to execute the queries. Should all the statements complete successfully, then the transaction is committed.

Use HugSQL

The major advantage of using HugSQL is that it allows us to write the SQL queries in separate files instead of having to embed strings in our code. This has a number of advantages, such as allowing us to use SQL tools to edit the queries. We already got a preview of HugSQL when we developed our guestbook application in Chapter 1, *Getting Your Feet Wet*, on page 1.

Getting Things Done with HugSQL

HugSQL provides a flexible DSL for generating the functions for running SQL queries. We'll start by seeing how we can define a single query in a file and then create a function from it using the def-db-fns macro. Let's place the query in the resources/find_user.sql file in our project.

---
db-examples/resources/users.sql

```
-- :name add-user! :! :n
-- :doc  adds a new user
INSERT INTO users
(id, pass)
VALUES (:id, :pass)
```

HugSQL uses specially formatted SQL comments as metadata for defining functions that interact with the database. The name of the function that runs the query is defined using the -- :name comment.

The name of the function is followed by flags indicating the SQL command and the result. The preceding query uses the :! flag to indicate that the function modifies the data, and the :n key to indicate that it returns the number of rows that were affected.

HugSQL supports the following command flags and defaults to :? when none is specified.

- :query or :?—Indicates a query with a result set

- :execute or :!—Can be used for any statement

- :returning-execute or :<!—Is used to indicate an INSERT ... RETURNING query

- :insert or :i!—Will attempt to return the generated keys

The result flag is used to indicate the type of result that is returned by the query. The result defaults to :raw when none is specified.

- :one or :1—A result with a single row

- :many or :*—A result with multiple rows

- :affected or :n—The number of affected rows

- :raw—The result generated by the underlying database adapter

The only things to note about the SQL statement itself are the placeholder keys for the VALUES. HugSQL uses these keys to look up the parameters in the input map when the generated function is called.

Now that we've defined a query, let's create a new namespace called db-examples.hugsql with the following content:

---
db-examples/src/db_examples/hugsql.clj

```
(ns db-examples.hugsql
  (:require [db-examples.core :refer [db]]
            [clojure.java.jdbc :as sql]
            [hugsql.core :as hugsql]))
```

```
(hugsql/def-db-fns "users.sql")
```

We can now call add-user! just like any other function, and the comment identified by the -- :doc flag is available as its doc string.

```
(add-user! db {:id "foo" :pass "bar"})
```

The function accepts the database connection as its first parameter, followed by the query map. Note that the keys in the map have the same names as those we defined earlier in the users.sql file. The connection we're using is the one that we defined earlier for our clojure.java.jdbc examples.

In case we wanted to return the fields from the record that was created, we could write the following query:

db-examples/resources/users.sql

```
-- :name add-user-returning! :i :1
-- :doc  adds a new user returning the id
INSERT INTO users
(id, pass)
VALUES (:id, :pass)
returning id
```

We have to rerun the def-db-fns macro to load the new query. Then we can run the generated function as follows:

```
(add-user-returning! db {:id "baz" :pass "bar"})
```

Note that support for the returning queries is database-driver dependent: some drivers do not facilitate returning the result of the insert query.

A tuple list can be used to do a multirecord insert. Let's update the users.sql file by adding the following query there:

db-examples/resources/users.sql

```
-- :name add-users! :! :n
-- :doc add multiple users
INSERT INTO users
(id, pass)
VALUES :t*:users
```

The :t* flag indicates that the users key is a vector of records to insert. Each record is described by a vector where the value matches the position of the parameter in the INSERT statement. We can now insert multiple users using the function we defined, as follows:

```
(add-users! db {:users
                [["bob" "Bob"]
                 ["alice" "Alice"]]})
```

We can now query the users by adding the following query:

db-examples/resources/users.sql

```
-- :name find-user :? :1
-- find the user with a matching ID
SELECT *
FROM users
WHERE id = :id
```

When we call the function, it should return a single map that represents the record when it's found and a nil result when it's not.

```
(find-user db {:id "bob"})
```

HugSQL supports in-list queries, where we can provide a vector of values as the parameter. The SQL query uses the :v* flag to indicate the value list parameter. Let's add a new file called resources/find_user.sql and place the following query there:

db-examples/resources/users.sql

```
-- :name find-users :? :*
-- find users with a matching ID
SELECT *
FROM users
WHERE id IN (:v*:ids)
```

The function parameters now consist of a map with the key :ids that points to a vector of IDs that we want to match.

```
(find-users db {:ids ["foo" "bar" "baz"]})
```

It's also worth noting that we can easily mix it with clojure.java.jdbc. For example, if we wanted to run queries in a transaction, then we'd use the with-db-transaction macro to wrap the calls to HugSQL-generated functions, as seen here:

db-examples/src/db_examples/hugsql.clj

```
(defn add-user-transaction [user]
  (sql/with-db-transaction [t-conn db]
    (if-not (find-user t-conn {:id (:id user)})
            (add-user! t-conn user))))

(add-user-transaction {:id "foobar"
                       :pass "I'm transactional"})
```

As we've seen, HugSQL is a very flexible library that allows us to define queries in a clean and intuitive way, without having to mix the SQL sources with our Clojure code. We've covered the core features of HugSQL, but it's worth noting that it provides many features that can facilitate for advanced use cases. I urge you to explore the official documentation to see what they are.

Generate Reports

In this section we'll cover how to generate reports from the data we collect in our database using the clj-pdf library.[8] Then we'll discuss how to serve the generated PDF to the browser using the appropriate response type.

Our application will have an employee table that will be populated with some sample data. We'll use this data to create a couple of different PDF reports, and we'll allow the users to select the type of report they wish to view. Let's create a new application called *reporting-example* using the Luminus template.

```
lein new luminus reporting-example +postgres
```

Now we open the project.clj file to add the clj-pdf dependency.

```
:dependencies [...
                [clj-pdf "2.2.0"]]
```

We also have to remember to update the database URL with the profiles.clj file as follows:

reporting-example/profiles.clj

```
{:profiles/dev
 {:env
  {:database-url
   "jdbc:postgresql://localhost/reporting?user=admin&password=admin"}}
 :profiles/test
 {:env
  {:database-url
   "jdbc:postgresql://localhost/report_test?user=admin&password=admin"}}}
```

Now let's update our migrations files, found in the resources/migrations folder. The "up" file creates the employee table, while the "down" file removes it.

```
CREATE TABLE employee
(name VARCHAR(50),
 occupation VARCHAR(50),
 place VARCHAR(50),
 country VARCHAR(50));

DROP TABLE employee;
```

With our migrations set up, run this command to initialize the database:

```
lein run migrate
```

---

8. https://github.com/yogthos/clj-pdf

Let's navigate to the namespace called reporting-example.db.core and see what we have there.

Luminus uses the conman library to handle external database connections. The library takes care of connection pooling and provides the connect! and disconnect! functions for managing the life cycle of the connection.[9]

When we generated our guestbook project, we used an embedded H2 database. In that case we created the data source that was passed to the conman/connect! function explicitly. Now that we're using an external database, the data source is specified declaratively using a map. The library knows how to create an instance of the PostgreSQL data source given this map.

Serializing and Deserializing Data Based on Its Type

You'll note that the namespace comes with a number of extend-protocol and extend-type definitions. Extending the IResultSetReadColumn protocol allows us to deserialize the column types returned by the database.

reporting-example/src/clj/reporting_example/db/core.clj

```
(defn to-date [sql-date]
  (-> sql-date (.getTime) (java.util.Date.)))

(extend-protocol jdbc/IResultSetReadColumn
  Date
  (result-set-read-column [v _ _] (to-date v))

  Timestamp
  (result-set-read-column [v _ _] (to-date v))

  Jdbc4Array
  (result-set-read-column [v _ _] (vec (.getArray v)))

  PGobject
  (result-set-read-column [pgobj _metadata _index]
    (let [type  (.getType pgobj)
          value (.getValue pgobj)]
      (case type
        "json" (parse-string value true)
        "jsonb" (parse-string value true)
        "citext" (str value)
        value))))
```

The java.sql.Date and java.sql.Timestamp types are converted into a java.util.Date type. The Jdbc4Array is deserialized into a vector. Finally, PGobject is serialized as either JSON or text based on its type.

Conversely, the extend-type allows us to serialize java.util.Date as a java.sql.Timestamp.

---

9.   https://github.com/luminus-framework/conman

reporting-example/src/clj/reporting_example/db/core.clj

```
(extend-type java.util.Date
  jdbc/ISQLParameter
  (set-parameter [v ^PreparedStatement stmt idx]
    (.setTimestamp stmt idx (Timestamp. (.getTime v)))))
(defn to-pg-json [value]
  (doto (PGobject.)
    (.setType "jsonb")
    (.setValue (generate-string value))))
(extend-protocol jdbc/ISQLValue
  IPersistentMap
  (sql-value [value] (to-pg-json value))
  IPersistentVector
  (sql-value [value] (to-pg-json value)))
```

Finally, the ISQLValue protocol allows us to serialize Clojure maps and vectors into PostgreSQL JSON types.

This allows us to keep all the type coercions in one place, instead of having to remember to do them each time we need to store or retrieve a value.

Now that we've looked at all the code that's been generated, let's start the REPL in this namespace and create the table that we'll be working with by running the following commands in it.

```
(require '[reporting-example.db.core :refer :all])
(mount.core/start #'reporting-example.db.core/*db*)

(in-ns 'reporting-example.db.core)
(jdbc/insert-multi!
  *db*
  :employee
  [:name :occupation :place :country]
  [["Albert Einstein", "Engineer", "Ulm", "Germany"]
   ["Alfred Hitchcock", "Movie Director", "London", "UK"]
   ["Wernher von Braun", "Rocket Scientist", "Wyrzysk", "Poland"]
   ["Sigmund Freud", "Neurologist", "Pribor", "Czech Republic"]
   ["Mahatma Gandhi", "Lawyer", "Gujarat", "India"]
   ["Sachin Tendulkar", "Cricket Player", "Mumbai", "India"]
   ["Michael Schumacher", "F1 Racer", "Cologne", "Germany"]])
```

Note we're passing the qualified reporting-example.db.core/*db* var to mount.core/start in the example. This ensures that mount only starts the specified state.

Finally, we write the query to read the records from the table.

```
reporting-example/resources/sql/queries.sql
```

```
-- :name read-employees :? :*
-- reads the list of employees
select * from employee
```

Let's run the conman/bind-connection statement to reinitialize the query functions and call the read-employees function it generates. We should see the following in the REPL console:

```
(conman/bind-connection *db* "sql/queries.sql")
```

```
(read-employees)
```

```
({:country "Germany",
  :place "Ulm",
  :occupation "Engineer",
  :name "Albert Einstein"}
 {:country "UK",
  :place "London",
  :occupation "Movie Director",
  :name "Alfred Hitchcock"}
 ...)
```

Notice that the result of calling read-employees is simply a list of maps where the keys are the names of the columns in the table. Let's see how we can use this to create a PDF with a table listing the employees in our database.

Generating the Reports

The clj-pdf library uses syntax similar to Hiccup's to define the elements in the document. The document itself is represented by a vector. The document vector must contain a map representing the metadata as its first element. The metadata is followed by one or more elements representing the document's content.

Let's create a namespace called reporting-example.reports and look at a few examples of creating PDF documents. We'll use the pdf function to create the reports and the template macro to format the input data. We'll also reference the reporting-example.db.core namespace so that we can call the read-employees function later on.

```
reporting-example/src/clj/reporting_example/reports.clj
```

```
(ns reporting-example.reports
  (:require [reporting-example.db.core :as db]
            [clj-pdf.core :refer [pdf template]]))
```

The pdf function accepts two arguments. The first can be either a vector representing the document or an input stream from which the elements are read.

The second can either be a string representing the output file name or an output stream.

Let's generate our first PDF by running the following code in the reporting-example.reports namespace:

```
(pdf
  [{:header "Wow, that was easy"}
   [:list
    [:chunk {:style :bold} "a bold item"]
    "another item"
    "yet another item"]
   [:paragraph "I'm a paragraph!"]]
  "doc.pdf")
```

As you can see, the report consists of vectors, each starting with a keyword identifying the type of element, followed by the metadata and the content. In the preceding report we have a list that contains three rows, followed by a paragraph. The PDF will be written to a file called doc.pdf in our project's root. The contents of the file should look like the following figure:

```
Wow that was easy
_____

- a bold item
- another item
- yet another item
I'm a paragraph!
```

Next, let's see how we can use the template macro to format the employee data into a nice table. This macro uses $ to create anchors to be populated from the data using keys of the same name.

The template returns a function that accepts a sequence of maps and applies the supplied template to each element in the sequence. In our case, since we're building a table, the template is simply a vector with the names of the keys for each cell in the row. Let's add the following template to the reporting-example.reports namespace:

reporting-example/src/clj/reporting_example/reports.clj

```
(def employee-template
  (template [$name $occupation $place $country]))
```

We should see the following output after running (employee-template (take 2 (db/read-employees))) in the REPL:

```
(["Albert Einstein" "Engineer" "Ulm" "Germany"]
 ["Alfred Hitchcock", "Movie Director", "London", "UK"])
```

It looks like our template works as expected. Let's use it to generate a report containing the full list of our employees:

```
(pdf
 [{:header "Employee List"}
  (into [:table
         {:border false
          :cell-border false
          :header [{:backdrop-color [0 150 150]} "Name" "Occupation" "Place" "Country"]}]
        (employee-template (db/read-employees)))]
 "report.pdf")
```

The resulting report should look like the following figure:

Of course, the template we used for this report is boring. Let's look at another example. Here we output the data in a list and style each element:

reporting-example/src/clj/reporting_example/reports.clj

```
(def employee-template-paragraph
  (template
    [:paragraph
     [:heading {:style {:size 15}} $name]
     [:chunk {:style :bold} "occupation: "] $occupation "\n"
     [:chunk {:style :bold} "place: "] $place "\n"
     [:chunk {:style :bold} "country: "] $country
     [:spacer]]))
```

Let's create a report using employee-template-paragraph by running the following:

```
(pdf
  [{}
   [:heading {:size 10} "Employees"]
   [:line]
   [:spacer]
   (employee-template-paragraph (db/read-employees))]
  "report.pdf")
```

Our new report should look like the following figure:

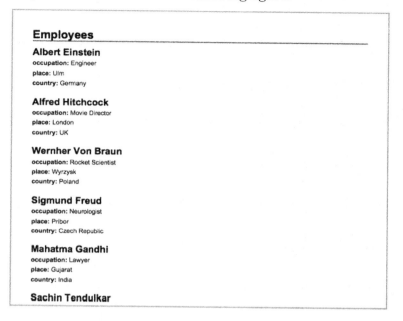

Displaying the Reports

Now that we've created a couple of reports on our data, let's see how we can serve them from our application. Let's write the functions to create the list and the table reports using the preceding examples:

reporting-example/src/clj/reporting_example/reports.clj

```
(defn table-report [out]
  (pdf
    [{:header "Employee List"}
     (into [:table
            {:border false
             :cell-border false
             :header [{:backdrop-color [0 150 150]} "Name" "Occupation" "Place"
                      "Country"]}]
           (employee-template (db/read-employees)))]
    out))

(defn list-report [out]
  (pdf
    [{}
     [:heading {:size 10} "Employees"]
     [:line]
     [:spacer]
     (employee-template-paragraph (db/read-employees))]
    out))
```

We update our page to provide links to both types of reports.

reporting-example/resources/templates/home.html

```
{% extends "base.html" %}
{% block content %}
  <div class="row">
    <div class="span12">
        <h1>Select report type:</h1>
        <ul class="nav nav-pills">
            <li class="btn btn-default">
                <a href="{{servlet-context}}/list">List reports</a>
            </li>
            <li class="btn btn-default">
                <a href="{{servlet-context}}/table">Table reports</a>
            </li>
        </ul>
        {% if error %}
        <h2>An error has occurred while generating the report:</h2>
        <div class="alert alert-danger">{{error}}</div>
        {% endif %}
    </div>
  </div>
{% endblock %}
```

Next, we navigate to reporting-example.routes.home and add some references needed to create the report route.

reporting-example/src/clj/reporting_example/routes/home.clj

```
(ns reporting-example.routes.home
  (:require [ring.util.response :as response]
            [compojure.core :refer [defroutes GET]]
            [reporting-example.reports :as reports]
            [reporting-example.layout :as layout]))
```

We also update the home function to serve the page without passing it any parameters.

reporting-example/src/clj/reporting_example/routes/home.clj

```
(defn home-page []
  (layout/render "home.html"))
```

Now we write a function to generate the response. We create an input stream using a supplied byte array and set it as the response. We also set the appropriate headers for the content type, the content disposition, and the length of the content.

reporting-example/src/clj/reporting_example/routes/home.clj

```
(defn write-response [report-bytes]
  (with-open [in (java.io.ByteArrayInputStream. report-bytes)]
```

```
(-> (response/response in)
    (response/header "Content-Disposition" "filename=document.pdf")
    (response/header "Content-Length" (count report-bytes))
    (response/content-type "application/pdf")) ))
```

Next we write another function to generate the report. This function creates a ByteArrayOutputStream that is used to store the report. Then it calls one of our report-generation functions with it. Once the report is generated, we call write-response with the contents of the output stream.

reporting-example/src/clj/reporting_example/routes/home.clj

```
(defn generate-report [report-type]
  (try
    (let [out (java.io.ByteArrayOutputStream.)]
      (condp = (keyword report-type)
        :table (reports/table-report out)
        :list  (reports/list-report out))
      (write-response (.toByteArray out)))
    (catch Exception ex
      (layout/render "home.html" {:error (.getMessage ex)}))))
```

Last but not least, we create a new route to serve our reports.

reporting-example/src/clj/reporting_example/routes/home.clj

```
(defroutes home-routes
  (GET "/" [] (home-page))
  (GET "/about" [] (about-page))
  (GET "/:report-type" [report-type] (generate-report report-type)))
```

You should now be able to navigate to http://localhost:3000 and select a link to one of the reports. When you click on the link, the corresponding report is served.

What You've Learned

This covers the basics of working with relational databases. You've now learned how to do the basic database queries and manage the connection life cycle, and you've written a reporting application that serves binary content in action. As we've covered in this chapter, database records are easily mapped to Clojure data structures. Therefore, the Clojure community largely sees object-relational mapping libraries as unnecessary.

In the next chapter we'll put together all the skills you've learned so far to write a picture-gallery application.

CHAPTER 8

Picture Gallery

In this chapter we'll bring together all the concepts you've learned thus far by building a picture gallery application. We'll write the application in the style of a single-page application (SPA).

Traditional applications rely on the server both to handle the business logic and to render the HTML for the UI. This can easily lead to tight coupling between the client and the server components. It also requires the server to do additional work that can be handled by the client instead.

Single-page applications rely on the client to handle all the presentation logic. The client typically communicates with the server using a RESTful API, thus providing a clear separation between client and server responsibilities.

This approach has a number of advantages: The user experience is improved since the entire page doesn't need to be reloaded to reflect changes. Also, the work of rendering the UI is amortized among the clients instead of having to be handled by the server. In addition, the client state is kept on the client, allowing the server to be written in a stateless fashion. Finally, the server API is easily testable and can be extended for different types of clients, such as native mobile apps.

The Development Process

We'll build our application by creating a brief outline of the features to work from and then filling in the details as we go along.

Luminus-based applications automatically start a network REPL when running in development mode. I recommend that you connect your editor to the REPL as you're working. This will allow you to get immediate feedback on the code you're writing. For example, if you're writing a function to pull some data from the database, try it right in the editor and see its output before hooking it up to the page.

What's in a Gallery

We'll identify the different use cases for our site and then start implementing the functionality needed to support each case. Let's go over a list of actions we'd like our site's users to be able to perform. Each of these use cases will constitute a particular workflow that we can complete independent of others.

Task A: Account Registration

For a user to put content on the site, she needs to have an account. To facilitate this, we need a registration form to collect some user details, such as a username and a password. Then we need to validate those and create a database entry for the user.

Task B: Login and Logout

Once a user creates an account, she should be able to log in using the credentials provided. We need to display a login form on our pages if the session does not contain a user. When the user logs in successfully, we want to display a logout button instead.

Task C: Uploading Pictures

With the preliminaries out of the way, we can focus on adding some core functionality. First we need to provide a way for users to upload content to the site. When a picture is uploaded, we need to create a thumbnail to display when listing the galleries. The thumbnail should then be saved along with the original image.

Task D: Displaying Pictures

Now that we can upload pictures, we need to display them. We'll display the thumbnails and use them as links to the full-sized pictures. Since our site is a multiuser one, we also need a way to list user galleries. This way visitors will be able to browse content grouped by the user who uploaded it.

Task E: Deleting Pictures

Users might wish to remove some of their uploads, and we'll provide an interface to do so. When a user chooses to delete a picture, she'll need a way to select it and then delete the picture along with the thumbnail.

Task F: Account Deletion

A user may also wish to remove her account: hopefully this scenario never comes up, but we'll facilitate it just in case. When an account is deleted, we'll have to remove the user from our database and remove all the pictures and thumbnails for that user.

Code Architecture

Now that we've identified what we want our site to do, we can begin thinking about how to implement it. It's a good idea to organize the code with maintainability in mind. As your application grows, it becomes increasingly important to be able to reason about parts of it in isolation.

The majority of the server-side code will be focused on providing service operations for the client side of the application. We can organize these services into namespaces that represent different types of workflows in the application. For example, we'll need namespaces for handling authentication and uploads and for displaying the galleries.

The client side of the application is primarily focused on presentation. Therefore, we'll need to create namespaces to represent different pages and UI components in the application. Ideally, we'd like to organize our UI to minimize shared state between different screens in the application. This will allow us to reason about the implementation of each screen independently.

The first step toward understanding the nature of our application is to consider its data model. Figuring out what data we wish to collect and how it will be used will help us understand the workflow and our use cases. Therefore, setting up our database and creating the necessary tables will be the first step in building our application.

If you've worked with a web framework in an object-oriented language, you're probably used to creating an object model and then mapping it to the database, either by writing SQL statements by hand or by using an object-relational mapping framework such as Hibernate to do that for you.[1]

In our application, the database will be our data model. As we saw in Chapter 7, *Database Access*, on page 117, the clojure.java.jdbc library represents tables as maps, where the keys represent the columns. Since it's idiomatic to use core data structures to represent the data in Clojure, we don't need to map the data to classes as we do for object-oriented languages. Following this rationale, we'll use our table definitions as the data model for the application.

---

1. http://www.hibernate.org/

Create the Application

Let's get started. To create the application, generate a new Luminus project called picture-gallery with authentication, Swagger, ClojureScript, and PostgreSQL database features.

```
lein new luminus picture-gallery +auth +swagger +cljs +postgres
```

As I mentioned earlier, I recommend that you develop the application interactively using the REPL. The env/dev/resources/config.edn file contains the development environment configuration. It declares a variable called :nrepl-port; that's used to allow us to connect the editor to the REPL once the application is started. The port is set to 7000 by default. All popular Clojure editors allow you to connect to a remote REPL and evaluate the code from the editor using it.

picture-gallery-a/env/dev/resources/config.edn

```
{:dev true
 :port 3000
 ;; when :nrepl-port is set the application starts the nREPL server on load
 :nrepl-port 7000}
```

Let's start the application in development mode:

```
cd picture-gallery
lein run
12:31:37.225 [main] DEBUG org.jboss.logging - Logging Provider: Slf4jLoggerProvider
15-Aug-23 12:31:38 INFO [picture-gallery.core] - nREPL server started on port 7000
15-Aug-23 12:31:38 INFO [picture-gallery.handler] -
-=[picture-gallery started successfully using the development profile]=-
12:31:38.290 INFO  [wunderboss.web.Web] (main) Registered web context /
15-Aug-23 12:31:38 INFO [picture-gallery.core] - server started on port: 3000
```

Once the server starts, the application is available at http://localhost:3000 and the nREPL accepts connections at localhost:7000, as seen in the server log. Let's now also start the Figwheel ClojureScript compiler in a separate terminal.

```
lein figwheel
```

Once Figwheel starts up, we can navigate the browser to http://localhost:3000 to see the default Luminus landing page as shown in the figure on page 141.

The page advises us that we have to set up our database and run the migrations. Let's look at accomplishing that task in the next section.

Configure the Database

The data model is a critical part of our application. We need to understand the type of data our application collects and how it's presented to the users.

picture-gallery   Home   About

Welcome to picture-gallery

Time to start building your site!

Learn more »

Welcome to ClojureScript

Database Configuration is Required

If you haven't already, then please follow the steps below to configure your database connection and run the necessary migrations.

- Create the database for your application.
- Update the connection URL in the `profiles.clj` file with your database name and login.
- Run `lein run migrate` in the root of the project to create the tables.
- Restart the application.

Managing Your Middleware

Request middleware functions are located under the `picture-gallery.middleware` namespace.

This namespace is reserved for any custom middleware for the application. Some default middleware is already defined here. The middleware is assembled in the `wrap-base` function.

Middleware used for development is placed in the `picture-gallery.dev-middleware` namespace found in the `env/dev/clj/` source path.

Here are some links to get started

1. HTML templating
2. Accessing the database
3. Setting response types
4. Defining routes
5. Adding middleware
6. Sessions and cookies
7. Security
8. Deploying the application

Since we're using a relational model for our application, we need to identify the relevant tables before we implement the workflows that rely on them.

Create the Database

We'll use a PostgreSQL database for our application. You can refer to Chapter 7, *Database Access*, on page 117, for details on configuring the database.

Let's start this database creation by creating a user called *gallery* with the password *pictures* and a new schema called picture_gallery_dev in the database. Do this by running the following commands in the psql shell:

```
CREATE USER gallery WITH PASSWORD 'pictures';
CREATE DATABASE picture_gallery_dev OWNER gallery;
```

Configure the Application

Now that our database is ready to use, let's open up the profiles.clj file in the root of our project and set the development database user credentials there. The template generates two separate profiles for development and testing.

```
{:profiles/dev
 {:env
  {:database-url "<dev database url>"}}
 :profiles/test
 {:env
  {:database-url "<test database url>"}}}
```

We need to set the :database-url in the :profiles/dev profile to the following string.

```
"jdbc:postgresql://localhost/picture_gallery_dev?user=gallery&password=pictures"
```

Now restart the app so that the new environment variables become available.

Define the Data Model

With the connection set up, we can now look at defining the necessary tables. We'll use the migration files found in the resources/migrations folder to track the tables that we add for our application.

Where to start? Think of the user tasks we identified. Since our first task is to implement user registration, we should try to identify the model for storing the user information. Each user needs to have a username and a password. Both of these variables can be strings.

Well, look at that. The application happens to already have generated migrations files for the users table. The "up" migrations file creates a table that's suitable for a typical user. Let's use that.

picture-gallery-a/resources/migrations/20150816001606-add-users-table.up.sql

```
CREATE TABLE users
(id VARCHAR(20) PRIMARY KEY NOT NULL,
 first_name VARCHAR(30),
 last_name VARCHAR(30),
 email VARCHAR(30),
 admin BOOLEAN,
 last_login TIME,
 is_active BOOLEAN,
 pass VARCHAR(200) NOT NULL);
```

Since the ID represents a unique user, it's set as a primary key. This prevents users with duplicate usernames from being created. Note: The password is hashed and thus necessitates a longer field to accommodate the length of the hashed string.

Let's run the migrations to create the table. You should see the following output indicating that the table was created successfully.

```
lein run migrate
2015-07-04 21:52:44.061:INFO::main: Logging initialized @10780ms
Jul 04, 2015 9:52:44 PM clojure.tools.logging$eval464$fn__470 invoke
INFO: Starting migrations
Jul 04, 2015 9:52:44 PM clojure.tools.logging$eval464$fn__470 invoke
INFO: creating migration table 'schema_migrations'
Jul 04, 2015 9:52:44 PM clojure.tools.logging$eval464$fn__470 invoke
INFO: Running up for [20150816001606]
Jul 04, 2015 9:52:44 PM clojure.tools.logging$eval464$fn__470 invoke
INFO: Up 20150728223411-add-users-table
Jul 04, 2015 9:52:44 PM clojure.tools.logging$eval464$fn__470 invoke
INFO: Ending migrations
(0)
```

With our users table in place, we're ready to move on to our first task of showing a registration page and providing a way to create user accounts.

Task A: Account Registration

User registration and authentication represent a self-contained workflow that is independent from the rest of our application's functionality. Each workflow in our application consists of complimentary client and server components. The server part is responsible for handling the business logic and providing an API for the client. The client side is responsible for managing the UI and the client application state.

Before we continue, we need to understand the workflow involved in user registration. The user has to enter some identifying information in a form and send that information to the server. The server routes this information to a handler function that decides whether a user account should be created based on the account-creation rules.

We need a form to collect the user information and call the server. The client then handles the result of the operation and notifies the user of the outcome.

Add Authentication Routes

Since we're building our application using the SPA style, most of our server routes consist of service operations. The application already has a picture-gallery.routes.services namespace generated by the +swagger profile. This namespace will contain the routes for all the services that we'll write going forward.

However, we don't want to pollute this namespace with all the different handler functions for each of the workflows, so we'll put these in their respective namespaces. The functions used for the authentication workflow will therefore live in the picture-gallery.routes.services.auth namespace.

Let's reference picture-gallery.db.core to access the database, ring.util.http-response to generate the appropriate response map, buddy.hashers to hash the password, and clojure.tools.logging to log any errors that might occur.

```
(ns picture-gallery.routes.services.auth
  (:require [picture-gallery.db.core :as db]
            [ring.util.http-response :as response]
            [buddy.hashers :as hashers]
            [clojure.tools.logging :as log]))
```

Our next step is to write a function that creates a user using the supplied parameter and notifies the client of the status of the operation. When the registration is successful, the function sets the :identity key in the session to indicate that the user is now logged in.

```
(ns picture-gallery.routes.services.auth
  (:require [picture-gallery.db.core :as db]
            [ring.util.http-response :as response]
            [buddy.hashers :as hashers]
            [clojure.tools.logging :as log]))

(defn register! [{:keys [session]} user]
  (try
    (db/create-user!
      (-> user
          (dissoc :pass-confirm)
          (update :pass hashers/encrypt)))
    (-> {:result :ok}
        (response/ok)
        (assoc :session (assoc session :identity (:id user))))
    (catch Exception e
```

```
(log/error e)
(response/internal-server-error
  {:result  :error
   :message "server error occurred while adding the user"}))))
```

The function attempts to store the user without doing any validation on the input. We already looked at handling input validation using the Bouncer library when we worked on the guestbook application in Chapter 2, *Luminus Web Stack*, on page 25. The next step is very similar to that. Registering users consists of collecting the user information we wish to store and creating a record in the database. In this case, we collect the username, a password, and a retyped password (to ensure the password was entered correctly the first time).

However, this time around we would also like to be able to notify the user of incorrect input before it's sent to the server. Since we're using ClojureScript on the front end, we can share the validation logic between the client and the server. Let's see how that's done.

Navigate to the source folder called src/cljc. This source path contains a namespace folder called picture_gallery. Clojure 1.7 introduced reader conditionals that can be used to output platform-specific code that interops with Java and JavaScript, respectively.[2] Using these extensions it's possible to write Clojure code that targets both platforms without having to duplicate the logic. Any code that we wish to cross-compile between different platforms should use the .cljc extension. It's used to indicate that the file can be cross-compiled between Clojure and ClojureScript.

The source paths are defined using the :source-paths key in the project.clj file. The top level defines the source folders for Clojure, while the one found under the :cljsbuild configuration specifies ones for ClojureScript. The :resource-paths key defines the paths for any noncode assets for the project.

picture-gallery-a/project.clj

```
:source-paths ["src/clj" "src/cljc"]
:resource-paths ["resources" "target/cljsbuild"]
```

We can create a new namespace called picture-gallery.validation. We will place it in a file called src/cljc/picture_gallery/validation.cljc. Notice the extension .cljc. The namespace references the Bouncer library, which itself cross-compiles between Clojure and ClojureScript, to provide a validation function for our application.

---

2. http://dev.clojure.org/display/design/Reader+Conditionals

picture-gallery-a/src/cljc/picture_gallery/validation.cljc

```
(ns picture-gallery.validation
  (:require [bouncer.core :as b]
            [bouncer.validators :as v]))

(defn registration-errors [{:keys [pass-confirm] :as params}]
  (first
    (b/validate
      params
      :id   v/required
      :pass [v/required
             [v/min-count 7 :message "password must contain at least 8 characters"]
             [= pass-confirm :message "re-entered password does not match"]])))
```

The registration-errors function accepts a map with the keys id, pass, and pass-confirm as its parameters. It then checks that the password contains at least seven characters and that it matches the retyped password.

We can now navigate back to the picture-gallery.routes.services.auth namespace and reference the validation namespace there as follows:

picture-gallery-a/src/clj/picture_gallery/routes/services/auth.clj

```
(ns picture-gallery.routes.services.auth
  (:require [picture-gallery.db.core :as db]
            [picture-gallery.validation :refer [registration-errors]]
            [ring.util.http-response :as response]
            [buddy.hashers :as hashers]
            [clojure.tools.logging :as log]))
```

Let's update the register function to validate the input. We use our newly created registration-errors function to check for errors and to return an error response to the client.

picture-gallery-a/src/clj/picture_gallery/routes/services/auth.clj

```
(if (registration-errors user)
  (response/precondition-failed {:result :error})
```

If no errors were found during validation, then we attempt to create the user and catch the exception. When the user is created successfully, we return the ok response to the client. In case of errors, we call the handle-registration-error function.

picture-gallery-a/src/clj/picture_gallery/routes/services/auth.clj

```
(defn handle-registration-error [e]
  (if (and
        (instance? java.sql.SQLException e)
        (-> e (.getNextException)
            (.getMessage)
```

```
          (.startsWith "ERROR: duplicate key value")))
  (response/precondition-failed
    {:result  :error
     :message "user with the selected ID already exists"})
  (do
    (log/error e)
    (response/internal-server-error
      {:result  :error
       :message "server error occurred while adding the user"})))))
```

The function checks whether the error indicates that the user ID is already taken and returns a custom error message if it is; otherwise it returns an internal server error.

The entire register! function should now look like this:

```
(defn register! [{:keys [session]} user]
  (if (registration-errors user)
    (response/precondition-failed {:result :error})
    (try
      (db/create-user!
        (-> user
            (dissoc :pass-confirm)
            (update :pass hashers/encrypt)))
      (-> {:result :ok}
          (response/ok)
          (assoc :session (assoc session :identity (:id user))))
      (catch Exception e
        (handle-registration-error e)))))
```

If any of these conditions fail, then the function returns the precondition-failed type response with a map that contains a :result key set to the value of :error.

Otherwise, the function attempts to create the user account in the database. Before the account is created, we need to remove the :pass-confirm key from the user map and encrypt the :pass key. When the record is created successfully, then we return the result of :ok. We'll catch any exceptions thrown when the account is being created and return the internal-server-error response if the operation fails.

Our function expects the create-user! function to be present in the picture-gallery.db.core namespace. This function is defined by the HugSQL library that was discussed in Chapter 7, *Database Access*, on page 117. Open the resources/sql/queries.sql file and update it as follows.

picture-gallery-a/resources/sql/queries.sql

```
-- :name create-user! :! :n
-- creates a new user record
INSERT INTO users
(id, pass)
VALUES (:id, :pass)

-- :name get-user :? :1
-- retrieve a user given the id
SELECT * FROM users
WHERE id = :id

-- :name delete-user! :! :n
-- delete a user given the id
DELETE FROM users
WHERE id = :id
```

We now have queries to add, to select, and to delete user accounts. Let's switch to the picture-gallery.db.core and run the (conman/bind-connection *db* "sql/queries.sql") command. This loads the query functions that we just defined.

Now test the register! function by navigating back to the picture-gallery.routes.services.auth namespace and running it with a test user in the REPL as follows:

```
(register! {} {:id "foo" :pass "12345678" :pass-confirm "12345678"})
```

We should see the result of {:result :ok}. If we run (db/get-user {:id "foo"}) next, we should see the user we just created as the result. We can also test the other cases by supplying an invalid user map and seeing how the function behaves in each case.

Once we're satisfied that the function is working properly, we navigate to the picture-gallery.routes.services namespace and replace the sample routes with the one needed for registration.

picture-gallery-a/src/clj/picture_gallery/routes/services.clj

```
(ns picture-gallery.routes.services
  (:require [picture-gallery.routes.services.auth :as auth]
            [ring.util.http-response :refer :all]
            [compojure.api.sweet :refer :all]
            [schema.core :as s]))

(s/defschema UserRegistration
  {:id            String
   :pass          String
   :pass-confirm  String})

(s/defschema Result
  {:result                  s/Keyword
   (s/optional-key :message) String})
```

```
(defapi service-routes
  {:swagger {:ui "/swagger-ui"
             :spec "/swagger.json"
             :data {:info {:version "1.0.0"
                           :title "Picture Gallery API"
                           :description "Public Services"}}}}
  (POST "/register" req
        :return Result
        :body [user UserRegistration]
        :summary "register a new user"
        (auth/register! req user)))
```

Since the Compojure-api library uses schemas to define the request and response for each service operation, we also have to add the UserRegistration and Result definitions. The first matches the parameters expected by the register! function, while the second describes the response produced by it.

Once we reload the namespace in the REPL, we should be able to navigate to http://localhost:3000/swagger-ui/ and test the service operation from the Swagger test UI as shown in the figure on page 150.

With the routes in place, we can focus our attention on the client-side code that is responsible for facilitating the registration workflow for the user. We need to create a form where users can enter their info, send the info to the server, and then be notified of the result.

Add the Registration UI

We want to display the form as a modal dialog in order to provide a smooth workflow that doesn't require the user to navigate to a separate page to register. Let's start by creating a modal component and testing it. Since the modal is a general-purpose component, we're likely to reuse it for other parts of the application as well. Let's create a picture-gallery.components.common namespace and create a modal component there.

picture-gallery-a/src/cljs/picture_gallery/components/common.cljs

```
(defn modal [header body footer]
  [:div
   [:div.modal-dialog
    [:div.modal-content
     [:div.modal-header [:h3 header]]
     [:div.modal-body body]
     [:div.modal-footer
      [:div.bootstrap-dialog-footer
       footer]]]]
   [:div.modal-backdrop.fade.in]])
```

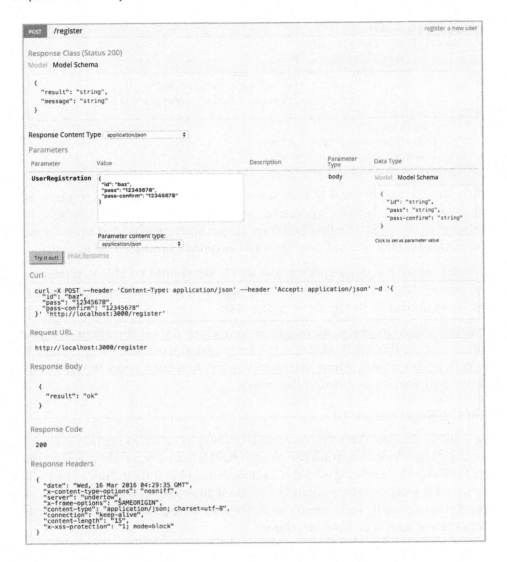

The modal component accepts the header, the body, and the footer as its arguments and then generates the markup for the Bootstrap modal dialog, placing the parameters in their appropriate places. Note that each of the arguments can also be a component itself, and the modal component simply specifies the layout for them.

In order to gray out the background, we're going to place the modal in a div followed by [:div.modal-backdrop.fade.in]. We also have to add the appropriate CSS in the resources/public/css/screen.css file.

picture-gallery-a/resources/public/css/screen.css

```
.modal-dialog {
    z-index: 100;
    margin: auto;
    position: absolute;
    top: 150px;
    left: 0;
    right: 0;
}
.modal-backdrop {
    z-index: 1;
}
```

We can now test that our modal works by referencing picture-gallery.components.common in picture-gallery.core and creating a new modal inside the page component.

```
(ns picture-gallery.core
  (:require ...
            [picture-gallery.components.common :as c])
  (:import goog.History))

...

(defn page []
  [:div
   ;;modal test
   [c/modal "I'm a Modal" [:p "this is the body"] "this is a footer"]
   [(pages (session/get :page))]])
```

When we look at the page in the browser, we should see something like this:

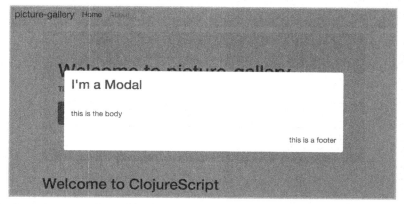

Now that we have a place for displaying our registration form, we can create a couple of additional helper functions for generating input fields. The form should collect the username, the password, and the password confirmation fields. Let's create the following helpers to facilitate that:

picture-gallery-a/src/cljs/picture_gallery/components/common.cljs

```
(defn input [type id placeholder fields]
  [:input.form-control.input-lg
   {:type        type
    :placeholder placeholder
    :value       (id @fields)
    :on-change   #(swap! fields assoc id (-> % .-target .-value))}])
(defn form-input [type label id placeholder fields optional?]
  [:div.form-group
   [:label label]
   (if optional?
     [input type id placeholder fields]
     [:div.input-group
      [input type id placeholder fields]
      [:span.input-group-addon
       "*"]])])
(defn text-input [label id placeholder fields & [optional?]]
  (form-input :text label id placeholder fields optional?))
(defn password-input [label id placeholder fields & [optional?]]
  (form-input :password label id placeholder fields optional?))
```

The input component creates an input HTML element with the given type. The component uses the id to look up the value in the fields atom that we supply and displays the value of the placeholder parameter as its placeholder text.

Next, we create a form-input component that creates a Bootstrap form group using the input component that we just created. The form group adds a label to the input and adds an asterisk next to the required inputs.

Finally, we create the text-input and the password-input components that create the types of inputs that we need in our form.

With that in place, let's create a namespace called picture-gallery.components.registration and proceed to write the form component there.

```
(ns picture-gallery.components.registration
  (:require [reagent.core :refer [atom]]
            [picture-gallery.components.common :as c]))

...

(defn registration-form []
  (let [fields (atom {})]
    (fn []
      [c/modal
       [:div "Picture Gallery Registration"]
       [:div
        [:div.well.well-sm
         [:strong "* required field"]]
```

```
[c/text-input "name" :id "enter a user name" fields]
[c/password-input "password" :pass "enter a password" fields]
[c/password-input "password" :pass-confirm "re-enter the password" fields]]
[:div
 [:button.btn.btn-primary "Register"]
 [:button.btn.btn-danger "Cancel"]]]))))
```

Now it's time to navigate back to picture-gallery.core and remove the code that loads the documents from the server: we won't be needing it. Don't worry about the rest of the code in the init! function for now.

picture-gallery-a/src/cljs/picture_gallery/core.cljs

```
(defn mount-components []
  (r/render [#'navbar] (.getElementById js/document "navbar"))
  (r/render [#'page] (.getElementById js/document "app")))

(defn init! []
  (load-interceptors!)
  (hook-browser-navigation!)
  (mount-components))
```

Next let's reference the picture-gallery.components.registration namespace and replace the test modal we created earlier with the registration modal.

```
(ns picture-gallery.core
  (:require ...
            [picture-gallery.components.registration :as reg])
  (:import goog.History))


...
(defn page []
  [:div
   ;;registration modal test
   [reg/registration-form]
   [(pages (session/get :page))]])
```

When we look at the page, we should see a nice registration form like the one in the figure on page 154.

Now that we've confirmed that our modal is working, let's make sure that we remove it from the page before moving on.

```
(defn page []
  [(pages (session/get :page))])
```

Our modal certainly looks nice, but it doesn't do much yet. Let's add some functionality to it. We already created an atom to store the data collected by the registration form; the next step is to send this data to the server via Ajax and handle the response.

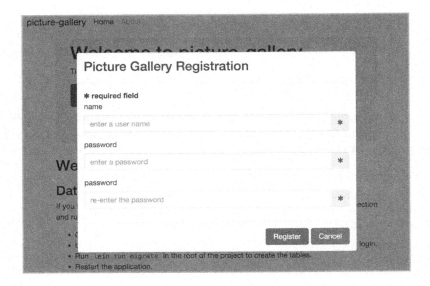

Calling the Server Using Ajax

As you'll recall from previous projects, we have to provide a CSRF token to the server in our requests. The resources/templates/home.html template contains a variable that holds this token. Recall that the csrf-token field is added to the context map by the picture-gallery.layout/render function. This value is assigned to the csrfToken variable when the page is rendered.

`picture-gallery-a/resources/templates/home.html`

```
<script type="text/javascript">
    var context = "{{servlet-context}}";
    var csrfToken = "{{csrf-token}}";
</script>
```

The project also contains a ClojureScript namespace called picture-gallery.ajax with the following code:

```
(ns picture-gallery.ajax
  (:require [ajax.core :as ajax]))

(defn default-headers [request]
  (-> request
      (update :uri #(str js/context %))
      (update
        :headers
        #(merge
          %
          {"Accept" "application/transit+json"
           "x-csrf-token" js/csrfToken}))))

(defn load-interceptors! []
```

```
(swap! ajax/default-interceptors
       conj
       (ajax/to-interceptor {:name "default headers"
                             :request default-headers})))
```

This namespace uses an interceptor to set the context and the default request headers for the application. The interceptors are applied to each request and provide a central way to set common parameters. The Accept header indicates that the server should return data encoded using the transit format. The x-csrf-token header sets the CSRF token that's found on the page.

The context variable in the preceding code is used when our application has a URL prefix. We may wish to use a context in a couple of scenarios.

The first scenario is when we're deploying the application to an application server such as Apache Tomcat. In this case, each application must have its own context path in order for the server to route requests accordingly.

The second scenario is when we wish to front multiple applications by a server such as Apache HTTP Server or Nginx without creating subdomains for each. The HTTP server would route requests to each application to a different URI.

Since the browser is not aware that our application has a context, the server has to provide that information when it generates the page. Luckily for us, the picture-gallery.layout namespace populates the :servlet-context key using the value bound to the *app-context* variable. Its value is in turn bound by the middleware found in the picture-gallery.middleware namespace.

picture-gallery-a/src/clj/picture_gallery/middleware.clj

```
(defn wrap-context [handler]
  (fn [request]
    (binding [*app-context*
              (if-let [context (:servlet-context request)]
                ;; If we're not inside a servlet environment
                ;; (for example when using mock requests), then
                ;; .getContextPath might not exist
                (try (.getContextPath ^ServletContext context)
                     (catch IllegalArgumentException _ context))
                ;; if the context is not specified in the request
                ;; we check if one has been specified in the environment
                ;; instead
                (:app-context env))]
      (handler request))))
```

The middleware checks for either the :servlet-context key in the request or the :app-context environment variable to populate the *app-context* variable. The

:servlet-context key is present when the application is deployed to an application server, such as Apache Tomcat.

The home.html template sets the value of the :servlet-context key as a JavaScript variable on the page.

picture-gallery-a/resources/templates/home.html

```
<script type="text/javascript">
    var context = "{{servlet-context}}";
    var csrfToken = "{{csrf-token}}";
</script>
```

Register the User

We're now ready to call the service operation to register the user using our registration form. Navigate back to the picture-gallery.components.registration namespace and add a register! function to call the service. Next, reference ajax.core, reagent.session, and picture-gallery.validation namespaces.

```
(ns picture-gallery.components.registration
  (:require ...
            [ajax.core :as ajax]
            [reagent.session :as session]
            [picture-gallery.validation :refer [registration-errors]]))

(defn register! [fields errors]
  (reset! errors (registration-errors @fields))
  (when-not @errors
    (ajax/POST "/register"
               {:params @fields
                :handler
                       #(do
                          (session/put! :identity (:id @fields))
                          (reset! fields {}))
                :error-handler
                       #(reset!
                         errors
                         {:server-error (get-in % [:response :message])})})))
```

We can now update our registration form to call the register! function when the Register button is clicked. We can also add an atom to hold the error that displays when it's populated by the :error-handler callback in the register! function.

```
(defn registration-form []
  (let [fields (atom {})
        error  (atom nil)]
    (fn []
      [c/modal
       [:div "Picture Gallery Registration"]
       [:div
```

```
    [:div.well.well-sm
     [:strong "* required field"]]
    [c/text-input "name" :id "enter a user name" fields]
    [c/password-input "password" :pass "enter a password" fields]
    [c/password-input "password" :pass-confirm "re-enter the password" fields]
    (when-let [error (:server-error @error)]
      [:div.alert.alert-danger error])]
   [:div
    [:button.btn.btn-primary
     {:on-click #(register! fields error)}
     "Register"]
    [:button.btn.btn-danger "Cancel"]]]])))
```

At this point we should be able to fill in some information and try to register the user from our form. If we do not see an error displayed in the form, we can check the database to confirm that the user was created.

The next step is to show the form conditionally. We can use the reagent.session provided by the reagent-utils library for this purpose.[3] Let's create a session key called :modal and display its value on the page whenever this key is populated. The modal can then be set in the session from anywhere in the app.

Now let's add a reference to the reagent.session namespace and update the Cancel button in our form to remove the :modal key from the session.

```
(ns picture-gallery.components.registration
  (:require [reagent.core :refer [atom]]
            [reagent.session :as session]
            [picture-gallery.components.common :as c]))

...

(defn registration-form []
  (let [fields (atom {})
        error  (atom nil)]
    (fn []
      [c/modal
       [:div "Picture Gallery Registration"]
       [:div
        [:div.well.well-sm
         [:strong "* required field"]]
        [c/text-input "name" :id "enter a user name" fields]
        [c/password-input "password" :pass "enter a password" fields]
        [c/password-input "password" :pass-confirm "re-enter the password" fields]
        (when-let [error (:server-error @error)]
          [:div.alert.alert-danger error])]
       [:div
        [:button.btn.btn-primary
         {:on-click #(register! fields error)}
```

---

3.   https://github.com/reagent-project/reagent-utils

```
    "Register"]
  [:button.btn.btn-danger
   {:on-click #(session/remove! :modal)}
   "Cancel"]]])))
```

Next let's add a component to the registration button that sets the registration-form as the modal in the session.

picture-gallery-a/src/cljs/picture_gallery/components/registration.cljs

```
(defn registration-button []
  [:a.btn
   {:on-click #(session/put! :modal registration-form)}
   "register"])
```

When the registration button is clicked, the registration modal is set in the session: when the Cancel button on the modal is clicked, it is removed.

Now let's navigate to the picture-gallery.core namespace, where we create a user menu component that we place in the navbar.

picture-gallery-a/src/cljs/picture_gallery/core.cljs

```
(defn user-menu []
  (if-let [id (session/get :identity)]
    [:ul.nav.navbar-nav.pull-xs-right
     [:li.nav-item
      [:a.dropdown-item.btn
       {:on-click #(session/remove! :identity)}
       [:i.fa.fa-user] " " id " | sign out"]]]
    [:ul.nav.navbar-nav.pull-xs-right
     [:li.nav-item [reg/registration-button]]]))
```

The component checks if an :identity key is present in the session. If it is, then it presents a Logout button that clears the identity from the session. Otherwise, it displays the registration-button that we just created.

We can now update the navbar component to add the user-menu to the navbar on the home page.

picture-gallery-a/src/cljs/picture_gallery/core.cljs

```
(defn navbar []
  (let [collapsed? (r/atom true)]
    (fn []
      [:nav.navbar.navbar-light.bg-faded
       [:button.navbar-toggler.hidden-sm-up
        {:on-click #(swap! collapsed? not)} "☰"]
       [:div.collapse.navbar-toggleable-xs
        (when-not @collapsed? {:class "in"})
        [:a.navbar-brand {:href "#/"} "picture-gallery"]
        [:ul.nav.navbar-nav
```

```
  [nav-link "#/" "Home" :home collapsed?]
  [nav-link "#/about" "About" :about collapsed?]]]
[user-menu]])))
```

You should now see a register button in the navbar, as in the following figure:

Now that we have the button hooked up, we also need to update the code to display the modal conditionally in our page component.

picture-gallery-a/src/cljs/picture_gallery/core.cljs

```
(defn modal []
  (when-let [session-modal (session/get :modal)]
    [session-modal]))
(defn page []
  [:div
   [modal]
   [(pages (session/get :page))]])
```

Note that the modal is written as a separate function instead of being added inline, as seen in the following example:

```
(defn page []
  [:div
   (when-let [session-modal (session/get :modal)]
     [session-modal])
   [(pages (session/get :page))]])
```

We separate the page and the modal components for one very important reason. When we put the modal inside the page component, then whenever the value of the :modal key in the session changes, it forces the entire page component to be re-rendered. That includes the current page selected from the session using the :page key and causes the state of the page to be lost.

When we split out the modal component into a separate function, then only that component is affected when the value of the :modal key changes. As a rule, you always want to ensure that the minimum necessary set of components is affected by a change in the application state.

We can now test that everything works as expected. When we click the register button, the registration modal should pop up. Conversely, when we click the Cancel button, it should disappear again.

Let's go back to the picture-gallery.components.registration namespace and add a few more finishing touches. Let's update the :handler callback in the register! function to remove the modal from the session and update the form to display the validation errors.

picture-gallery-a/src/cljs/picture_gallery/components/registration.cljs

```clojure
(ns picture-gallery.components.registration
  (:require [reagent.core :refer [atom]]
            [reagent.session :as session]
            [picture-gallery.components.common :as c]
            [ajax.core :as ajax]
            [picture-gallery.validation :refer [registration-errors]]))

(defn register! [fields errors]
  (reset! errors (registration-errors @fields))
  (when-not @errors
    (ajax/POST "/register"
               {:params @fields
                :handler
                        #(do
                           (session/put! :identity (:id @fields))
                           (reset! fields {})
                           (session/remove! :modal))
                :error-handler
                        #(reset!
                          errors
                          {:server-error (get-in % [:response :message])})})))
(defn registration-form []
  (let [fields (atom {})
        error  (atom nil)]
    (fn []
      [c/modal
       [:div "Picture Gallery Registration"]
       [:div
        [:div.well.well-sm
         [:strong "* required field"]]
        [c/text-input "name" :id "enter a user name" fields]
        (when-let [error (first (:id @error))]
          [:div.alert.alert-danger error])
        [c/password-input "password" :pass "enter a password" fields]
        (when-let [error (first (:pass @error))]
          [:div.alert.alert-danger error])
        [c/password-input "password" :pass-confirm "re-enter the password" fields]
        (when-let [error (:server-error @error)]
          [:div.alert.alert-danger error])]
       [:div
```

```
      [:button.btn.btn-primary
       {:on-click #(register! fields error)}
       "Register"]
      [:button.btn.btn-danger
       {:on-click #(session/remove! :modal)}
       "Cancel"]]])))
(defn registration-button []
  [:a.btn
   {:on-click #(session/put! :modal registration-form)}
   "register"])
```

With the error handling hooked up, the client can notify the user of the errors before calling the server.

This wraps up the user-registration workflow. We're now ready to tackle our next task: allowing users to log in and log out after creating an account.

Task B: Login and Logout

The actions for logging in and logging out are based on the state of the session. If a user identity is not present in the session, then we should present the user with a login form. Conversely, when there is an identity present, we should present an option for the user to log out.

To log in, the user submits her username and password using a form on the page. These are checked against the stored credentials. If they match, we put her identity in the session.

When the user logs in, we send the credentials using basic HTTP authentication.[4] The specification states that the username and the password are joined using the : separator. The string is then encoded using base 64, and the authorization method Basic() is prepended. The string is then set as the Authorization header in the request. The resulting header might look as follows:

```
Authorization: Basic QWxhZGRpbjpvcGVuIHNlc2FtZQ==
```

Let's start by adding the necessary service routes in the picture-gallery.routes.services namespace under the service-routes route group.

picture-gallery-b/src/clj/picture_gallery/routes/services.clj

```
(POST "/login" req
      :header-params [authorization :- String]
      :summary "log in the user and create a session"
      :return Result
      (auth/login! req authorization))
```

---

4.   https://en.wikipedia.org/wiki/Basic_access_authentication

```
(POST "/logout" []
      :summary "remove user session"
      :return Result
      (auth/logout!))
```

The login route receives a POST() request at the /login URI with the authorization credentials as header parameters using the :header-params key. These are passed to the login! function in the picture-gallery.routes.services.auth namespace that we'll write shortly. The result of the function will be sent back to the client.

Let's also write a logout route that calls the picture-gallery.routes.services.auth/logout! function. The logout route doesn't require any parameters, since all we have to do is remove the user session from memory when the user logs out.

Let's write the login! and logout! functions in the picture-gallery.routes.services.auth namespace, starting with the login function. The login function has to decode the base 64 string and then split the username and password using the : character. Let's write a helper function called decode-auth for that.

picture-gallery-b/src/clj/picture_gallery/routes/services/auth.clj

```
(defn decode-auth [encoded]
  (let [auth (second (.split encoded " "))]
    (-> (.decode (java.util.Base64/getDecoder) auth)
        (String. (java.nio.charset.Charset/forName "UTF-8"))
        (.split ":"))))
```

Use the decoded username and password to query the database to check if the user exists and if the supplied password matches the hashed one that was created when the user registered. This is done by the authenticate function.

picture-gallery-b/src/clj/picture_gallery/routes/services/auth.clj

```
(defn authenticate [[id pass]]
  (when-let [user (db/get-user {:id id})]
    (when (hashers/check pass (:pass user))
      id)))
```

Now we can write the login! function that uses the two functions we just defined to handle the login operation.

picture-gallery-b/src/clj/picture_gallery/routes/services/auth.clj

```
(defn login! [{:keys [session]} auth]
  (if-let [id (authenticate (decode-auth auth))]
    (-> {:result :ok}
        (response/ok)
        (assoc :session (assoc session :identity id)))
    (response/unauthorized {:result :unauthorized
                            :message "login failure"})))
```

The function accepts the request and the authentication string as its parameters. It attempts to log the user in using this string. If the login is successful, then we return the result "OK" and set the :identity key in the session that was provided in the request. Otherwise, we return the unauthorized response with the message stating that the login failed.

The logout! function returns a result "OK" and sets the :session in the response to nil. Setting the session explicitly to nil causes the Ring session middleware to remove the existing session.

picture-gallery-b/src/clj/picture_gallery/routes/services/auth.clj

```
(defn logout! []
  (-> {:result :ok}
      (response/ok)
      (assoc :session nil)))
```

Once again, navigate to the Swagger test page to test that our service operations work correctly. We'll need to generate a credentials string encoded in base 64 to test the login! operation. Generate this string in the REPL as follows:

```
(str "Basic "
     (.encodeToString
       (java.util.Base64/getEncoder)
       (.getBytes "user:pass")))
```

When you paste the result in the authorization field on the test page, you'll see the server response. You should see a 200 response when the credentials are correct and a 401 response otherwise as ahown in the figure on page 164.

You can test the logout! function the same way to see if it works correctly. Once you're satisfied that the service routes are working, let's turn to the client UI.

The login workflow looks similar to the registration workflow we developed earlier. Create a modal that collects the username and password. These are sent to the server via Ajax. If the server responds that the authentication was successful, then we set the username as the :identity in the session. Otherwise, we display an error to the user to indicate the login attempt was rejected.

Let's create a new ClojureScript namespace under the src/cljs folder called picture-gallery.components.login. We write separate functions to encode the credentials, call the server, display the registration modal, and display a button that puts the modal in the session.

The namespace declaration must include the following references. Most of these we've seen before, and the only new reference is the goog.crypt.base64. Since ClojureScript leverages the Google Closure library, the namespaces it

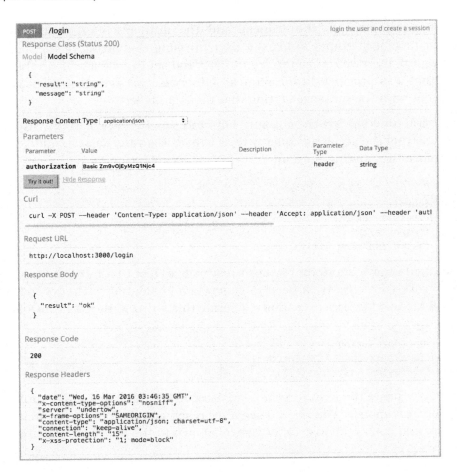

provides can be included the same way that ones written in ClojureScript can. The goog.crypt.base64 namespace provides a encodeString function that can be used to encode the username and the password as a base 64 string.

picture-gallery-b/src/cljs/picture_gallery/components/login.cljs

```
(ns picture-gallery.components.login
  (:require [reagent.core :refer [atom]]
            [reagent.session :as session]
            [goog.crypt.base64 :as b64]
            [clojure.string :as string]
            [ajax.core :as ajax]
            [picture-gallery.components.common :as c]))
```

We can create the encode-auth function to generate the authorization header using the b64/encodeString function.

```
picture-gallery-b/src/cljs/picture_gallery/components/login.cljs
```

```
(defn encode-auth [user pass]
  (->> (str user ":" pass) (b64/encodeString) (str "Basic ")))
```

Next, let's write the login! function that calls the server and sends it the credentials supplied in the fields atom. The fields are sent using the Authorization header after being encoded using the encode-auth function we just wrote. The success handler removes the modal from the session, sets the :identity key to the username, and clears out the form atom. Instead, the error handler populates the error atom with the error message from the server.

```
(defn login! [fields error]
  (let [{:keys [id pass]} @fields]
    (reset! error nil)
    (ajax/POST "/login"
               {:headers        {"Authorization" (encode-auth (string/trim id) pass)}
                :handler         #(do
                                    (session/remove! :modal)
                                    (session/put! :identity id)
                                    (reset! fields nil))
                :error-handler #(reset! error (get-in % [:response :message]))}))))
```

Now write the login-form function that creates a modal similar to the one we used for registration. Let's use the helper functions from the picture-gallery.components.common namespace to define the text and password-input fields.

```
picture-gallery-b/src/cljs/picture_gallery/components/login.cljs
```

```
(defn login-form []
  (let [fields (atom {})
        error (atom nil)]
    (fn []
      [c/modal
       [:div "Picture Gallery Login"]
       [:div
        [:div.well.well-sm
         [:strong "* required field"]]
        [c/text-input "name" :id "enter a user name" fields]
        [c/password-input "password" :pass "enter a password" fields]
        (when-let [error @error]
          [:div.alert.alert-danger error])]
       [:div
        [:button.btn.btn-primary
         {:on-click #(login! fields error)}
         "Login"]
        [:button.btn.btn-danger
         {:on-click #(session/remove! :modal)}
         "Cancel"]]])))
```

All that's left to do is to create a component that inserts the login modal into the session.

picture-gallery-b/src/cljs/picture_gallery/components/login.cljs

```
(defn login-button []
  [:a.btn
   {:on-click #(session/put! :modal login-form)}
   "login"])
```

Let's navigate to the picture-gallery.core namespace. This is where we reference the ajax.core and the picture-gallery.components.login.

```
(ns picture-gallery.core
  (:require ...
            [ajax.core :as ajax]
            [picture-gallery.components.login :as l])
  (:import goog.History))
```

With that done, let's update our user-menu to display both the login-button and the registration-button components. The logout button now calls the server /logout() route and removes the :identity from the session in its handler.

picture-gallery-b/src/cljs/picture_gallery/core.cljs

```
(defn user-menu []
  (if-let [id (session/get :identity)]
    [:ul.nav.navbar-nav.pull-xs-right
     [:li.nav-item
      [:a.dropdown-item.btn
       {:on-click #(ajax/POST
                    "/logout"
                    {:handler (fn [] (session/remove! :identity))})}
       [:i.fa.fa-user] " " id " | sign out"]]]
    [:ul.nav.navbar-nav.pull-xs-right
     [:li.nav-item [l/login-button]]
     [:li.nav-item [reg/registration-button]]]))
```

With that in place, we should now be able to log in to our application and see the username displayed in the navbar menu. Once logged in to the app, we should see the signout link displayed in the navbar instead:

picture-gallery Home About   foo | sign out

Welcome to picture-gallery

TODO: display pictures

However, we're not quite done yet. If we refresh the page, we lose the client session state and the client side of the app reverts back to the default state, asking the user to log in again. In order to fix this, the server has to provide the client with the information about its session state when the page loads.

If you recall, when the user logs in, we set the :identity key in the session.

picture-gallery-b/src/clj/picture_gallery/routes/services/auth.clj

```
(defn login! [{:keys [session]} auth]
  (if-let [id (authenticate (decode-auth auth))]
    (-> {:result :ok}
        (response/ok)
        (assoc :session (assoc session :identity id)))
    (response/unauthorized {:result :unauthorized
                            :message "login failure"})))
```

A middleware function called wrap-identity in the picture-gallery.middleware namespace then binds it to the picture-gallery.layout/*identity* dynamic variable.

picture-gallery-b/src/clj/picture_gallery/middleware.clj

```
(defn wrap-identity [handler]
  (fn [request]
    (binding [*identity* (get-in request [:session :identity])]
      (handler request))))
```

We can now update the render function in the picture-gallery.layout namespace to set the :identity key in the context map that's passed to Selmer when rendering pages. We can use this variable to provide the client part of the application with information about the state of the user session.

picture-gallery-b/src/clj/picture_gallery/layout.clj

```
(defn render
  "renders the HTML template located relative to resources/templates"
  [template & [params]]
  (content-type
    (ok
      (parser/render-file
        template
        (assoc params
          :page template
          :csrf-token *anti-forgery-token*
          :servlet-context *app-context*
          :identity *identity*)))
    "text/html; charset=utf-8"))
```

To do this, we need to open up the resources/templates/home.html file and create a JavaScript variable called identity. This variable is set to the value of the :identity key in the context map.

picture-gallery-b/resources/templates/home.html

```
<script type="text/javascript">
    var context = "{{servlet-context}}";
    var csrfToken = "{{csrf-token}}";
    var identity = {{identity|json|safe}};
</script>
```

Now when the page loads and an :identity key is in the session, its value is populated on the page and becomes available to the client. All that's left to do is to take the value of the js/identity and set it as the :identity key in the client session in the init! function.

picture-gallery-b/src/cljs/picture_gallery/core.cljs

```
(defn init! []
  (load-interceptors!)
  (hook-browser-navigation!)
  (session/put! :identity js/identity)
  (mount-components))
```

The page now correctly preserves the session state when it's refreshed in the browser.

We need to do one last thing before we're finished with the login workflow. The session middleware on the server defaults to timing sessions out after half an hour of inactivity. However, the client code is not aware of the timeout event. Once the user is logged in, the page behaves the same way whether the server session is active or not.

Let's fix this by writing a session-timer function that checks the session status periodically and logs the user out if the session stays inactive for too long.

We track the session status using a :user-event variable that is set any time a user action is initiated. In our case, the action would be represented by Ajax calls to the server. Let's open up the picture-gallery.ajax namespace to add a new interceptor that sets this variable in the session.

picture-gallery-b/src/cljs/picture_gallery/ajax.cljs

```
(ns picture-gallery.ajax
  (:require [ajax.core :as ajax]
            [reagent.session :as session]))
```

picture-gallery-b/src/cljs/picture_gallery/ajax.cljs

```
(defn user-action [request]
  (session/put! :user-event true)
  request)

(defn load-interceptors! []
  (swap! ajax/default-interceptors
```

```
into
[(ajax/to-interceptor {:name "default headers"
                       :request default-headers})
 (ajax/to-interceptor {:name "user action"
                       :request user-action})]]))
```

Now any time we make an Ajax call, both the client and the server know about the user action. The next step is to go back to the picture-gallery.components.login namespace and write the timeout function. The function checks whether there's an :identity key in the session and then checks if a user event has occurred. In case of an event, we remove the :user-event variable from the session and schedule the next check using the timeout-ms variable. In case no event occurred, we remove the :identity key from the session.

picture-gallery-b/src/cljs/picture_gallery/components/login.cljs

```
(def timeout-ms (* 1000 60 30))

(defn session-timer []
  (when (session/get :identity)
    (if (session/get :user-event)
      (do
        (session/remove! :user-event)
        (js/setTimeout #(session-timer) timeout-ms))
      (session/remove! :identity))))
```

We can now update the handler in the login! function to start the session-timer when the user logs in successfully.

picture-gallery-b/src/cljs/picture_gallery/components/login.cljs

```
(defn login! [fields error]
  (let [{:keys [id pass]} @fields]
    (reset! error nil)
    (ajax/POST "/login"
               {:headers     {"Authorization"
                              (encode-auth (when id (string/trim id)) pass)}
                :handler     #(do
                               (session/remove! :modal)
                               (session/put! :identity id)
                               (js/setTimeout session-timer timeout-ms)
                               (reset! fields nil))
                :error-handler #(reset! error (get-in % [:response :message]))})))
```

With this code in place, we can ensure that the client times out sessions at the same time the server does. We're now ready to take a look at the core workflow of our application related to uploading and displaying pictures.

Task C: Uploading Pictures

Once again, our workflow consists of two parts. We have to implement the service operation that handles file uploads, and then we have to provide the UI for the user to upload the file. In addition to saving the file, it would also be nice to generate a thumbnail for it. This allows us to show image previews on the gallery page without having to retrieve full-sized images. The files will be stored in the database and associated with their owner via the username.

We'll start by implementing the server workflow and then testing it using the Swagger UI page. Once it's working the way we need, we can turn our attention to implementing the client side of the workflow.

Updating the Model

We need to update our database to handle file uploads. Let's create a new table called files and then write a query function that populates it. The first step is to create a new migrations file by running the following command:

```
lein migratus create add-files-table
```

The command uses the Migratus plugin to create the "up" and "down" migrations files in the resources/migrations folder under the root of the application.

The next step is to write the statement to create the files table in the "up" migration file. The table tracks the owner, the type of file, the name of the file, and the file content.

picture-gallery-c/resources/migrations/20150819224308-add-files-table.up.sql

```sql
CREATE TABLE files
(owner VARCHAR(20) NOT NULL,
 type  VARCHAR(50) NOT NULL,
 name  VARCHAR(50) NOT NULL,
 data  BYTEA,
 PRIMARY KEY(owner, name));
```

The "down" migration file removes the table created by the "up" migration statement.

picture-gallery-c/resources/migrations/20150819224308-add-files-table.down.sql

```sql
DROP TABLE files;
```

We can now run the following command to update the database tables:

```
lein run migrate
```

The next step is to write a statement for saving files in our database and place it in the resources/sql/queries.sql file.

picture-gallery-c/resources/sql/queries.sql

```
-- :name save-file! :! :n
-- saves a file to the database
INSERT INTO files
(owner, type, name, data)
VALUES (:owner, :type, :name, :data)
```

The SQL statement accepts the parameters that match the :owner, :type, :name, and :data keys in the parameter map and creates a new row in the files table.

Handling the Upload

Since we're creating a new workflow, we should create a new namespace for it. Let's make a picture-gallery.routes.services.upload namespace for handling the task of saving the files by adding the following references to the namespace declaration:

picture-gallery-c/src/clj/picture_gallery/routes/services/upload.clj

```
(ns picture-gallery.routes.services.upload
  (:require [picture-gallery.db.core :as db]
            [ring.util.http-response :refer :all]
            [clojure.tools.logging :as log])
  (:import [java.awt.image AffineTransformOp BufferedImage]
           [java.io ByteArrayOutputStream FileInputStream]
           java.awt.geom.AffineTransform
           javax.imageio.ImageIO
           java.net.URLEncoder))
```

We can break down the server operations into a series of tasks and then write the corresponding functions to accomplish each of these tasks. The first function to write is the save-image! function. It handles the top-level workflow of saving the image and generating the response.

A good way to figure out what helper functions we need is to stub them out in our top-level function and then implement them once we understand the workflow a little better.

```
(defn scale-image [file thumb-size])
```

```
(defn image->byte-array [image])
```

picture-gallery-c/src/clj/picture_gallery/routes/services/upload.clj

```
(defn save-image! [user {:keys [tempfile filename content-type]}]
  (try
    (let [db-file-name (str user (.replaceAll filename "[^a-zA-Z0-9-_\|\.]" ""))]
      (db/save-file! {:owner user
                      :type  content-type
                      :name  db-file-name
                      :data  (file->byte-array tempfile)})
      (db/save-file! {:owner user
                      :type  "image/png"
                      :data  (image->byte-array
                               (scale-image tempfile thumb-size))
                      :name  (str thumb-prefix db-file-name)}))
    (ok {:result :ok})
    (catch Exception e
      (log/error e)
      (internal-server-error "error"))))
```

The function accepts the user identity stored in the session and the file
description sent from the client as a map. The file is described by a map that
in turn contains the following keys:

- :tempfile—The file itself
- :filename—The name of the file being uploaded
- :content-type—The content type of the file being uploaded
- :size—The size of the file in bytes

The keys that are of particular interest to us are called filename and tempfile.
Let's try to store the file in the database by converting the content of the
:tempfile key into a byte array. Then let's create a thumbnail by scaling the
tempfile and storing it with a thumb-prefix prepended to its name. If both operations succeed, we return the status "OK"; otherwise we return a server error.

Now let's define the constants for the prefix and the size of the thumbnail at
the top of the namespace.

picture-gallery-c/src/clj/picture_gallery/routes/services/upload.clj

```
(def thumb-size 150)

(def thumb-prefix "thumb_")
```

Then we write a function to convert the file to a byte array. The function creates an input stream from the file and copies its contents into a byte array
output stream. The output stream is then converted to a byte array that's
returned.

```
(defn file->byte-array [x]
  (with-open [input  (FileInputStream. x)
              buffer (ByteArrayOutputStream.)]
    (clojure.java.io/copy input buffer)
    (.toByteArray buffer)))
```

Next we need to work on scaling the image. Here we leverage the AffineTransform class provided by the Java standard library to create a scale operation, and we use AffineTransformOp to do the transformation. The filter method on the transform-op uses the original image to produce the scaled image we require.

```
(defn scale [img ratio width height]
  (let [scale         (AffineTransform/getScaleInstance
                        (double ratio) (double ratio))
        transform-op (AffineTransformOp.
                        scale AffineTransformOp/TYPE_BILINEAR)]
    (.filter transform-op img (BufferedImage. width height (.getType img)))))
```

Let's test that our scale function works correctly. Copy an image file with the name image.jpg into our project's root and run the following from the REPL:

```
(require '[clojure.java.io :as io])

(ImageIO/write
  (let [image        (ImageIO/read (io/input-stream "image.jpg"))
        scale-factor (/ thumb-size
                        (max (.getWidth org-image)
                             (.getHeight org-image)))]
    (scale image scale-factor thumb-size thumb-size))
  "jpeg"
  (File. "scaled.jpg"))
```

If the function works correctly, then we should end up with a scaled.jpg in the same folder, with a size of 150 pixels by 150 pixels.

We can now write a scale-image function to read the uploaded file's image data using the ImageIO class. Once we have an image, we can grab its width and height values and then scale it to the height defined by the thumb-size constant.

```
(defn scale-image [file thumb-size]
  (let [img        (ImageIO/read file)
        img-width  (.getWidth img)
        img-height (.getHeight img)
        ratio      (/ thumb-size img-height)]
    (scale img ratio (int (* img-width ratio)) thumb-size)))
```

The scale-image can now also be tested from the REPL. It's a good idea to test it with a few images that have different dimensions to ensure that they all scale correctly.

```
(ImageIO/write
  (scale-image (io/input-stream "image.jpg") thumb-size)
  "jpeg"
  (File. "scaled.jpg"))
```

We also need to write an image->byte-array function to take the scaled thumbnail image and convert it to a byte array stored in the database.

picture-gallery-c/src/clj/picture_gallery/routes/services/upload.clj

```
(defn image->byte-array [image]
  (let [baos (ByteArrayOutputStream.)]
    (ImageIO/write image "png" baos)
    (.toByteArray baos)))
```

The function writes the image to a byte array output stream using the ImageIO/write method from the Java standard library. The contents of the output stream are then returned as a byte array.

With these functions in place, we can now navigate to the picture-gallery.routes.services namespace and create a route for file uploads. However, we don't want to add this route to the service-routes we have already defined, since it shouldn't be publicly accessible.

Instead, let's create a new set of routes called restricted-service-routes and place the route there. We also need to reference the upload namespace in order to use it.

```
(ns picture-gallery.routes.services
  (:require [picture-gallery.routes.services.auth :as auth]
            [picture-gallery.routes.services.upload :as upload]
            ...))
```

The route accepts a POST() request containing the multipart params. This map contains the :file key that in turn points to a map containing the file description we discussed earlier. We take this map and pass it to the save-image! function we just wrote, along with the user identity from the session. We have to use the TempFileUpload type for the parameters, so we reference that in our namespace as well.

```
(ns picture-gallery.routes.services
  (:require ...
            [compojure.api.upload :refer [wrap-multipart-params TempFileUpload]]))
```

picture-gallery-c/src/clj/picture_gallery/routes/services.clj

```clojure
(defapi restricted-service-routes
  {:swagger {:ui "/swagger-ui-private"
             :spec "/swagger-private.json"
             :data {:info {:version "1.0.0"
                           :title "Picture Gallery API"
                           :description "Private Services"}}}}
  (POST "/upload" req
        :multipart-params [file :- TempFileUpload]
        :middleware [wrap-multipart-params]
        :summary "handles image upload"
        :return Result
        (upload/save-image! (:identity req) file)))
```

We now have to remember to add the new restricted-service-routes to the app-routes declaration in the picture-gallery.handler namespace.

```clojure
(ns picture-gallery.handler
  (:require ...
            [picture-gallery.routes.services
             :refer [service-routes restricted-service-routes]]
            ...))
```

picture-gallery-c/src/clj/picture_gallery/handler.clj

```clojure
(def app-routes
  (routes
    #'service-routes
    (wrap-routes #'restricted-service-routes middleware/wrap-auth)
    (wrap-routes #'home-routes middleware/wrap-csrf)
    (route/not-found
      (:body
        (error-page {:status 404
                     :title "page not found"})))))
```

With all that in place, you should now restart the application (if it's already running) and then navigate to the Swagger UI page to test our newly implemented upload functionality. You can test uploading some files and check the database to confirm that the entries were indeed created there. (Note that you have to use the localhost:3000/swagger-ui-private/index.html#/default this time around, since the upload routes are found under the private routes.) Our next logical step is to see how we can display these files in the browser.

Creating the Upload UI

Now that the services are implemented and working, it's time to add the UI component that allows users to do image uploads. Let's create a new namespace called picture-gallery.components.upload. The namespace will contain a form that allows the user to select a file to upload and a function that will handle the upload.

Since we're uploading a file, we must use the multipart/form-data encoding for the form. This type of form can't be created directly through JavaScript. Luckily, the Google Closure library that ClojureScript is built on top of provides a way to create an iFrame that can be used to submit the file. Let's take a look at how this all works. Let's start by including the needed references in our namespace declaration.

picture-gallery-c/src/cljs/picture_gallery/components/upload.cljs

```
(ns picture-gallery.components.upload
  (:require [goog.events :as gev]
            [reagent.core :as reagent :refer [atom]]
            [reagent.session :as session]
            [picture-gallery.components.common :as c])
  (:import goog.net.IframeIo
           goog.net.EventType
           [goog.events EventType]))
```

Note the imports for IframeIO and EventType. These are needed to generate the iFrame and submit the file. These have to be accessed through interop similar to the way Java classes are accessed in Clojure. We call the upload-file! function that handles the upload as follows:

picture-gallery-c/src/cljs/picture_gallery/components/upload.cljs

```
(defn upload-file! [upload-form-id status]
  (reset! status nil)
  (let [io (IframeIo.)]
    (gev/listen
      io goog.net.EventType.SUCCESS
      #(reset! status [:div.alert.alert-success "file uploaded successfully"]))
    (gev/listen
      io goog.net.EventType.ERROR
      #(reset! status [:div.alert.alert-danger "failed to upload the file"]))
    (.setErrorChecker io #(= "error" (.getResponseText io)))
    (.sendFromForm
      io
      (.getElementById js/document upload-form-id)
      "/upload")))
```

The function accepts the form ID for the element where the iFrame should be created and an atom to set the status of the Ajax request. The form creates the IframeIo object and then adds the listeners for the events when the upload succeeds as well as when it fails. Each listener sets the appropriate status in the atom. The function calls sendFromForm on the io object and passes it the DOM element pointed to by the upload-form-id.

Since the event to submit the form is triggered by the user pressing the button, the form has to be mounted in the browser DOM in order for the user to access it. Therefore, we don't have to worry about the life cycle of the DOM component in this instance.

The form itself looks similar to the registration and login forms we've written in the previous tasks. Once again, we use a modal to display the content of the form and an atom to track its state.

picture-gallery-c/src/cljs/picture_gallery/components/upload.cljs

```clojure
(defn upload-form []
  (let [status (atom nil)
        form-id "upload-form"]
    (fn []
      [c/modal
       [:div "Upload File"]
       [:div
        (when @status @status)
        [:form {:id       form-id
                :enc-type "multipart/form-data"
                :method   "POST"}
         [:fieldset.form-group
          [:label {:for "file"} "select an image for upload"]
          [:input.form-control {:id "file" :name "file" :type "file"}]]]
        [:button.btn.btn-primary
         {:on-click #(upload-file! form-id status)}
         "Upload"]
        [:button.btn.btn-danger.pull-right
         {:on-click #(session/remove! :modal)}
         "Cancel"]]])))
```

Finally, let's add a button component that we place in the navbar when the user is logged in.

picture-gallery-c/src/cljs/picture_gallery/components/upload.cljs

```clojure
(defn upload-button []
  [:a.btn
   {:on-click #(session/put! :modal upload-form)}
   "upload image"])
```

Let's navigate back to the picture-gallery.core namespace, where we reference the upload namespace and add the button to the user-menu component.

```clojure
(ns picture-gallery.core
  (:require ...
            [picture-gallery.components.upload :as u])
  (:import goog.History))
```

picture-gallery-c/src/cljs/picture_gallery/core.cljs

```clojure
(defn user-menu []
  (if-let [id (session/get :identity)]
    [:ul.nav.navbar-nav.pull-xs-right
     [:li.nav-item [u/upload-button]]
     [:li.nav-item
      [:a.dropdown-item.btn
       {:on-click #(ajax/POST
                     "/logout"
                     {:handler (fn [] (session/remove! :identity))})}
       [:i.fa.fa-user] " " id " | sign out"]]]
    [:ul.nav.navbar-nav.pull-xs-right
     [:li.nav-item [l/login-button]]
     [:li.nav-item [reg/registration-button]]]))
```

You should now be able to log in and see the upload link in the menu. When a user clicks the link, the freshly minted upload form pops up to allow the user to upload the file:

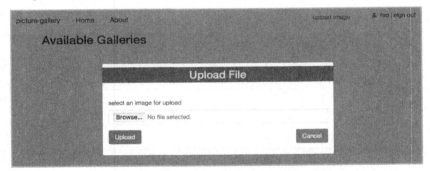

If you select an image file and upload it, then you should be able to check the database to confirm that the upload was handled successfully, as you did when you tested the service using Swagger UI.

Now that we have some pictures in the database, it's time to look at how we can display them on the page.

Task D: Displaying Pictures

We now have all the pieces in place to start working on the gallery portion of the application. Each gallery consists of the images that the user uploaded to our server. Since the images can be large, we'd like instead to display the thumbnails that we generate for each image on the page. When clicked, a thumbnail will display the full-size picture.

Displaying a Gallery for a User

The first thing we need to do is write a query to select the names of the thumbnail files for a particular user and then send those to the client. The client can then create image links for each thumbnail that point to the actual image. We also have to write a function that retrieves the image from the database and serves it using the appropriate MIME type. Let's start by writing the queries in the resources/sql/queries.sql file:

picture-gallery-d/resources/sql/queries.sql

```
-- :name list-thumbnails
-- selects thumbnail names for the given gallery owner
SELECT owner, name FROM files
 WHERE owner = :owner
  AND name LIKE 'thumb\_%'

-- :name get-image :? :1
-- retrieve image data by name
SELECT type, data FROM files
WHERE name = :name
AND owner = :owner
```

Next let's create a new namespace called picture-gallery.routes.services.gallery with the following references:

picture-gallery-d/src/clj/picture_gallery/routes/services/gallery.clj

```
(ns picture-gallery.routes.services.gallery
  (:require [picture-gallery.layout :refer [error-page]]
            [picture-gallery.db.core :as db]
            [ring.util.http-response :refer :all])
  (:import java.io.ByteArrayInputStream))
```

With that done, let's add the get-image and list-thumbnails functions to accomplish the tasks we've outlined:

picture-gallery-d/src/clj/picture_gallery/routes/services/gallery.clj

```
(defn get-image [owner name]
  (if-let [{:keys [type data]} (db/get-image {:owner owner :name name})]
    (-> (ByteArrayInputStream. data)
        (ok)
        (content-type type))
    (error-page {:status 404
                 :title "page not found"})))

(defn list-thumbnails [owner]
  (ok (db/list-thumbnails {:owner owner})))
```

The get-image function accepts the owner and the name of the image as its parameters and then runs the SQL query to retrieve the content type along with the image data. The function then initializes a ByteArrayInputStream using the data and sets the content type to the type of the image. In case the image cannot be found, an error page is generated instead. All the list-thumbnails function does is wrap the database query with the ok response.

We can now reference the picture-gallery.routes.services.gallery in the picture-gallery.routes.services namespace and create new routes using these functions.

```
(ns picture-gallery.routes.services
  (:require ...
            [picture-gallery.routes.services.gallery :as gallery]))
```

picture-gallery-d/src/clj/picture_gallery/routes/services.clj

```
(GET "/gallery/:owner/:name" []
     :summary "display user image"
     :path-params [owner :- String name :- String]
     (gallery/get-image owner name))
(GET "/list-thumbnails/:owner" []
     :path-params [owner :- String]
     :summary "list thumbnails for images in the gallery"
     :return [Gallery]
     (gallery/list-thumbnails owner))
```

The route for retrieving the image uses a RESTful format, where we generate the URI for the image specifically using the */gallery/:owner/:name* format. We then use the name and owner parameters to look up the image using the function we just wrote. The route for listing the thumbnails returns the list of image names for the specified owner.

We also need to create a schema description for the response that consists of a collection of gallery descriptions. The gallery consists of a map with the :owner and the :name keys to specify the gallery owner and the image name.

```
(s/defschema Gallery
  {:owner String
   :name  String})
```

Once again, navigate to the Swagger UI test page and confirm that both functions behave as desired. When you specify a username for the list-thumbnails() route, you should see the list of thumbnail file descriptions for that user as shown in the figure on page 181.

Similarly, when you specify one of the image names in the gallery() route, then you should see the actual image returned in the response as shown in the figure on page 182.

We're now ready to implement the client-side UI for this part of the application. The gallery is on a separate page in our application, and we should create a

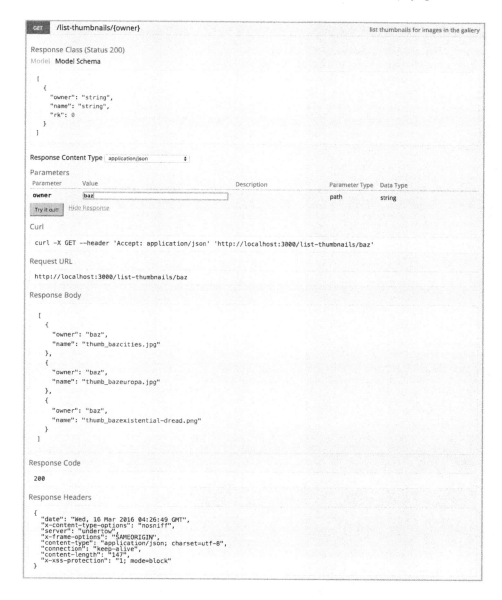

namespace for it called picture-gallery.components.gallery. The gallery page should consist of a grid of thumbnails where the user can click on an individual thumbnail to see the image at its original size.

Since we may have a lot of images in a particular gallery, we'll partition the list of images into sublists and navigate those using a pager, as we did with the cat API viewer in Chapter 6, *Writing RESTful Web Services*, on page 101. Let's start by adding the following references in our namespace declaration:

picture-gallery-d/src/cljs/picture_gallery/components/gallery.cljs

```
(ns picture-gallery.components.gallery
  (:require [reagent.core :refer [atom]]
            [reagent.session :as session]
            [ajax.core :as ajax]
            [clojure.string :as s]
            [picture-gallery.components.common :as c]))
```

As usual, we start by writing the top-level functions and then work our way through the helper functions that we need. The topmost function is going to be the gallery-page. This function is responsible for rendering the page with the thumbnails.

picture-gallery-d/src/cljs/picture_gallery/components/gallery.cljs

```
(defn gallery-page []
  (let [page (atom 0)]
    (fn []
      [:div.container
       (when-let [thumbnail-links (partition-links (session/get :thumbnail-links))]
         [:div.row>div.col-md-12
          [pager (count thumbnail-links) page]
          [gallery (thumbnail-links @page)]])])))
```

The function uses an atom to track the position in the thumbnail pager. The thumbnails should be present in the session atom under the :thumbnail-links key. When the key is populated, the function renders the pager and the selected gallery partition. Let's partition the links using the partition-links function that follows:

picture-gallery-d/src/cljs/picture_gallery/components/gallery.cljs

```
(defn partition-links [links]
  (when (not-empty links)
    (vec (partition-all 6 links))))
```

The function partitions the collection of links into groups of six and then coerces the result into a vector so we can address each group by its index.

The pager function displays the navigation links based on the number of groups generated by the partition-links function. The logic in the pager is the same as the one for displaying links from the Cat API viewer we developed in Chapter 6, *Writing RESTful Web Services*, on page 101 . When a page is selected, the page atom is updated with its index. When the first page is selected, the back navigation button is disabled. Conversely, when the last page is selected, the forward navigation button is disabled.

picture-gallery-d/src/cljs/picture_gallery/components/gallery.cljs

```
(defn pager [pages page]
  (when (> pages 1)
    (into
      [:div.text-xs-center>ul.pagination.pagination-lg]
      (concat
        [[:li.page-item>a.page-link.btn.btn-primary
          {:on-click #(swap! page back pages)
           :class    (when (= @page 0) "disabled")}
          [:span "«"]]]
```

```
(map (partial nav-link page) (range pages))
[[:li.page-item>a.page-link.btn.btn-primary
  {:on-click #(swap! page forward pages)
   :class    (when (= @page (dec pages)) "disabled")}
  [:span "»"]]])))))
```

Let's also extract the logic for updating the selected page index into the following helper function:

picture-gallery-d/src/cljs/picture_gallery/components/gallery.cljs

```
(defn forward [i pages]
  (if (< i (dec pages)) (inc i) i))
(defn back [i]
  (if (pos? i) (dec i) i))
(defn nav-link [page i]
  [:li.page-item>a.page-link.btn.btn-primary
   {:on-click #(reset! page i)
    :class    (when (= i @page) "active")}
   [:span i]])
```

The gallery function is responsible for displaying the table using the links for the particular partition. Let's further partition the links into sets of three per row and then create a column for each thumbnail within the row.

picture-gallery-d/src/cljs/picture_gallery/components/gallery.cljs

```
(defn gallery [links]
  [:div.text-xs-center
   (for [row (partition-all 3 links)]
     ^{:key row}
     [:div.row
      (for [link row]
        ^{:key link}
        [thumb-link link])])])
```

Each link contains the owner and the name keys. We use these to construct the preview for the image. This is done by the thumb-link function.

picture-gallery-d/src/cljs/picture_gallery/components/gallery.cljs

```
(defn thumb-link [{:keys [owner name]}]
  [:div.col-sm-4>img
   {:src      (str js/context "/gallery/" owner "/" name)
    :on-click #(session/put!
                :modal
                (image-modal
                  (str js/context "/gallery/" owner "/"
                       (s/replace name #"thumb_" ""))))}])
```

The function creates a td that contains the thumbnail with a preview of the image. The thumbnail in turn creates a modal that displays the original image when clicked.

Note that the thumb-link function uses the js/context variable as part of the URL that it constructs. This is done for the same reason we added the js/context in the picture-gallery.ajax namespace. Should the application be run with a context, such as when deploying to an application server, then it needs to be prepended explicitly on the client.

The modal contains a div with the image and another div for the background. When the image is clicked, the modal is removed from the session, allowing us to navigate back to the gallery. The background div uses the modal-back-drop.fade.in classes to darken the rest of the page.

picture-gallery-d/src/cljs/picture_gallery/components/gallery.cljs

```
(defn image-modal [link]
  (fn []
    [:div
     [:img.image.panel.panel-default
      {:on-click #(session/remove! :modal)
       :src link}]
     [:div.modal-backdrop.fade.in]]))
```

We also need to add a bit of CSS in order to have our modal show up in the center of the page. Note that we need to add the image.panel.panel-default classes to the image tag. Next, we set the following style for the image class in screen.css:

picture-gallery-d/resources/public/css/screen.css

```
.image {
    z-index: 100;
    position: absolute;
    margin: auto;
    left: 0;
    right: 0;
    padding:20px;
}
```

The image should now show up in a panel at the center of the screen. Finally, let's write a function to fetch the image links via Ajax to load the gallery thumbnail data.

picture-gallery-d/src/cljs/picture_gallery/components/gallery.cljs

```
(defn fetch-gallery-thumbs! [owner]
  (ajax/GET (str "/list-thumbnails/" owner)
            {:handler #(session/put! :thumbnail-links %)}))
```

We're now ready to hook up the gallery display on the home page. Navigate back to picture-gallery.core to add the required functionality. The first thing we have to do is reference the namespace we just created.

```
(ns picture-gallery.core
  (:require ...
            [picture-gallery.components.gallery :as g])
  (:import goog.History))
```

Next let's add the gallery-page function to the map of available pages.

picture-gallery-d/src/cljs/picture_gallery/core.cljs

```
(def pages
  {:home    #'home-page
   :gallery #'g/gallery-page
   :about   #'about-page})
```

With the page added, we can update the client-side routes to call the fetch-gallery-thumbs! function to load the thumbnails and set the page to :gallery when the user navigates to the /gallery/:owner URI.

picture-gallery-d/src/cljs/picture_gallery/core.cljs

```
(secretary/defroute "/" []
                    (session/put! :page :home))
(secretary/defroute "/gallery/:owner" [owner]
                    (g/fetch-gallery-thumbs! owner)
                    (session/put! :page :gallery))
(secretary/defroute "/about" []
                    (session/put! :page :about))
```

You can now test navigating to a particular gallery page to see the thumbnails displayed there. For example, if you had a user foo, then you should be able to navigate to http://localhost:3000/#/gallery/foo to see the gallery for that user, as seen in the following figure:

The next step is to display the list of galleries for all the users on the home page. To do that, we'd like to grab an image for each user in the database and display these in the table. When users click on a particular image, they will be taken to the gallery page associated with the owner of the image.

Displaying All Available Galleries

We first have to update our SQL queries to add a function that pulls a unique image for each user from the database.

picture-gallery-d/resources/sql/queries.sql

```
-- :name select-gallery-previews :? :*
-- selects a thumbnail for each user gallery
WITH summary AS (
    SELECT f.owner,
           f.name,
           ROW_NUMBER() OVER(PARTITION BY f.owner
                                  ORDER BY f.name DESC) AS rk
      FROM files f WHERE name like 'thumb\_%')
SELECT s.*
  FROM summary s
 WHERE s.rk = 1
```

With the function added, we either have to rerun (conman/bind-connection conn "sql/queries.sql") from the picture-gallery.db.core namespace in the REPL or restart the application to load the new query. Next, we have to write a service function that wraps the gallery previews in an ok response.

picture-gallery-d/src/clj/picture_gallery/routes/services/gallery.clj

```
(defn list-galleries []
  (ok (db/select-gallery-previews)))
```

Finally, we need to create a route for the list-galleries function in the picture-gallery.routes.services namespace.

picture-gallery-d/src/clj/picture_gallery/routes/services.clj

```
(GET "/list-galleries" []
     :summary "lists a thumbnail for each user"
     :return [Gallery]
     (gallery/list-galleries))
```

The query that we run produces an additional :rk key when grouping the results. Since the result is otherwise identical to the Gallery schema we've already defined, let's add this as an optional key, allowing us to use it for both list-thumbnails and the list-galleries routes.

picture-gallery-d/src/clj/picture_gallery/routes/services.clj

```
(s/defschema Gallery
  {:owner                 String
   :name                  String
   (s/optional-key :rk) s/Num})
```

Once again, you can test that you're getting the right data by navigating to the Swagger UI page and calling the list-galleries route that you just created:

Back on the client side, we can now update the picture-gallery.core namespace to fetch the available galleries and display them on the home page.

picture-gallery-d/src/cljs/picture_gallery/core.cljs

```
(defn galleries [gallery-links]
  [:div.text-xs-center
   (for [row (partition-all 3 gallery-links)]
     ^{:key row}
     [:div.row
      (for [{:keys [owner name]} row]
        ^{:key (str owner name)}
        [:div.col-sm-4
         [:a {:href (str "#/gallery/" owner)}
          [:img {:src (str js/context "/gallery/" owner "/" name)}]]])])])

(defn list-galleries! []
```

```
  (ajax/GET "/list-galleries"
           {:handler #(session/put! :gallery-links %)}))
(defn home-page []
  (list-galleries!)
  (fn []
    [:div.container
     [:div.row
      [:div.col-md-12>h2 "Available Galleries"]]
     (when-let [gallery-links (session/get :gallery-links)]
       [:div.row>div.col-md-12
        [galleries gallery-links]])]))
```

The galleries function partitions the links into sets of three and then proceeds to render them as image links in a table. Next the list-galleries! function fetches the galleries via Ajax and sets them as the :gallery-links key in the session. Finally, the home-page function calls list-galleries! and renders the galleries component when the :gallery-links is populated in the session with the gallery data.

When you reload the page, it should now display the galleries using the thumbnails. If you select a particular thumbnail, then the gallery page associated with it should be displayed.

Task E: Deleting Pictures

It's reasonable for users to want to remove images they no longer wish to display. Therefore, we need to provide a way for users to select images they wish to remove and tell the application about it. To delete a picture, we'll have to remove both the original image and the generated thumbnail from the database.

Since the images can only be removed by the owner, we'll check if the ID of the owner of the page matches the user in the session. When this is the case, we'll display a button next to the image that will allow the user to delete it.

Implementing the Server Route

First we need to write the service operation for deleting images from the database. Let's open up the queries.sql file and add the query for deleting files. The query uses a combination of the username and the filename to identify the file that needs to be deleted.

picture-gallery-e/resources/sql/queries.sql

```
-- :name delete-file! :! :n
-- deletes the file with the given name and owner
DELETE FROM files
WHERE name = :name
AND owner = :owner
```

Next let's open up the picture-gallery.routes.services.gallery namespace and add the delete-image! function. This function deletes both the original image and the thumbnail that we generated when the image was uploaded.

picture-gallery-e/src/clj/picture_gallery/routes/services/gallery.clj

```
(defn delete-image! [owner thumb-name image-name]
  (db/delete-file! {:owner owner :name thumb-name})
  (db/delete-file! {:owner owner :name image-name})
  (ok {:result :ok}))
```

With the delete-image! function added, let's navigate to the picture-gallery.routes.services namespace and add the route for deleting the image. Declare the route under restricted-service-routes since it shouldn't be publicly available.

picture-gallery-e/src/clj/picture_gallery/routes/services.clj

```
(DELETE "/image/:thumbnail" {:keys [identity]}
        :path-params [thumbnail :- String]
        :summary "delete the specified file from the database"
        :return Result
        (gallery/delete-image!
          identity thumbnail (clojure.string/replace thumbnail #"thumb_" "")))
```

The route accepts a DELETE() request from the client and looks for the thumbnail name in the path params of the request. It then parses out the full image name and passes them both to the delete-image! function along with the user identity from the request.

Note that we use the identity found in the server session when deleting the image, even though the client already sent us the image name that it would like to delete. Doing this ensures that a malicious client would not be able to delete an image that belongs to a different user.

Implementing the UI

With the service functionality added, we can now focus on adding the UI portion of the workflow. Navigate to the picture-gallery.components.gallery namespace, where we put the logic for rendering gallery thumbnails.

Since deletion of images is a destructive operation, we want to add a confirmation dialog before actually deleting the image. Let's write a delete-image-button function that looks as follows:

picture-gallery-e/src/cljs/picture_gallery/components/gallery.cljs

```
(defn delete-image-button [owner name]
  (session/put!
    :modal
    (fn []
      [c/modal
        [:h2 "Remove " name "?"]
        [:div [:img {:src (str "/gallery/" owner "/" name)}]]
        [:div
          [:button.btn.btn-primary
            {:on-click #(delete-image! name)}
            "delete"]
          [:button.btn.btn-danger
            {:on-click #(session/remove! :modal)}
            "Cancel"]]])))
```

The function creates a modal asking the user to confirm the deletion of the specified image. Should the user choose to cancel, we remove the modal from the session; otherwise we call the delete-image! function that follows:

picture-gallery-e/src/cljs/picture_gallery/components/gallery.cljs

```
(defn delete-image! [name]
  (ajax/DELETE (str "/image/" name)
          {:handler #(do
                       (session/update-in!
                         [:thumbnail-links]
                         (fn [links]
                           (remove
                             (fn [link] (= name (:name link)))
                             links)))
                       (session/remove! :modal))}))
```

The delete-image! function calls the /delete-image() route that we defined earlier and passes it the name of the thumbnail as part of the URL. The handler updates the :thumbnail-links key to remove the link with the name of the image from the list. This ensures that the image is also removed in the UI once it's deleted by the server.

We can now update the thumb-link function to check whether the :identity key in the session matches the owner of the image and then display a button that triggers the modal for deleting the image.

`picture-gallery-e/src/cljs/picture_gallery/components/gallery.cljs`

```clojure
(defn thumb-link [{:keys [owner name]}]
  [:div.col-sm-4
   [:img
    {:src      (str js/context "/gallery/" owner "/" name)
     :on-click #(session/put!
                  :modal
                  (image-modal (str js/context
                                    "/gallery/" owner "/"
                                    (s/replace name #"thumb_" ""))))}]
   (when (= (session/get :identity) owner)
     [:div.text-xs-center>div.btn.btn-danger
      {:on-click #(delete-image-button owner name)}
      [:i.fa.fa-times]])])
```

Thus:

One last task on our list is to allow users to delete their accounts from our app. Now let's take a look at how that's accomplished.

Task F: Account Deletion

When a user decides to delete her account, we need to delete all the user-related information from the database, as well as all the user's files.

Implementing Account-Deletion Service Operations

The first thing to do is to write the queries to delete the user along with the files associated with them. Add the following code to the queries.sql file:

`picture-gallery-f/resources/sql/queries.sql`

```sql
-- :name delete-user! :! :n
-- deletes the user account
DELETE FROM users
WHERE id = :id

-- :name delete-user-images! :! :n
```

```
-- deletes all the images for the specified user
DELETE FROM files
WHERE owner = :owner
```

Since account deletion is a single operation, these queries have to be run atomically, meaning that either both queries complete successfully or neither query is run. In other words, these queries have to be run in a transaction. Open up the picture-gallery.db.core namespace and add this function there:

picture-gallery-f/src/clj/picture_gallery/db/core.clj

```
(defn delete-account! [id]
  (conman/with-transaction [*db*]
    (delete-user! {:id id})
    (delete-user-images! {:owner id})))
```

The function uses the conman/with-transaction macro, which takes the database connection and creates a transaction using it. Since the functions that it calls have been generated using the conman/bind-connection macro, they default to using the transactional connection without t-conn being explicitly passed to them.

The next step is to define the service handler function in the picture-gallery.routes.services.auth namespace. The function accepts the identity of the user that is logged in, calls the delete-account! function that you just wrote, and sets the response session to nil to indicate that the user is no longer logged in.

picture-gallery-f/src/clj/picture_gallery/routes/services/auth.clj

```
(defn delete-account! [identity]
  (db/delete-account! identity)
  (-> {:result :ok}
      (response/ok)
      (assoc :session nil)))
```

With that in place, you're ready to add the service route for deleting the account. Again, this route should be placed under the restricted-service-routes definition in the picture-gallery.routes.services namespace.

picture-gallery-f/src/clj/picture_gallery/routes/services.clj

```
(DELETE "/account" {:keys [identity]}
    (auth/delete-account! identity))
```

That's all you need to do on the server side. Now let's turn our attention to the client and implement the UI components that allow the user to delete her account.

Implementing Account Deletion UI Components

To keep things simple, let's place the account deletion under the user menu
in the navbar component. However, the current menu is starting to get a little
busy. Let's refactor it so that when the user is logged in, she's able to click
on her name and see a drop-down with the options to delete the account and
log out.

picture-gallery-f/src/cljs/picture_gallery/core.cljs

```clojure
(defn user-menu []
  (if-let [id (session/get :identity)]
    [:ul.nav.navbar-nav.pull-xs-right
      [:li.nav-item
       [u/upload-button]]
      [:li.nav-item
       [account-actions id]]]
    [:ul.nav.navbar-nav.pull-xs-right
      [:li.nav-item [l/login-button]]
      [:li.nav-item [reg/registration-button]]]))
```

The menu now uses the account-actions component. The component manages
the state of the drop-down and populates it with the buttons to handle the
two actions just described.

picture-gallery-f/src/cljs/picture_gallery/core.cljs

```clojure
(defn account-actions [id]
  (let [expanded? (r/atom false)]
    (fn []
      [:div.dropdown
       {:class   (when @expanded? "open")
        :on-click #(swap! expanded? not)}
       [:button.btn.btn-secondary.dropdown-toggle
        {:type :button}
        [:span.glyphicon.glyphicon-user] " " id [:span.caret]]
       [:div.dropdown-menu.user-actions
        [:a.dropdown-item.btn
         {:on-click
           #(session/put!
             :modal reg/delete-account-modal)}
         "delete account"]
        [:a.dropdown-item.btn
         {:on-click
           #(ajax/POST
             "/logout"
             {:handler (fn [] (session/remove! :identity))})}
         "sign out"]]])))
```

The component uses an atom to check whether the menu is expanded or not. The atom state is flipped whenever the list item containing the username is clicked. When that happens, the user should see a drop-down menu that contains the buttons to delete the account and to log out.

When someone clicks a username, a drop-down menu shows up below the button. However, the menu ends up at the edge of the screen, and the content is only partially displayed. We can fix this by adding a bit of CSS to offset the drop-down.

picture-gallery-f/resources/public/css/screen.css

```
.user-actions {
  margin-left: -80px;
}
```

Since account deletion is a destructive operation, let's use the confirmation modal, as we did when deleting images. Let's place the modal in the picture-gallery.components.registration namespace. Navigate there and add this code:

picture-gallery-f/src/cljs/picture_gallery/components/registration.cljs

```
(defn delete-account-modal []
  (fn []
    [c/modal
     [:h2.alert.alert-danger "Delete Account!"]
     [:p "Are you sure you wish to delete the account and associated gallery?"]
     [:div
      [:button.btn.btn-primary
       {:on-click (fn []
                    (delete-account!)
                    (session/remove! :modal))}
       "Delete"]
      [:button.btn.btn-danger
       {:on-click (fn [] (session/remove! :modal))}
       "Cancel"]]]))
```

The modal confirms that the user is sure she wishes to perform this action and then calls the delete-account! function when the Delete Account! button is clicked. The Cancel button simply removes the modal from the session.

picture-gallery-f/src/cljs/picture_gallery/components/registration.cljs

```
(defn delete-account! []
  (ajax/DELETE "/account"
               {:handler #(do
                            (session/remove! :identity)
                            (session/put! :page :home))}))
```

The function calls the /account() route we just wrote using the DELETE() HTTP method and then removes the :identity key from the session in the callback handler. At this point the account should be removed from the database and the session cleared from the server. Since the :identity key is no longer in the client session, the user is now presented with the login and registration options instead of the user menu.

Now that our application is fully functional, we can have a bit of fun by using a JavaScript library to set the background color of the image modal based on the average image colors. This exercise will illustrate how we can interact with JavaScript code that isn't aware of the React virtual DOM, as well as illustrate the nuances of using external JavaScript libraries when doing advanced ClojureScript compilation.

Adding Some Color

Let's take a look at how we can use the AlbumColors library to create a three-color palette using the image colors.[5] We'll then use these colors to set a background gradient for the DOM node containing the image.

Let's start by adding the library JavaScript file to our project.[6] Save the file in the resources/public/vendor/js folder as color.js.

Next we'll add the new JavaScript file to the resources/templates/home.html template file in order to load it on the page.

picture-gallery-colors/resources/templates/home.html

```
<!-- scripts and styles -->
{% style "/assets/bootstrap/css/bootstrap.min.css" %}
{% style "/assets/font-awesome/css/font-awesome.min.css" %}
{% style "/css/screen.css" %}
{% script "/vendor/js/colors.js" %}
```

We can now start using this library to figure out the colors for the image background. Let's navigate to the picture-gallery.components.gallery namespace and update the code to do that.

The AlbumColors library works by taking a link to an image and returning a vector of three colors, each in turn represented by a vector of RGB values. For example, the output might look as follows: [[254, 254, 254], [2, 138, 14], [4, 171, 21]]. Since we'd like to use the output to create a gradient background for the image, we can start by writing a couple of helper functions to do that.

---

5.   https://github.com/chengyin/albumcolors
6.   https://raw.githubusercontent.com/chengyin/albumcolors/master/albumcolors.js

picture-gallery-colors/src/cljs/picture_gallery/components/gallery.cljs

```
(defn rgb-str [[r g b] mask]
  (str "rgba(" r "," g "," b "," mask ")"))
(defn set-background! [style [c1 c2 c3]]
  (set! (.-background style)
        (str "linear-gradient("
             (rgb-str c3 0.8) ","
             (rgb-str c2 0.9) ","
             (rgb-str c1 1) ")")))
```

The set-background! function accepts a JavaScript-style object and the three colors generated by calling AlbumColors. It then proceeds to generate the style string using these. The rgb-str function is used to generate the string to represent each color.

Our next problem is that we need to get access to the actual DOM node that's mounted in the browser in order to set the style. Recall that Reagent internally uses a virtual DOM and that the elements aren't guaranteed to be mounted in the browser DOM at any one time. Therefore, in order to work with the actual browser DOM node, we have to use a different approach.

Luckily, each component has a life cycle that Reagent lets us hook into. The life cycle consists of the following states.

- :component-did-mount
- :get-initial-state
- :component-will-receive-props
- :should-component-update
- :component-will-mount
- :component-will-update
- :component-did-update
- :component-will-unmount
- :render

The states that are of particular interest to us are :component-did-mount and :render. The handler for the first state is called whenever the component is mounted in the browser DOM, and the handler for the second state is called when Reagent attempts to render the component. When we specified the component using a function (as we've been doing up to now), only the :render state was being used.

However, once we hook into the :component-did-mount state, then we're able to manipulate the browser DOM directly. This is precisely what we need to do in order to accomplish our task. Let's modify the image-modal component to split out the image component into a separate function.

picture-gallery-colors/src/cljs/picture_gallery/components/gallery.cljs

```clojure
(defn image-modal [thumb-link link]
  (fn []
    [:div
     [image-panel thumb-link link]
     [:div.modal-backdrop.fade.in]]))
```

We also want to update the component to accept the thumb-link argument that we use to calculate the average image color. Since the original image could be large, it may take a long time to process. The thumbnail images, on the other hand, are always guaranteed to be a fixed size, making them perfect for this task. We also have to remember to update the thumb-link component to pass the second argument to the image-modal.

picture-gallery-colors/src/cljs/picture_gallery/components/gallery.cljs

```clojure
(defn thumb-link [{:keys [owner name]}]
  [:div.col-sm-4
   [:img
    {:src      (str js/context "/gallery/" owner "/" name)
     :on-click #(session/put!
                  :modal
                  (image-modal
                    (str js/context "/gallery/" owner "/" name)
                    (str js/context "/gallery/" owner "/"
                      (s/replace name #"thumb_" ""))))}]
   (when (= (session/get :identity) owner)
     [:div.text-xs-center>div.btn.btn-danger
      {:on-click #(delete-image-button owner name)}
      [:i.fa.fa-times]])])
```

The image-panel function calls reagent/create-class to generate the component. The function accepts a map keyed on the life cycle events that we just discussed. Let's provide callback functions for the :component-did-mount and the :render events.

picture-gallery-colors/src/cljs/picture_gallery/components/gallery.cljs

```clojure
(defn image-panel-did-mount [thumb-link]
  (fn [div]
    (.getColors
      (js/AlbumColors. thumb-link)
      (fn [colors]
        (-> div reagent/dom-node .-style (set-background! colors))))))

(defn render-image-panel [link]
  (fn []
    [:img.image.panel.panel-default
```

```
    {:on-click #(session/remove! :modal)
     :src link}])))
(defn image-panel [thumb-link link]
  (reagent/create-class {:render       (render-image-panel link)
                         :component-did-mount (image-panel-did-mount thumb-link)}))
```

The render-image-panel callback looks just like a regular Reagent component. However, the image-panel-did-mount function returns a function that expects a mounted Reagent component as its input. This component contains the actual DOM node that was generated by Reagent when it was mounted.

The function returned by the image-panel-did-mount closure creates a JavaScript object representing the colors for the link by calling AlbumColors with the thumb-link as its parameter. It then calls the .getColors method on this object and passes it an anonymous callback function that's responsible for setting the background color on div.

The callback uses the reagent/dom-node function to extract the div DOM element. Next, it grabs the style property and passes it to the set-background! function that we wrote earlier, along with the generated colors.

With these changes in place, we should now be able to see a background color gradient around the image, as seen in the following figure:

Now let's try packaging our app for deployment and running it. Note that we'll have to specify the database URL as an environment variable when we run the packaged application. In development mode, the variable was populated from the profiles.clj configuration file. However, once we run the packaged application, all configuration must come from the environment. Using the "bash" shell, run the following commands:

```
export DATABASE_URL="jdbc:postgresql://localhost/picture_gallery_dev?..."
lein uberjar
java -jar target/uberjar/picture-gallery.jar
```

Unfortunately, once the app starts up, the page won't render. If you check the browser console, you'll see an error that looks like the following:

```
Uncaught TypeError: Object [object Object] has no method 'Le'
```

This error is not terribly descriptive and doesn't give much to go on. It says that we tried to call a method named Le on some object and that the method doesn't exist.

The hint here is that we never defined a method called Le. What's happening is that the advanced optimizer is munging the function names when it compiles the JavaScript. This isn't a problem for functions we've defined ourselves, as they're guaranteed to get consistent naming throughout. However, we're now calling a function from the AlbumColors JavaScript library. The compiler munges its name as well, and the resulting name will obviously not be found.

Luckily, there's a simple solution to this problem. The Google Closure compiler provides a way to protect function names in external libraries by declaring them in an externs file. Let's create a new file called externs.js under the resources directory of our project and declare the functions whose names we wish to protect in it:

picture-gallery-colors/resources/externs.js

```
var AlbumColors = {};
AlbumColors.getColors = function() {};
```

Once that's done, let's reference this file in the :externs vector under the :cljsbuild profile as follows:

picture-gallery-colors/project.clj

```
:cljsbuild
{:builds
 {:app
  {:source-paths ["src/cljc" "src/cljs"]
   :compiler
   {:output-to "target/cljsbuild/public/js/app.js"
    :output-dir "target/cljsbuild/public/js/out"
    :externs ["react/externs/react.js"
              "resources/externs.js"]
    :pretty-print true}}}}
```

Now if we clean and recompile our ClojureScript, everything should work as expected.

```
lein uberjar
java -jar target/uberjar/picture-gallery.jar
15-Oct-02 22:05:33 Nyx INFO [picture-gallery.handler] -
-=[picture-gallery started successfully]=-
22:05:33.833 INFO  [wunderboss.web.Web] (main) Registered web context /
15-Oct-02 22:05:33 Nyx INFO [picture-gallery.core] - server started on port: 3000
```

The preceding example illustrates how we can generate an externs file by hand. However, this can be tedious if you're using a lot of external libraries in your application. A simpler way is to use the library itself as the externs file. This approach will work in most cases; however, it will also generate a lot of warnings during compilation. You can suppress those like this:

```
:cljsbuild
{:builds
 {:app
  {:source-paths ["src/cljs" "src/cljc"]
   :compiler
   {:output-to "target/cljsbuild/public/js/app.js"
    :output-dir "target/cljsbuild/public/js/out"
    :externs ["react/externs/react.js"
              "resources/public/vendor/js/colors.js"]
    :closure-warnings {:externs-validation :off
                       :non-standard-jsdoc :off}
    :pretty-print true}}}}
```

With the preceding configuration, the ClojureScript compiler tries to infer the externs automatically, and any warnings are suppressed in the output.

What You've Learned

Congratulations! You now have a working application that you can package and deploy in production. In the next chapter, we'll look at adding tests and packaging the application for running in different types of environments.

CHAPTER 9

Finishing Touches

In this chapter we'll take a look at adding tests and packaging the application for deployment.

Unit Tests

There are many schools of thought on how, what, and when to test. This is a very sensitive subject for many people. As such, I will simply give an overview of the basic tools available for testing and leave it up to you to decide how and when to use them.

The Test API

Clojure provides built-in support for testing via the clojure.test namespace. When a new project is created, a test package is generated along with it.

Let's take a quick look at what the clojure.test API looks like and how to work with it. The simplest way to write tests is to create assertions using the is macro. The following are a few examples of how it works:

```
(is (= 4 (+ 2 2)))

(is (= 5 (+ 2 2)))

FAIL in  (:1)
    expected: (= 5 (+ 2 2))
    actual: (not (= 5 4))
false

(is (even? 2))

(is (instance? String 123))
FAIL in (:1)
expected: (instance? String 123)
  actual: java.lang.Long
false
```

As you can see, the is macro can take any expression. If the expression fails, the macro prints the expression along with the actual result and then returns false; otherwise it returns true.

We can also group our tests together by using the testing macro. This macro accepts a string name for the group of tests followed by the assertions.

```
(testing "Collections"
  (is (coll? {}))
  (is (coll? #{}))
  (is (coll? []))
  (is (coll? '())))
```

Finally, we can define tests by using the deftest macro:

```
(deftest collections-test
  (testing "Collections"
    (is (coll? {}))
    (is (coll? #{}))
    (is (coll? []))
    (is (coll? '()))))
```

The tests defined using deftest can be called like regular functions. You can also run all the tests in the read-evaluate-print loop by calling run-tests. All tests in the application's test folder can be run via Leiningen by calling lein test. The API contains a number of other helpers as well, but I hope that the preceding examples will prove sufficient for you to get started.

Finally, it's worth mentioning that there are a number of test frameworks for Clojure, such as Midje and Speclj.[1,2] Furthermore, test frameworks are available specifically for testing web applications. The two popular choices to explore are Peridot and Kerodon.[3,4]

These frameworks provide many features not found in the core testing API. If your testing needs go beyond the basics we explored here, these will make excellent tools in your Clojure toolbox.

Testing the Application

Our app has two types of routes. Some routes serve the user-interface (UI) portion of the application to be rendered by the browser, and others expose service end points accessed via Ajax by the client part of the application.

---

1. https://github.com/marick/Midje
2. http://speclj.com/
3. https://github.com/xeqi/peridot
4. https://github.com/xeqi/kerodon

We'll look at writing tests for both types of routes in our application.

Luminus includes a library called *ring-mock* by default.[5] The library provides a number of helper functions for generating mock requests.

We already have a test harness defined for our application. You can find it under the test/clj/picture_gallery/test/ directory. The test handler is called handler.clj. If we open it up, we can see that it defines a test called test-app.

picture-gallery-tests/test/clj/picture_gallery/test/handler.clj

```
(deftest test-app
  (testing "main route"
    (let [response (app (request :get "/"))]
      (is (= 200 (:status response)))))
  (testing "not-found route"
    (let [response (app (request :get "/invalid"))]
      (is (= 404 (:status response))))))
```

The ring.mock.request/request function is used to generate the request. It accepts a keyword indicating the request method, followed by the target URI and an optional parameter map that isn't used in the example.

```
(request <method> <url> <optional params>)
```

The request is then passed to the picture-gallery.handler/app function that is the main entry point for our application. The result of calling app with the mock request is a Ring-style response discussed in Chapter 2, *Luminus Web Stack*, on page 25.

The first test checks that the app responds with the status 200 when we request the / URI. The second test checks that status 404 is returned for a nonexistent URI.

So far so good. Now let's see what's involved in creating a test for the login service operation. We'd like to call the /login URL and pass it the user ID and the password. However, the login credentials must be passed in as an encoded Authorization header.

We can implement the first test by writing a function that generates the header value given the username and the password.

---

5.   https://github.com/ring-clojure/ring-mock

picture-gallery-tests/test/clj/picture_gallery/test/handler.clj

```clojure
(defn encode-auth [user pass]
  (->> (str user ":" pass)
       (.getBytes)
       (.encodeToString (java.util.Base64/getEncoder))
       (str "Basic ")))
```

Next, let's write a login-request function that generates the request and sets the header using the ring.mock.request/header function.

picture-gallery-tests/test/clj/picture_gallery/test/handler.clj

```clojure
(defn login-request [id pass]
  (-> (request :post "/login")
      (header "Authorization" (encode-auth id pass))))
```

That leaves us with one last problem. The authenticate function in the picture-gallery.routes.services.auth/ namespace calls (db/get-user {:id id}) from the picture-gallery.db.core namespace. This function fetches the user credentials from the database. However, we wish to test the request handler and not the model.

In some languages it's possible to use monkey patching to get around this problem. This approach allows you to simply redefine the offending function at runtime with your own version. The downside of this approach is that the change is global and therefore might interact poorly with code that expects the original version.

Clojure provides a with-redefs macro that redefines vars within the scope of its body. This approach gives us the ability to make runtime modifications in a safer fashion, where we know precisely the scope of the code that is affected.

For our purposes, we'll redefine the get-users function with a mock function for the scope of our tests. It's handy that we didn't have to plan for this when writing our application's business logic. Let's look at how this works in action. Let's first define a mock function that returns a test user.

picture-gallery-tests/test/clj/picture_gallery/test/handler.clj

```clojure
(defn mock-get-user [{:keys [id]}]
  (if (= id "foo")
    {:id "foo"
     :pass (hashers/encrypt "bar")}))
```

We also need to reference buddy.hashers for it to encrypt the password.

```clojure
[buddy.hashers :as hashers]
```

We can now redefine the picture-gallery.db.core/get-user with the mock function before running our test:

```
(with-redefs [picture-gallery.db.core/get-user mock-get-user]
  (app (login-request "foo" "bar")))
```

We can see that the response contains the status of 200. The response body is an input stream, and we'll want to get data out of it. Let's write a function to parse out the response data.

picture-gallery-tests/test/clj/picture_gallery/test/handler.clj

```
(defn parse-response [body]
  (-> body slurp (parse-string true)))
```

Since we need to parse the response body into a Clojure data structure, we need to reference the parse-string function from the Cheshire library in our namespace declaration.

```
[cheshire.core :refer [parse-string]]
```

We can now check that the response has the following data:

```
(with-redefs [picture-gallery.db.core/get-user mock-get-user]
  (-> (login-request "foo" "bar") app :body parse-response))
;;{:result "ok"}
```

If we provide incorrect credentials, we'll see a different response instead:

```
(with-redefs [picture-gallery.db.core/get-user mock-get-user]
  (-> (login-request "foo" "xxx") app :body parse-response))
;;{:result "unauthorized", :message "login failure"}
```

We can now wrap this up in an actual test that checks that the application responds correctly in both scenarios.

picture-gallery-tests/test/clj/picture_gallery/test/handler.clj

```
(deftest test-login
  (testing "login success"
    (with-redefs [picture-gallery.db.core/get-user mock-get-user]
      (let [{:keys [body status]} (app (login-request "foo" "bar"))]
        (is
         (= 200 status))
        (is
         (= {:result "ok"}
            (parse-response body))))))
  (testing "password mismatch"
    (with-redefs [picture-gallery.db.core/get-user mock-get-user]
      (let [{:keys [body status]} (app (login-request "foo" "baz"))]
        (is
         (= {:result "unauthorized" :message "login failure"}
            (parse-response body)))
        (is
         (= 401 status))))))
```

Database Testing

Now that we've seen some basics of testing, let's take a look at how we can test our app against a database. If you recall, the profiles.clj file contains two separate database-connection URLs. One is specified under the :profiles/dev key and is used during development. The other is specified under the :profiles/test key and will be used for testing.

It's good practice to create a separate schema for testing that's independent of the one used for development. This allows you to ensure that the data quality in this schema is not affected by anything you do during development, such as creating or removing users.

Let's create a new schema called *picture_gallery_test* and navigate to the picture-gallery.test.db.core namespace in the test source path. The namespace contains a default test harness that looks like this:

```
(use-fixtures
  :once
  (fn [f]
    (mount/start
      #'picture-gallery.config/env
      #'picture-gallery.db.core/*db*)
    (migrations/migrate ["migrate"] (select-keys env [:database-url]))
    (f)))
(deftest test-users
  (jdbc/with-db-transaction [t-conn *db*]
    (jdbc/db-set-rollback-only! t-conn)
    (is (= 1 (db/create-user!
               t-conn
               {:id         "1"
                :first_name "Sam"
                :last_name  "Smith"
                :email      "sam.smith@example.com"
                :pass       "pass"})))
    (is (= {:id         "1"
            :first_name "Sam"
            :last_name  "Smith"
            :email      "sam.smith@example.com"
            :pass       "pass"
            :admin      nil
            :last_login nil
            :is_active  nil}
           (db/get-user t-conn {:id "1"}))))))
```

The fixtures are used to initialize the database connection and run any out-standing migrations before the tests are run. The test-users test attempts to create a user in the database within a transaction and tests that the user was created successfully. The transaction is rolled back after the test runs, ensuring that the database is in a clean state for the next test.

The default test that we have fails because our create-user! function only populates the :id and the :pass keys.

```
-- :name create-user!
-- creates a new user record
INSERT INTO users
(id, pass)
VALUES (:id, :pass)
```

Update the test in this way to make it pass by setting the expected values:

```
(is (= {:id        "1"
        :first_name nil
        :last_name  nil
        :email      nil
        :pass       "pass"
        :admin      nil
        :last_login nil
        :is_active  nil}
       (db/get-user {:id "1"}))))
```

Using a test schema allows us to test our application end-to-end. I recommended this approach for any integration and validation testing.

Package the Application

Our application is now ready to be packaged and deployed. Let's see how to accomplish this using Leiningen and go over some of the things to be aware of, depending on how you wish to run the application in production.

Up to this point we've been running our application by calling lein run to start up the HTTP server in development mode. In this mode the server watches the files for changes and reloads them as needed. This obviously causes a significant performance hit. Since we should optimize our application for performance when we deploy in production, we'll need to package it differently. Let's look at the two most popular ways to run Clojure web applications in production, along with the benefits and the drawbacks of these approaches.

The first approach is to create a standalone executable with an embedded HTTP server such as Immutant. This way the application will not have any external dependencies, aside from having the Java Runtime Environment installed on the system.

The downside of this approach is that we'll have to manage the configuration for each application individually. We'll have to configure things like logging, database connections, SSL configuration, and so on. It also means that each application will have more overhead because we need to spawn an independent instance of the JVM for it.

The second approach is to create a WAR (which stands for web application archive) that can be deployed to an application server such as Apache Tomcat. With this approach we can do all the environment-specific configuration on the application server.

The application server can also host multiple applications on a shared domain. This allows us to have less overhead per application and the ability to provide a common configuration for all the applications deployed on the server. The container can keep track of database connection settings, logging configurations, managing HTTPS listeners, and so on.

The downside of this approach is that the application server will have higher overhead than embedded Jetty. The application server's configuration is often more complex as well. The work involved may not be justified, depending on how you plan to manage your application in production.

Another problem with using application servers is that a single application can bring down the whole domain and affect all the applications deployed to the server. Running applications as standalone instances avoids this problem by design.

The good news is that it's equally easy to package the application for either type of deployment. If you start with one approach, you can switch to the other with minimal effort.

Standalone Deployment

Here we'll take a closer look at what's involved in deployment as a standalone application.

Running as an UberJar

When we wish to package the application for standalone deployment, we simply run the following from the application's root:

```
lein uberjar
```

If you recall, when the application is running standalone, then the environment variables declared in profiles.clj are no longer available. Thus, we have to specify the database connection variable before running the package application.

Luminus uses a library called *cprop* for configuration management.[6] The library provides a number of options for specifying the configuration settings.

The first option is to include the configuration directly in the JAR. The library will look for a config.edn file on the classpath and read the configuration from there. Alternatively, we can specify the location of the EDN configuration file using an environment variable called *conf*. When multiple configurations are found, they will be merged into a single configuration map when the application starts. The keys found in the external configuration will overwrite the keys in the one packaged in the JAR. Finally, we can specify the configuration keys as environment variables. Environment variables have precedence over the former two options. Since we only have a single configuration key in our case, let's specify it as an environment variable.

```
export DATABASE_URL="jdbc:postgresql://localhost/picture_gallery_dev?..."
```

The resulting artifact will be created in the target folder. We can now run this JAR by invoking java -jar target/picture-gallery.jar. Once the server starts, you can see it running by browsing to localhost:3000. We also have to remember to provide the database connection environment variable for the application to use.

```
export DATABASE_URL="jdbc:postgresql://localhost/picture_gallery_dev?..."
java -jar target/uberjar/picture-gallery.jar
```

The server runs on port 3000 by default. To override the default port, use the $PORT environment variable.

Running with HTTP Kit

The UberJar we created uses an embedded Immutant server. However, it's possible to swap out Immutant for a different container. One such container is HTTP Kit.

HTTP Kit is a Ring-compliant event-driven server for Clojure that aims to be a drop-in replacement for Immutant. HTTP Kit uses the nonblocking I/O model to handle requests. This allows for extremely high throughput.

Luminus provides adapter libraries for all the major Clojure HTTP servers. To use HTTP Kit, we first have to reference its adapter in our project.clj dependencies. We also have to reference *ring-ttl-session* since we are no longer using the Immutant session middleware.

```
:dependencies [... [luminus-http-kit "0.1.3"]
                   [ring-ttl-session "0.3.0"]]
```

---

6. https://github.com/tolitius/cprop

Now let's proceed to update our picture-gallery.middleware to use the ttl-memory-store. We need to replace the reference to [immutant.web.middleware :refer [wrap-session]] with [ring-ttl-session.core :refer [ttl-memory-store]].

```
(ns picture-gallery.middleware
  (:require ...
            ;removed: [immutant.web.middleware :refer [wrap-session]]
            [ring-ttl-session.core :refer [ttl-memory-store]]))
```

Let's update the wrap-base function to use the new session store as follows:

```
(defn wrap-base [handler]
  (-> ((:middleware defaults) handler)
      wrap-auth
      wrap-formats
      wrap-webjars
      wrap-flash
      (wrap-defaults
        (-> site-defaults
            (assoc-in [:security :anti-forgery] false)
            (assoc-in [:session :store] (ttl-memory-store (* 60 30)))))
      wrap-context
      wrap-internal-error))
```

We can now compile the application as a standalone executable and run it using the HTTP Kit server. Recall that the database URL needs to be present in the environment if it's not already.

```
lein uberjar
java -jar target/uberjar/picture-gallery.jar
```

That's all there is to it. Thanks to Ring architecture, the application is largely insulated from the implementation details of the underlying HTTP server being used.

Running as a Daemon

We can run our application as a daemon on *nix systems. For example, to daemonize it on Ubuntu, we could create an upstart configuration.[7] To do that we'll make a configuration file, /etc/init/gallery.conf, where we'll add these settings:

```
## Upstart config file (use 'start gallery', 'stop gallery')
## stdout and stderr will be captured in /var/log/upstart/gallery.log
author "Me"
description "Start the Picture Gallery web app on its default port"
start on (local-filesystems and net-device-up IFACE!=lo)
exec java -Dconf=/srv/gallery.edn -jar /srv/picture-gallery.jar

## Try to restart up to 10 times within 5 min:
```

---

7.   http://upstart.ubuntu.com/

```
respawn limit 10 300
```

Note that we're using a gallery.edn configuration file to supply the configuration for the application. The contents of the file should be an EDN map containing the :database-url key.

```
{:database-url
 "jdbc:postgresql://localhost/picture_gallery_dev?user=gallery&password=pictures"}
```

When the conf environment variable is set, then the cprop library looks for the EDN configuration file specified and reads it as part of the configuration.

Application-Server Deployment

Now that we know how to run our application standalone, let's see how that compares to running it on an application server.

Tomcat Deployment

Before starting this section, you will need to download a copy of the Tomcat server and extract the archive locally.

Tomcat is started by running bin/catalina.sh start under the Tomcat directory. You can see the server logs under logs/catalina.out. When the server starts, you should see something like the following in your log:

```
May 5, 2013 11:12:25 AM org.apache.catalina.core.AprLifecycleListener init
INFO: The APR-based Apache Tomcat Native library, which allows optimal performance
in production environments, was not found on the java.library.path:
.:/Library/Java/Extensions:/System/Library/Java/Extensions:/usr/lib/java
May 5, 2013 11:12:25 AM org.apache.coyote.AbstractProtocol init
INFO: Initializing ProtocolHandler ["http-bio-3000"]
...
```

Stopping the server is equally simple. To do that you run bin/catalina.sh stop.

One of the features that the application server provides is managing JDBC connections. Let's configure the server to provide the connection for the picture gallery database.

We'll start by adding the jar file for the database driver to the lib folder in the Tomcat root directory. The driver can be found in the Maven cache folder located at ~/.m2/repository/org/postgresql/postgresql/9.4-1201-jdbc41/. This driver was downloaded by Leiningen when we added it as a dependency for our application. Note that the specific version of the driver available may be different from the one used in the book.

With the driver in place, we have to create a resource definition for the database. Let's open up the conf/server.xml file and add the following XML in the GlobalNamingResources section:

```
<Resource name="jdbc/picture-gallery"
          auth="Container"
          type="javax.sql.DataSource"
          maxTotal="100"
          maxIdle="30"
          maxWaitMillis="10000"
          username="gallery"
          password="pictures"
          driverClassName="org.postgresql.Driver"
          url="jdbc:postgresql://localhost/picture_gallery_dev"/>
```

We also have to expose this resource to the applications deployed on the server by creating a resource link in the conf/context.xml file. The resource link looks like the following:

```
<ResourceLink name="jdbc/picture-gallery"
              global="jdbc/picture-gallery"
              type="javax.sql.DataSource" />
```

Using a JNDI Database Connection

We want to update the app to use this resource instead of managing its own connection. Let's first navigate to the picture-gallery.db.core namespace and change the connection settings as follows:

picture-gallery-war/src/clj/picture_gallery/db/core.clj

```
(def ^:dynamic *db* {:name "java:comp/env/jdbc/picture-gallery"})

(conman/bind-connection *db* "sql/queries.sql")
```

We no longer have to manage the life cycle of the connection, because the application server does that for us. Instead, we just have to refer to the JNDI name we gave the resource when we configured it. Note that the name has to be prefixed with the *java:comp/env/* context in order to be found.

Since we changed the *db* atom to use a JNDI connection, we'll have to supply it manually when we're running the application in development mode. We need to add the [directory-naming/naming-java "0.8"] dependency in the dependencies under the :project/dev profile. Then we can open up the picture-gallery.core namespace and add the following code there:

picture-gallery-war/env/dev/clj/picture_gallery/core.clj

```
(defn start-app [args]

  (System/setProperty "java.naming.factory.initial"
                      "org.apache.naming.java.javaURLContextFactory")
```

```
(System/setProperty "java.naming.factory.url.pkgs"
                    "org.apache.naming")
(doto (new javax.naming.InitialContext)
  (.createSubcontext "java:")
  (.createSubcontext "java:comp")
  (.createSubcontext "java:comp/env")
  (.createSubcontext "java:comp/env/jdbc")
  (.bind "java:comp/env/jdbc/picture-gallery"
        (doto (org.postgresql.ds.PGSimpleDataSource.)
          (.setServerName "localhost")
          (.setDatabaseName "picture_gallery_dev")
          (.setUser "gallery")
          (.setPassword "pictures")))))

(logger/init (:log-config env))
(doseq [component (-> args
                      (parse-opts cli-options)
                      mount/start-with-args
                      :started)]
  (log/info component "started"))
((:init defaults))
(.addShutdownHook (Runtime/getRuntime) (Thread. stop-app)))
```

This creates a naming context and binds an instance of the driver to it. With this code in place, the app should work the same as it did when we started using lein run.

To deploy our application as a WAR, we need to use the uberwar plugin:

picture-gallery-war/project.clj

```
:plugins [[lein-environ "1.0.1"]
          [migratus-lein "0.2.6"]
          [lein-cljsbuild "1.1.1"]
          [lein-uberwar "0.1.0"]]

:uberwar {:handler picture-gallery.handler/app
          :init picture-gallery.handler/init
          :destroy picture-gallery.handler/destroy
          :name "picture-gallery.war"}
```

The plugin uses the :uberwar configuration key and allows us to specify the hooks to the functions that should be run during the application life cycle. The :handler is the entry point for the application that routes the requests. The :init function that runs the application is loaded, and the :destroy function runs when it's shut down. The :name key specifies the name of the resulting archive.

We'll have to add these functions in the picture-gallery.handler namespace to ensure that mount is called to start the stateful resources when the application runs on the application server.

picture-gallery-war/src/clj/picture_gallery/handler.clj

```clojure
(ns picture-gallery.handler
  (:require [compojure.core :refer [routes wrap-routes]]
            [picture-gallery.layout :refer [error-page]]
            [picture-gallery.routes.home :refer [home-routes]]
            [picture-gallery.routes.services
              :refer [service-routes restricted-service-routes]]
            [compojure.route :as route]
            [picture-gallery.middleware :as middleware]
            ;;additional dependencies for init/destroy
            [mount.core :as mount]
            [clojure.tools.logging :as log]
            [picture-gallery.env :refer [defaults]]))

(defn init
  "init will be called once when
   app is deployed as a servlet on
   an app server such as Tomcat
   put any initialization code here"
  []
  (doseq [component (:started (mount/start))]
    (log/info component "started"))
  ((:init defaults)))

(defn destroy
  "destroy will be called when your application
   shuts down, put any clean up code here"
  []
  (log/info "picture-gallery is shutting down...")
  (doseq [component (:stopped (mount/stop))]
    (log/info component "stopped"))
  (log/info "shutdown complete!"))
```

Since we're going to be running the application on a server, we no longer need to include the HTTP Kit server as a dependency in production. Let's move this dependency to the :dependencies key under the :project/dev profile. Our development dependencies should now look like this:

picture-gallery-war/project.clj

```clojure
:dependencies [[prone "1.0.2"]
               [ring/ring-mock "0.3.0"]
               [ring/ring-devel "1.4.0"]
               [pjstadig/humane-test-output "0.7.1"]
               [com.cemerick/piggieback "0.2.2-SNAPSHOT"]
               [lein-doo "0.1.6"]
               [lein-figwheel "0.5.0-6"]
               [mvxcvi/puget "1.0.0"]
               [directory-naming/naming-java "0.8"]
               [org.webjars/webjars-locator-jboss-vfs "0.1.0"]
               [luminus-http-kit "0.1.3"]]]
```

We'll now have to move the src/clj/picture_gallery/core.clj file to the env/dev/clj/picture_gallery/core.clj location. Since the HTTP Kit dependency is available only during development, any code referencing it has to be moved to the dev source path.

Now that we've removed the HTTP server from the production dependencies, we can run the following command to build the application for deployment.

```
lein uberwar
```

This produces the WAR artifact that can be run on the server. Deploying the application consists of copying the generated archive to the webapps directory under Tomcat. When the application is deployed, it will have a context relative to the server's root. By default the context is inferred from the archive name. Let's deploy the archive we created as picture-gallery.war.

```
cp target/uberjar/picture-gallery.war \
~/tomcat/webapps/picture-gallery.war
```

We can look at the logs/catalina.out log to see whether our WAR was deployed successfully. Any logs from our application can also be found in this log since it captures stdout and since our default logging configuration has it as one of its appenders.

The application should now be available at http://localhost:8080/picture-gallery.

The approaches we've discussed require us to manage our own server. An alternative is to deploy the application on a cloud service. In particular, Heroku provides explicit support for running Clojure applications. In the following section we'll look at how to deploy our application there.

Heroku Deployment

Heroku is a cloud service with a free hosting option. Before we start using Heroku, we need to make sure we have Git and Heroku Toolbelt installed.[8,9]

Heroku uses the command specified in a file called Procfile to start up the application. This file must be placed in the project's root directory.

In order to run a Clojure application on Heroku, we need a Procfile that specifies the command that starts the application. Luminus generates this file for us by default:

```
web: java $JVM_OPTS -cp target/picture-gallery.jar \
    clojure.main -m picture-gallery.core
```

---

8. http://git-scm.com/
9. https://toolbelt.heroku.com/

Next we need to initialize a Git repository for our application by running the following commands:

```
git init
git add .
git commit -m "init"
```

Once our repository is created, we can test the application by running foreman start. If the application starts up fine, then we're ready to deploy it to the cloud by running the following command:

```
heroku create
```

To add PostgreSQL support for the application, we run this command:

```
heroku addons:add heroku-postgresql
```

You can find the connection settings for the database on your Heroku dashboard. You'll need to add these to your database configuration in the application. We're now ready to push our application to Heroku.

```
git push heroku master
```

Once the upload completes, Heroku will attempt to build and deploy your application. If this process completes successfully, you should be able to browse to the application URL specified in your administration console.

What You've Learned

This concludes the design, implementation, and deployment of our site. We covered many aspects of creating a real-world application during our journey, such as handling static resources, database access, and Ajax.

Although our site is functional, it clearly could use some improvements. You may wish to consider implementing paging for large galleries, creating multiple galleries per user, uploading multiple images in batches, and setting the visibility of uploaded images. I encourage you to try to implement these features on your own to test your knowledge of the material.

The skills you've learned by building applications throughout the book should allow you to create a wide variety of web applications using Clojure. It is my hope that you'll be able to apply these skills in building real-world applications going forward.

Clojure Primer

Since numerous books for learning Clojure are already available, I'll keep this overview short. Even if you're not familiar with Clojure, I hope you'll find that most of the code in this book is easy to follow. Instead of looking at syntax in depth, I'd like to briefly go over the way Clojure programs are structured and some of the unique aspects of the language.

All the mainstream languages belong to the same family. Once you learn one of these languages, very little effort is involved in learning another. Generally, all you have to do is learn some syntax sugar and the useful functions in the standard library to become productive. You may find a new concept here and there, but most of your existing skills are easily transferable.

This is not the case with Clojure. Being a Lisp dialect, it comes from a different family of languages and requires learning new concepts in order to use it effectively. However, I assure you that Clojure is not inherently more difficult to understand, and with a bit of practice you might even feel it's quite the opposite.

A Functional Perspective

Clojure is a functional language. This makes it extremely well positioned for writing modern applications. As the application grows, it's imperative to be able to reason about parts of the application in isolation. It's equally important to have code that is testable and reusable. Let's take a look at the aspects of functional programming that facilitate these qualities.

Managing State

Functional languages are ideal for writing large applications because they eschew global state and favor immutability as the default. When the data is predominantly immutable, we can safely reason about parts of the application in isolation.

"Immutable data structures" might sound like a strange idea at first. However, many of the benefits associated with functional languages are directly facilitated by them. Let's look at what makes these data structures such a powerful tool.

In most languages, data can be passed around either by value or by reference. Passing data by value is safe since we know that any changes we make to the data will not have any effect outside the function. However, it's also prohibitively expensive in many cases, so any substantial amount of data is passed around by reference. This makes code more difficult to reason about, as you have to know all the places where a piece of data is referenced to update it safely.

Immutable data structures provide us with a third option. Every time a change is made to a data structure, a new revision is created. The price we pay when altering the data is proportional to the size of the change. When a piece of data is no longer referenced, it simply gets garbage-collected.

Instead of having to manually track every reference to a piece of data, we can offload this work to the language runtime. This allows us to effectively "copy" data any time we make a change without having to worry about where it comes from or what the scope of our change will be.

Having such data structures facilitates writing pure functions. A pure function is simply a function that has no side effects. Since such functions can be reasoned about in isolation, the applications written using such functions are composed of individual self-contained components. This type of code is referred to as being referentially transparent.

Achieving Code Reuse

Object-oriented languages tend to have strong coupling between the data and the functions that operate on it. In this scenario we can't easily reuse methods written in one class when we have a similar problem that we need to solve in another.

This problem does not exist in a functional language because the logic and the data are kept separate. The language provides a small set of common data structures, such as lists, maps, and sets. All the functions operate on these data structures; and when we come to a new problem, we can easily reuse any function we write.

Each function represents a certain transformation that we wish to apply to our data. When we need to solve a problem, we simply have to understand the sequence of transformations and map those to the appropriate functions. This style of code is referred to as *declarative*.

Declarative code separates what is being done from how it is done. For example, when we wish to iterate over a collection, we use an iterator function. The logic that we want to execute on each step of the iteration is passed in as a parameter.

One important advantage of this style is that we benefit from having code reuse at the function level. An iterator function can be written once to handle the edge cases and boundary checks. We can now reuse this logic without having to worry about remembering to do these checks time and again.

Leveraging Multiprocessing

Functional code also makes it easier to tackle the difficult problems of parallelism and concurrency. While there is no silver bullet for addressing either problem, the language can certainly make it easier to reason about them.

Since pure functions depend solely on their arguments, they do not rely on any shared state and can be safely computed in parallel. This means we can easily parallelize many algorithms to take advantage of the extra cores. An example of this is mapping a function over the items in a collection. We can start by writing a version using the map function. Should we discover that each operation takes a significant amount of time, then we can simply switch to using pmap to run the operations in parallel.

Meanwhile, the immutable data structures provide an excellent tool for managing shared state. Clojure provides a Software Transactional Memory (STM) API based on these data structures. With transactional memory we no longer have to worry about manual locking when dealing with threads. Additionally, the data only needs to be locked for writing. Since the existing data is immutable, it can be read safely even while an update is happening.

Data Types

Clojure provides a number of data types, most of which are unsurprising:

- Vars provide mutable storage locations. These can be bound and rebound on a per-thread basis.

- Booleans can have a value of true or false; nil values are also treated as false.

- Numbers can be integers, doubles, floats, or fractions.

- Symbols are used as identifiers for variables.
- Keywords are symbols that reference themselves and are denoted by a colon; these are often used as keys in maps.
- Strings are denoted by double quotes and can span multiple lines.
- Characters are denoted by a preceding backslash.
- Regular expressions are strings prefixed with a hash symbol.

In addition to the data types, Clojure provides a rich set of standard collections. These include lists, vectors, maps, and sets.

- List: (1 2 3)
- Vector: [1 2 3]
- Map: {:foo "a" :bar "b"}
- Set: #{"a" "b" "c"}

Interestingly, Clojure logic is written using its data structures. Using the same syntax for both data and logic allows for powerful metaprogramming features. We can manipulate any piece of Clojure code just like we would any other data structure. This feature makes it trivial to template the code for recurring patterns in your problem domain. In Clojure, code is data and data is code.

Using Functions

Function calls in Clojure work the same as any mainstream languages such as Python. The main difference is that the function name comes after the parenthesis in the Clojure version.

```
functionName(param1, param2)
```

```
(function-name param1 param2)
```

This difference can be explained very simply. The function call is just a list containing the function name and its parameters. In Clojure, a list is a special type of data structure reserved for creating callable expressions. To create a list data structure, we have to call the list function:

```
(list 1 2 3)
```

Anonymous Functions

As the name implies, anonymous functions are simply functions that aren't bound to a name. Let's take a look at the following function that accepts a single argument and prints it.

```
(fn [arg] (println arg))
```

The function is defined by using the fn form followed by the vector containing its argument and the body. We could call the preceding function by setting it as the first item in a list and its argument as the second.

```
((fn [arg] (println arg)) "hello")
=>"hello"
```

Clojure provides syntactic sugar for defining anonymous functions using the # notation. With it we can rewrite our function more concisely:

```
#(println %)
```

Here, the % symbol indicates an unnamed argument. If the function accepted multiple arguments, then each one would be followed by a number indicating its position. This can be seen in the next example:

```
#(println %1 %2 %3)
```

The preceding anonymous function accepts three arguments and prints them out in order. This type of function is useful when you need to perform a one-off operation that doesn't warrant defining a named function. These functions are often used in conjunction with the higher-order functions that we'll look at in a moment.

Named Functions

Named functions are simply anonymous functions bound to a symbol used as an identifier. Clojure provides a special form called def that's used for creating global variables. It accepts a name and the body to be assigned to it. We can create a named function by using def as follows:

```
(def square (fn ([x] (* x x))))
```

Since creating these variables is such a common operation, Clojure provides a special form called defn that does this for us:

```
(defn square [x]
  (* x x))
```

The first argument to defn is the name of the function being defined. It is followed by a vector containing the arguments and the body of the function. In the preceding code, we passed in a single item for the body; however, we could pass as many items as we like.

```
(defn bmi [height weight]
  (println "height:" height)
  (println "weight:" weight)
  (/ weight (* height height)))
```

Here we define a function to calculate BMI using the height and weight parameters. The body consists of two print statements and a call to divide the weight by the square of the height. All the expressions are evaluated from the inside out. In the last statement, (* height height) is evaluated, then the weight is divided by the result and returned. In Clojure, mathematical operators (such as / and *) are regular functions, so we call them using the prefix notation as we would with any other function.

Note that only the result from the last expression is returned from the function; the results of all the other expressions are discarded. Therefore, any intermediate expressions should strictly be used for side effects, as is the case with the preceding println calls.

Clojure uses a single-pass compiler. For this reason, the functions must be declared before they are used. In the case where we need to refer to a function before it's been defined, we must use the declare macro to provide a forward declaration.

```
(declare down)

(defn up [n]
  (if (< n 10)
    (down (+ 2 n))
    n))
(defn down [n]
  (up (dec n)))
```

As you might have noticed, the code structure is a tree. This tree is called the *abstract syntax tree*, or AST for short. This is the same AST that the compiler sees when compiling the code. By being able to see the AST directly, we can visualize the relationships between pieces of logic.

Since we write our code in terms of data, we have fewer syntactic hints than in most languages. For example, we have no explicit return statements. Instead, the last expression of the function body is returned implicitly. This might take a little getting used to if you're accustomed to seeing a lot of annotations in your code. To aid readability, functions are often kept short (five lines or less is a good rule of thumb), while indentation and spacing are used for grouping code visually.

Clojure makes no distinction between functions and variables. You can assign a function to a label, pass it as a parameter, or return a function from another function. Functions that can be treated as data are referred to as being *first-class* because they don't have any additional restrictions attached to them.

Higher-Order Functions

Functions that take other functions as parameters are called higher-order functions. One example of such a function is map:

```
(map #(* % %) [1 2 3 4 5])
=>(1 4 9 16 25)
```

Here we pass in two parameters to the map function. The first parameter is an anonymous function that squares its argument and the second is a collection of numbers. The map function visits each item in the collection and squares it. One advantage of using higher-order functions is that we don't have to worry about boundary conditions, such as nil checks. The iterator function handles these for us.

Another example of a higher-order function is filter(). This function goes through a collection and keeps only the items matching the condition specified.

```
(filter even? [1 2 3 4 5])
=>(2 4)
```

You can, of course, chain these functions together to solve problems:

```
(filter even?
  (map #(* 3 %) [1 2 3 4 5]))
=>(6 12)
```

Here we multiply each item by 3 and then we use filter() to keep only the even items from the resulting sequence.

Thanks to higher-order functions, you should practically never have to write loops or explicit recursion. When you need to iterate over a collection, use a function such as map or filter instead. Since Clojure has a rich standard library, practically any data transformation can be achieved by a combination of several higher-order functions.

Instead of having to learn a lot of different language features and syntax, you simply have to learn the functions in the standard library. Once you learn to associate data transformations with specific functions, many problems can be solved by simply putting them together in the right order.

Here is a real-world example of this idea. The problem is to display a formatted address given the fields representing it. Commonly an address has a unit number, a street, a city, a postal code, and a country. We'll have to examine each of these pieces, remove the nil and empty ones, then insert a separator between them.

Let's say we have a table in our database that contains the following fields:

```
unit        | street         | city    | postal_code | country
""          | "1 Main Street" | Toronto | nil         | Canada
```

Given the preceding data as strings, we would like to output the following formatted string:

```
1 Main Street, Toronto, Canada
```

All we have to do is find the functions for the tasks of removing empty fields, interposing the separator, and concatenating the result into a string:

```
(defn concat-fields [& fields]
  (clojure.string/join ", " (remove empty? fields)))

(concat-fields "" "1 Main Street" "Toronto" nil "Canada")
=> "1 Main Street, Toronto, Canada"
```

The & notation in the preceding parameter definition states that the function accepts a variable number of arguments. The arguments are represented by a list inside the function body.

Notice that we didn't have to specify how to do any of the tasks when writing our code. Most of the time we simply say what we're doing by composing the functions representing the operations we wish to carry out. The resulting code also handles all the common edge cases:

```
(concat-fields) => ""
(concat-fields nil) => ""
(concat-fields "") => ""
```

Closures

We've now seen how we can declare functions, name them, and pass them as parameters to other functions. One last thing we can do is write functions that return other functions as their result. One use for this is to provide the functionality facilitated by constructors in object-oriented languages.

Let's say we wish to greet our guests warmly. We can write a function that accepts the greeting string as its parameter and returns a function that takes the name of the guest and prints a customized greeting for that guest:

```
(defn greeting [greeting-string]
  (fn [guest]
    (println greeting-string guest)))

(let [greet (greeting "Welcome to the wonderful world of Clojure")]
  (greet "Jane")
  (greet "John"))
```

The inner function in the greeting has access to the greeting-string value since the value is defined in its outer scope. The greeting function is called a *closure* because it closes over its parameters—in our case the greeting-string—and makes them available to the function that it returns.

You'll also notice that we're using a form called let to bind the greet symbol and make it available to any expressions inside it. The let form serves the same purpose as declaring variables in imperative languages.

Threading Expressions

By this point you've probably noticed that nested expressions can be difficult to read. Fortunately, Clojure provides a couple of helper forms to deal with this problem. Let's say we have a range of numbers, and we want to increment each number, interpose the number 5 between them, and then sum the result. We could write the following code to do that:

```
(reduce + (interpose 5 (map inc (range 10))))
```

It's a little difficult to tell what's happening in the preceding example at a glance. With a few more steps in the chain, we'd be really lost. On top of that, if we wanted to rearrange any of the steps, such as interposing 5 before incrementing, then we'd have to re-nest all our expressions. An alternative way to write this expression is to use the ->> form:

```
(->> (range 10) (map inc) (interpose 5) (reduce +))
```

Here, we use ->> to thread the operations from one to the next. This means that we implicitly pass the result of each expression as the last argument of the next one. To pass it as the first argument, we'd use the -> form instead.

Being Lazy

Many Clojure algorithms use lazy evaluation, where the operations aren't performed unless their result actually needs to be evaluated. Laziness is crucial for making many algorithms work efficiently. For example, you might think the preceding example is very inefficient since we have to iterate over the sequence each time to create the range, map across it, interpose the numbers, and reduce the result.

However, this is not actually the case. The evaluation of each expression happens on demand. The first value in the range is generated and passed to the function, then the next, and so on, until the sequence is exhausted. This is similar to the approach that languages like Python take with their iterator mechanics.

Structuring the Code

One nontrivial difference between Clojure and imperative languages is the way the code is structured. In imperative style, it's a common pattern to declare a shared mutable variable and modify it by passing it different functions. Each time we access the memory location, we see the result of the code that previously worked with it. For example, if we have a list of integers and we wish to square each one and then print the even ones, the following Python code would be perfectly valid:

```python
l = range(1, 6)

for i, val in enumerate(l) :
  l[i] = val * val

for i in l :
  if i % 2 == 0 :
    print i
```

In Clojure this interaction has to be made explicit. Instead of creating a shared memory location and then having different functions access it sequentially, we chain functions together and pipe the input through them:

```clojure
(println
  (filter #(= (mod % 2) 0)
    (map #(* % %) (range 1 6))))
```

Or, as we've covered, we could use the ->> macro to flatten the operations:

```clojure
(->> (range 1 6)
     (map #(* % %))
     (filter #(= (mod % 2) 0))
     (println))
```

Each function returns a new value instead of modifying the existing data in place. You may think that this can get expensive, and it would be with a naïve implementation, where the entirety of the data is copied with every change.

In reality, Clojure is backed by persistent data structures that create in-memory revisions of the data.[1] Each time a change is made, a new revision is created proportional to the size of the change. With this approach we only pay the price of the difference between the old and the new data structures while ensuring that any changes are inherently localized.

---

1. http://en.wikipedia.org/wiki/Persistent_data_structure

Destructuring Data

Clojure has a powerful mechanism called destructuring for declaratively accessing values in data structures. If you know the data structure's type, you can describe it using a literal notation in the binding. Let's look at some examples of what this means.

```
(let [[small big] (split-with #(< % 5) (range 10))]
  (println small big))

=>(0 1 2 3 4) (5 6 7 8 9)
```

Here we use the split-with function to split a range of ten numbers into a sequence containing two elements: numbers less than 5 and numbers greater than or equal to 5. The split-with function returns a sequence containing two elements: the first is the sequence of items that are less than 5, and the other is the sequence that is greater than or equal to 5. Since we know the result's format, we can write it in a literal form as [small big] and then use these named elements within the let binding.

We can use this type of destructuring in function definitions as well. Let's say we have a function called print-user that accepts a vector with three items. It names the items name, address, and phone, respectively.

```
(defn print-user [[name address phone]]
  (println name address phone))
(print-user ["Bob" "12 Jarvis street, Toronto" "416-987-3417"])
```

We can also specify variable arguments as a sequence in cases where a variable number of arguments can be supplied. This is done by using the ampersand followed by the name for the argument list.

```
(defn foo [& args]
  (println args))

(foo "a" "b" "c")
=>(a b c)
```

Since the variable arguments are stored in a sequence, it can be destructured like any other.

```
(defn foo [first-arg & [second-arg]]
  (println (if second-arg
             "two arguments were passed in"
             "one argument was passed in")))
(foo "bar")
=>"one argument was passed in"

(foo "bar" "baz")
=>"two arguments were passed in"
```

Destructuring can also be applied to maps. When destructuring a map, we create a new map where we supply the names for the local bindings pointing to the keys from the original map:

```clojure
(let [{foo :foo bar :bar} {:foo "foo" :bar "bar"}]
  (println foo bar)
```

It's possible to destructure a nested data structure as well. As long as you know the data's structure, you can simply write it out.

```clojure
(let [{[a b c] :items id :id} {:id "foo" :items [1 2 3]}]
  (println id " has the following items " a b c))
```

Finally, since extracting keys from maps is a very common operation, Clojure provides syntactic sugar for this task.

```clojure
(defn login [{:keys [user pass]}]
 (and (= user "bob") (= pass "secret"))))

(login {:user "bob" :pass "secret"})
```

Another useful destructuring option allows us to extract some keys while preserving the original map.

```clojure
(defn register [{:keys [id pass repeat-pass] :as user}]
  (cond
    (nil? id) "user id is required"
    (not= pass repeat-pass) "re-entered password doesn't match"
    :else user))
```

Namespaces

When writing real-world applications, we need tools to organize our code into separate components. Object-oriented languages provide classes for this purpose. The related methods are all defined in the same class. In Clojure, we group our functions into namespaces instead. Let's look at how a namespace is defined.

```clojure
(ns colors)

(defn hex->rgb [[_ & rgb]]
    (map #(->> % (apply str "0x") (Long/decode))
         (partition 2 rgb)))

(defn hex-str [n]
  (-> (format "%2s" (Integer/toString n 16))
      (clojure.string/replace " " "0"))))

(defn rgb->hex [color]
  (apply str "#" (map hex-str color)))
```

Preceding, we have a namespace called colors containing three functions called hex->rgb, hex-str, and rgb->hex. The functions in the same namespace can call each other directly. However, if we wanted to call these functions from a different namespace we would have to reference the colors namespace there first.

Clojure provides two ways to do this: we can use either the :use or the :require keyword.

The :use Keyword

When we reference a namespace with :use, all its vars become implicitly available, as if they were defined in the namespace that references it.

```
(ns myns
  (:use colors))

(hex->rgb "#33d24f")
```

This approach has two downsides. We don't know where the function was originally defined, making it difficult to navigate the code, and if we reference two namespaces that use the same name for a function, we'll get an error.

We can address the first problem by selecting the functions we wish to use explicitly using the :only keyword in our :use declaration.

```
(ns myns
  (:use [colors :only [rgb->hex]]))

(defn hex-str [c]
  (println "I don't do much yet"))
```

This way we document where rgb->hex comes from and we're able to declare our own hex-str function in the myns namespace without conflicts. Note that rgb->hex still uses the hex-str function defined in the colors namespace.

The :require Keyword

The approach of using the :require keyword to reference the namespace provides us with more flexible options. Let's look at each of these.

We can require a namespace without providing any further directives. In this case, any calls to vars inside it must be prefixed with the namespace declaration indicating their origin.

```
(ns myns
  (:require colors))

(colors/hex->rgb "#324a9b")
```

This approach is explicit about the origin of the vars being referenced and ensures that we won't have conflicts when referencing multiple namespaces. One problem is that when our namespace declaration is long, it gets tedious to have to type it out any time we wish to use a function declared inside it. To address this problem, the :require statement provides the :as directive, allowing us to create an alias for the namespace.

```
(ns myotherns
  (:require [colors :as c]))

(c/hex->rgb "#324a9b")
```

We can also require functions from a namespace by using the :refer keyword. This is synonymous with the :use notation we saw earlier. To require all the functions from another namespace, we can write the following:

```
(ns myns
  (:require [colors :refer :all]))
```

If we wish to select what functions to require by name, we can instead write this:

```
(ns myns
  (:require [colors :refer [rgb->hex]]))
```

As you can see, a number of options are available for referencing vars declared in other namespaces. If you're not sure what option to pick, then requiring the namespace by name or alias is the safest route.

Dynamic Variables

Clojure provides support for declaring dynamic variables that can have their value changed within a particular scope. Let's look at how this works.

```
(declare ^:dynamic *foo*)

(println *foo*)
=>#<Unbound Unbound: #'bar/*foo*>
```

Here we declare *foo* as a dynamic var and don't provide any value for it. When we try to print *foo*, we get an error indicating that this var has not been bound to any value. Let's look at how we can assign a value to *foo* using a binding.

```
(binding [*foo* "I exist!"]
  (println *foo*))
=>"I exist!"
```

We set *foo* to a string with value "I exist!" inside the binding. When the println function is called within the binding, we no longer get an error when trying to print its value.

This technique can be useful when dealing with resources such as file streams, database connections, or scoped variables. In general, the use of dynamic variables is discouraged since they make code more opaque and difficult to reason about. However, they have legitimate uses, and it's worth knowing how they work.

Polymorphism

One useful aspect of object orientation is polymorphism; while polymorphism happens to be associated with that style, it's in no way exclusive to object-oriented programming. Clojure provides two common ways to achieve runtime polymorphism. Let's look at each of these in turn.

Multimethods

Multimethods provide an extremely flexible dispatching mechanism using a selector function associated with one or more methods. The multimethod is defined using defmulti, and each method is defined using defmethod. For example, if we had different shapes and we wanted to write a multimethod to calculate the area, we could do the following:

```clojure
(defmulti area :shape)
(defmethod area :circle [{:keys [r]}]
  (* Math/PI r r))

(defmethod area :rectangle [{:keys [l w]}]
  (* l w))

(defmethod area :default [shape]
  (throw (Exception. (str "unrecognized shape: " shape))))

(area {:shape :circle :r 10})
=> 314.1592653589793

(area {:shape :rectangle :l 5 :w 10})
=> 50
```

Preceding, the dispatch function uses a keyword to select the appropriate method to handle each type of map. This works because keywords act as functions and when passed a map return the value associated with them. The dispatch function can be as sophisticated as we like, however.

```clojure
(defmulti encounter
  (fn [x y] [(:role x) (:role y)]))

(defmethod encounter [:manager :boss] [x y]
  :promise-unrealistic-deadlines)

(defmethod encounter [:manager :developer] [x y]
  :demand-overtime)
```

```
(defmethod encounter [:developer :developer] [x y]
  :complain-about-poor-management)

(encounter {:role :manager} {:role :boss})
=> :promise-unrealistic-deadlines
```

Protocols allow defining an abstract set of functions that can be implemented by a concrete type. Let's look at an example protocol:

```
(defprotocol Foo
  "Foo doc string"
  (bar [this b] "bar doc string")
  (baz [this] [this b] "baz doc string"))
```

As you can see, the Foo protocol specifies two methods, bar and baz. The first argument to the method is the object instance followed by its parameters. Note that the baz method has multiple arity. We can now create a type that implements the Foo protocol using the deftype macro:

```
(deftype Bar [data]
  Foo
  (bar [this param]
    (println data param))
  (baz [this]
    (println (class this)))
  (baz [this param]
    (println param)))
```

Here we create type Bar that implements protocol Foo. Each method prints out some of its parameters. Let's see what it looks like when we create an instance of Bar and call its methods:

```
(let [b (Bar. "some data")]
  (.bar b "param")
  (.baz b)
  (.baz b "baz with param"))

some data param
Bar
baz with param
```

The first method call prints out the data Bar was initialized with and the parameter that was passed in. The second method call prints out the object's class, while the last method call demonstrates the other arity of baz.

We can also use protocols to extend the functionality of existing types, including existing Java classes. For example, we can use extend-protocol to extend the java.lang.String class with the Foo protocol:

```
(extend-protocol Foo String
(bar [this param] (println this param)))

(bar "hello" "there")
=>"hello there"
```

The preceding examples illustrate the basic principles of how protocols can be used to write polymorphic code. However, protocols have many other uses as well, and I encourage you to discover these on your own.

What About Global State?

While predominantly immutable, Clojure provides support for shared mutable data as well via its STM library.[2] The STM ensures that all updates to mutable variables are done atomically. There are two major kinds of mutable types: the atom and the ref. The atom is used in cases where we need to do uncoordinated updates, and the ref is used when we might need to do multiple updates as a transaction.

Let's look at an example of defining an atom and using it.

```
(def global-val (atom nil))
```

We've defined an atom called global-val, and its current value is nil. We can now read its value by using the deref function, which returns the current value.

```
(println (deref global-val))
=>nil
```

Since this is a common operation, there is a shorthand for deref: the @ symbol. So writing (println @global-val) is equivalent to the preceding example.

Let's look at two ways of setting a new value for our atom. We can either use reset! and pass in the new value, or we can use swap! and pass in a function that accepts the current value and updates it.

```
(reset! global-val 10)
(println @global-val)
=>10
(swap! global-val inc)
(println @global-val)
=>11
```

Note that both swap! and reset! end in exclamation points (!); this convention indicates that these functions operate on mutable data.

---

2.   http://clojure.org/concurrent_programming

We define a ref the same way we define an atom, but the two are used rather differently. Let's take a quick look at a concrete example of how a ref is used.

```
(def names (ref []))

(dosync
  (ref-set names ["John"])
  (alter names #(if (not-empty %)
                  (conj % "Jane") %)))
```

The preceding code defines a ref called names and then opens a transaction using a dosync statement. Inside the transaction, the names are set to a vector with the value "John". Next, the alter function is called to check if names is not empty and to add "Jane" to the vector of names when that's the case.

Note that since this is happening inside a transaction, the check for emptiness depends on the existing state along with any state built up within the same transaction. If we tried to add or remove a name in a different transaction, it would have no visible effect on ours. In case of a collision, one of the transactions would end up being retried.

Writing Code That Writes Code for You

Because Clojure is a dialect of Lisp, it provides a powerful macro system. Macros allow for templating of repetitive blocks of code and for deferring evaluation, among numerous other uses. A macro works by treating code as data instead of evaluating it. This allows us to manipulate the code tree just like any other data structure.

Macros execute before compile time, and the compiler sees the result of macro execution. Because of this level of indirection, macros can be difficult to reason about, and thus it's best not to use them when a function will do the job.

However, macros have legitimate uses, and it's worth understanding how they work. In this book we use very few macros, so we'll only touch on their syntax superficially.

Let's look at a concrete example of a macro and see how it differs from the regular code we saw previously. Imagine that we have a web application with a session atom that might contain a user. We might want to load certain content only if a user is present in the session and not otherwise.

```
(def session (atom {:user "Bob"}))

(defn load-content []
  (if (:user @session)
    "Welcome back!"
    "please log in"))
```

This works, but it's tedious and error-prone to write our if statement every single time. Since our condition's logic stays the same, we can template this function as follows:

```clojure
(defmacro defprivate [name args & body]
  `(defn ~(symbol name) ~args
    (if (:user @session)
      (do ~@body)
      "please log in")))
```

The macros are defined using the defmacro special form. The major difference between defn and defmacro is that the parameters passed to defmacro are not evaluated by default.

To evaluate the parameter, we use the tilde, as we're doing with ~(symbol name). Using the ~ notation indicates that we'd like to replace the name with the value it refers to. This is called *unquoting*.

The ~@ notation used in (do ~@body) is called *unquote splicing*. This notation is used when we're dealing with a sequence. The contents of the sequence are merged into the outer form during the splicing. In this case body consists of a list representing the function's body. The body must be wrapped in a do block because the if statement requires having no more than two arguments.

The backtick (`) sign means that we wish to treat the following list as data instead of executing it. This is the opposite of unquoting, and it's referred to as *syntax-quoting*.

As I mentioned earlier, the macros are executed before evaluation time. To see what the macro will be rewritten as when the evaluator sees it, we can call macroexpand-1.

```clojure
(macroexpand-1 '(defprivate foo [greeting] (println greeting)))

(clojure.core/defn foo [greeting]
  (if (:user (clojure.core/deref session))
    (do (println greeting))
    "please log in"))
```

You can see that (defprivate foo (println "bar")) gets rewritten with a function definition that has the if statement inside. This resulting code is what the evaluator sees, and it's equivalent to what we would have to write by hand otherwise. Now we can simply define a private function using our macro, and it will check for us automatically.

```clojure
(defprivate foo [message] (println message))

(foo "this message is private")
```

The preceding example might seem a little contrived, but it demonstrates the power of being able to easily template repetitions in code. This allows you to create a notation that expresses your problem domain using the language natural to it.

The Read-Evaluate-Print Loop

Another big aspect of working in Clojure is the read-evaluate-print loop (REPL). In many languages you write the code, and then you run the entire program to see what it does. In Clojure, most development is done interactively using the REPL. In this mode we can see each piece of code we write in action as soon as it's written.

In nontrivial applications it's often necessary to build up a particular state before you can add more functionality. For example, a user has to log in and query some data from the database, and then you need to write functions to format and display this data. With a REPL you can get the application to the state where the data is loaded and then write the display logic interactively without having to reload the application and build up the state every time you make a change.

This method of development is particularly satisfying because you see immediate feedback when making changes. You can easily try things out and see what approach works best for the problem you're trying to solve. This encourages experimentation and refactoring of the code as you go, which in turn helps you to write better and cleaner code.

Calling Out to Java

One last thing that we'll cover is how Clojure embraces its host platform to benefit from the rich ecosystem of existing Java libraries. In some cases we may wish to call a Java library to accomplish a particular task that doesn't have a native Clojure implementation. Calling Java classes is very simple and follows the standard Clojure syntax fairly closely.

Importing Classes

When we wish to use a Clojure library, we employ :use and :require statements. However, when we wish to import a Java class, we have to use the :import statement.

```
(ns myns
  (:import java.io.File))
```

We can also group multiple classes from the same package in a single import, as follows:

```
(ns myns
 (:import [java.io File FileInputStream FileOutputStream]))
```

Instantiating Classes

To create an instance of a class, we can call new just as we would in Java.

```
(new File ".")
```

We could also use a common shorthand for creating new objects:

```
(File. ".")
```

Calling Methods

Once we have an instance of a class, we can call methods on it. The notation is similar to making a regular function call. When we call a method, we pass the object its first parameter, followed by any other parameters that the method accepts.

```
(let [f (File. ".")]
 (println (.getAbsolutePath f)))
```

Here we've created a new file object f and we've called .getAbsolutePath on it. Notice that methods have a period (.) in front of them to differentiate them from regular Clojure functions. If we wanted to call a static function or a variable in a class, we would use the / notation, as follows:

```
(str File/separator "foo" File/separator "bar")
```

```
(Math/sqrt 256)
```

We can also chain multiple method calls together using the double period (..) notation as our shorthand. Say we wanted to get the string indicating the file path and then get its bytes; we could write the code for that in two ways:

```
(.getBytes (.getAbsolutePath (File. ".")))
```

```
(.. (File. ".") getAbsolutePath getBytes)
```

The second notation looks more natural and is easier to read. Although there is other syntactic sugar for working with Java, the preceding is sufficient for following the material we cover in this book.

Summary

This concludes our tour of Clojure basics. Altogether we touched on only a small portion of the overall language. But if you understand the preceding examples, then you should have no trouble following any of the code in the rest of the book. Once you have your development environment up and running, don't hesitate to try out the examples shown here in the REPL and play around with them until you feel comfortable moving on.

Authentication with OAuth

In this appendix we'll cover how to use the clj-oauth library to authenticate users via Twitter.[1]

Why Use OAuth

Delegating authentication to a third-party service has numerous benefits. It can make it easier for users to use your service because they can use their existing accounts. Conversely, it offloads user management to the third party, making your application simpler. Let's take a look at what's involved in allowing users to log in to the application using their existing Twitter accounts.

Create the Application

Let's create a new Luminus project called *oauth-example* by running this:

```
lein new luminus oauth-example
```

Next, let's add the clj-oauth dependency in the project.clj file.

```
:dependencies [...
               [clj-oauth "1.5.5"]]
```

We're ready to implement the Twitter Oauth workflow. Create a new namespace called oauth-example.twitter-oauth and add these references in its declaration:

oauth-example/src/clj/oauth_example/twitter_oauth.clj

```
(ns oauth-example.twitter-oauth
  (:require [oauth.client :as oauth]
            [oauth-example.config :refer [env]]))
```

We need the oauth.client namespace for handling the OAuth calls and the oauth-example.config/env for reading the secret tokens for the application.

---

1. https://github.com/mattrepl/clj-oauth

With that in place, we define the constants for the Twitter OAuth URLs; these are used to fetch the tokens and call the authorization service.

oauth-example/src/clj/oauth_example/twitter_oauth.clj

```
(def request-token-uri
  "https://api.twitter.com/oauth/request_token")

(def access-token-uri
  "https://api.twitter.com/oauth/access_token")

(def authorize-uri
  "https://api.twitter.com/oauth/authenticate")
```

Now we call the oauth.client/make-consumer function to create a consumer instance. The client functions will require the consumer and your access keys that will be provided by Twitter. These should not be embedded in the application and therefore will come from the environment. We expect the :twitter-consumer-key and the :twitter-consumer-secret variables to be set in order to provide these keys. We can now define functions to generate the callback URI, fetch the tokens, and generate the redirect URI.

oauth-example/src/clj/oauth_example/twitter_oauth.clj

```
(defn oauth-callback-uri
  "Generates the Twitter oauth request callback URI"
  [{:keys [headers]}]
  (str (headers "x-forwarded-proto")
       "://" (headers "host")
       "/oauth/twitter-callback"))

(defn fetch-request-token
  "Fetches a request token."
  [request]
  (->> request
       oauth-callback-uri
       (oauth/request-token consumer)
       :oauth_token))

(defn fetch-access-token
  [request_token]
  (oauth/access-token consumer request_token (:oauth_verifier request_token)))

(defn auth-redirect-uri
  "Gets the URI the user should be redirected to when authenticating with Twitter."
  [request-token]
  (str (oauth/user-approval-uri consumer request-token)))
```

That's all we need to do to facilitate authentication via Twitter. Now let's go to the oauth-example.routes.home namespace and add the routes that enable the authentication workflow. We start by referencing the oauth-example.twitter-oauth that we just wrote.

oauth-example/src/clj/oauth_example/routes/home.clj

```clojure
(ns oauth-example.routes.home
  (:require [oauth-example.layout :as layout]
            [compojure.core :refer [defroutes GET]]
            [ring.util.http-response :refer [ok found]]
            [clojure.java.io :as io]
            [clojure.tools.logging :as log]
            [oauth-example.twitter-oauth :as tw]))
```

Now let's write functions to handle initiating the workflow as well as the callback from Twitter.

oauth-example/src/clj/oauth_example/routes/home.clj

```clojure
(defn twitter-init
  "Initiates the Twitter OAuth"
  [request]
  (-> (tw/fetch-request-token request)
      tw/auth-redirect-uri
      found))

(defn twitter-callback
  "Handles the callback from Twitter."
  [request_token {:keys [session]}]
  ; oauth request was denied by user
  (if (:denied request_token)
    (-> (found "/")
        (assoc :flash {:denied true}))
    ; fetch the request token and do anything else you wanna do if not denied.
    (let [{:keys [user_id screen_name]} (tw/fetch-access-token request_token)]
      (log/info "successfully authenticated as" user_id screen_name)
      (-> (found "/")
          (assoc :session
            (assoc session :user-id user_id :screen-name screen_name))))))
```

The twitter-init function calls the fetch-request-token function we just wrote, passes its result to the auth-redirect-uri function, and redirects to the URI it generates.

The twitter-callback function handles the callback from Twitter that contains the result of the authentication attempt by the user. If the user fails to log in, then the request_token contains the :denied key. In this case we stick the :denied key in a flash session and redirect the user back to the home page. If a user successfully logs in, then we call the fetch-access-token function we wrote earlier. It gives us the :user_id and the :screen_name keys. Let's log that the user authenticated successfully and put the user identity in the session. The user is then redirected to the home page. Now we need to update the home-page function to accept options for rendering the home page.

oauth-example/src/clj/oauth_example/routes/home.clj

```clojure
(defn home-page [opts]
  (layout/render "home.html" opts))
```

Finally, we create two routes to handle the authentication workflow and pass the correct options to the home-page function.

oauth-example/src/clj/oauth_example/routes/home.clj

```clojure
(defroutes home-routes
  (GET "/" {:keys [flash session]} (home-page (or flash session)))
  (GET "/about" [] (about-page))
  (GET "/oauth/twitter-init" req (twitter-init req))
  (GET "/oauth/twitter-callback" [& req_token :as req] (twitter-callback req_token req)))
```

The only thing left to do is to update the HTML page to add a Twitter sign-in button and display the result. Let's open up the resources/templates/home.html template and update it as follows.

oauth-example/resources/templates/home.html

```html
{% extends "base.html" %}
{% block content %}
  <div class="jumbotron">
    <h1>Welcome to oauth-example</h1>
    <p>Time to start building your site!</p>
    <p>
      <a class="btn btn-primary btn-lg" href="http://luminusweb.net">
      Learn more &raquo;
      </a>
    </p>
  </div>

  <div class="row">
    <div class="span12">

      {% if denied %}
        <h2>Failed to sign in!</h2>
      {% endif %}

      {% if screen-name %}
        <h2>Welcome {{screen-name}}</h2>
      {% else %}
        <a href="/oauth/twitter-init">
          <img src="img/sign-in-with-twitter-gray.png" alt="Sign in with Twitter">
          </img>
        </a>
      {% endif %}
      </h2>
    </div>
  </div>
{% endblock %}
```

When the denied key is present in the context, then we inform the user that access was denied. When the screen-name is present, then we greet the user. Otherwise, we display the sign-in button.

We've now finished all the tasks necessary for our application to allow the users to sign in using Twitter. Next, let's see what we need to do on the other end in order for Twitter to accept login requests via our app.

Set Up the Twitter Application

In order to use Twitter sign-in functionality, you must have an application hosted on a public-facing server. In case you don't already have a publicly available server, you can set up a free hosted application using Heroku.[2]

Using Twitter sign-in functionality requires you to create a Twitter account and configure the application. Once you've registered with Twitter, then you have to go to the https://apps.twitter.com/ URL and create a new application there.

Make sure that you fill out the Callback URL section. This is the /oauth/twitter-callback route that we defined earlier. Twitter will call this route with the result of the authentication attempt. Note that you have to supply the full URL that includes the server; e.g., https://myapp.herokuapp.com/oauth/twitter-callback.

Once you've created the application, go to its settings and make sure that the "Allow this application to be used to sign in with Twitter" option is checked.

Now you need to navigate to the Keys and Access Tokens section. This is where you can find the Consumer Key (API Key) and the Consumer Secret (API Secret) fields. You need to take these values and set them as the environment variables on the server where you deploy the application, as seen here:

```
export TWITTER_CONSUMER_KEY="Qwr35oKzkiAtoFEalDb2Atlza"
export TWITTER_CONSUMER_SECRET="aTFbBkCwyNeYzWPeX9Y7HzpBZtyrw7uYyuXeWvRu"
```

With the keys in place, you should be able to navigate to the home page and sign in via Twitter by clicking the sign-in button. This will redirect you to the official Twitter authentication page. Note that if you're already signed in to Twitter in the browser, then the page will redirect you back to your app without requiring an additional sign-in. Otherwise you'll be prompted to sign in using your Twitter credentials. When you're redirected back, then you'll either see your username displayed or a notification that access was denied by Twitter.

---

2. https://www.heroku.com/

Document-Oriented Database Access

A SQL database may not always be a good fit for your application. Many applications do not require a relational schema. If the application simply needs a persistence layer to store and retrieve records, then a document store may be a good fit.

Picking the Right Database

In addition to the features offered by a particular database, you need to consider three main aspects when picking a document-based database. These are consistency, availability, and partition tolerance, as defined by the CAP theorem.[1] Since these goals are at odds with one another, you'll have to decide on the two that are most important to you.

Consistency

When we have consistency, each client has the same view of the data. This aspect comes into play when you have a database cluster with multiple nodes. In a consistent database, each node is guaranteed to have the same view of the data.

Some databases, such as CouchDB,[2] provide eventual consistency. This means that while each node in the cluster is self-consistent, it's not guaranteed to be serving up the latest data.

Availability

Availability means the database doesn't have a global lock. A client connected to any node can read and write freely. However, the data is guaranteed to

---

1. http://en.wikipedia.org/wiki/CAP_theorem
2. http://couchdb.apache.org/

propagate through the cluster eventually. The downside of this approach is that clients are not guaranteed to see the latest data at all times.

CouchDB uses this model to allow high-availability clustering. Note that the clusters should always have an odd number of nodes. This allows CouchDB to use a quorum to decide what record will be kept in case of a conflict. This can occur if two clients are updating a record while connected to different nodes. One of the clients will end up with a revision conflict in this scenario.

Partition Tolerance

A partition-tolerant database works well across physical network partitions. This means that if your cluster experiences a serious network outage, the nodes are able to resync automatically when the network becomes available.

Using CouchDB

CouchDB values availability and partition tolerance. This makes it ideal for creating clusters where you want high throughput without a bottleneck.

In this section we'll cover how to use CouchDB from Clojure to accomplish basic tasks such as storing, retrieving, and deleting documents.

As a prerequisite to working with the following examples, you'll need to either set up a local instance of CouchDB or use one of their free services, such as Iris Couch.[3] After the database is set up, create a new table using its web user interface, accessible at http://hostname:5984/_utils. Let's call this table clutchtest.

Clutch Library

The easiest way to access CouchDB from Clojure is to use the Clutch library.[4] Clutch provides a very simple and intuitive interface. To use the library, we must first add its dependency to our project. The latest version at the time of writing is [com.ashafa/clutch "0.4.0"].

Connecting to the Database

To use clutch, we must require it in our namespace declaration.

```
(:require [com.ashafa.clutch :as couch])
```

Then we have to define our connection URL. Since CouchDB is accessible over HTTP, our URL can be a simple string specifying the database address.

---

3. http://www.iriscouch.com/
4. https://github.com/clojure-clutch/clutch

```
(def db "http://localhost:5984/clutchtest")
```

We could also add authentication to the URL directly in our connection string.

```
(def db "http://user:pass@localhost:5984/clutchtest")
```

Or we could use the URL library to create a URL and attach the credentials to it as a map.[5]

```
(def db (assoc (cemerick.url/url "https://localhost:5984/" "clutchtest")
               :username "user"
               :password "pass"))
```

Now that we have the connection created, let's look at how to store documents in our database.

Storing Documents

All interaction with the database must happen inside the with-db macro. This macro ensures that the connection is closed properly after we're done.

To store a document in the database, we can call the put-document function and pass it a Clojure map representing our document.

```
(couch/with-db db
  (couch/put-document {:foo "bar"}))
```

The preceding code creates a new document in our database with a randomly generated ID assigned to it. To assign a specific ID to a document, we must include the :_id key in our map.

```
(couch/with-db db
  (couch/put-document
    {:_id "user" :username "foo" :pass "$dfsdf#23434"}))
```

:_rev key When we wish to update an existing document, we must also include the revision of the current document in the map. For example, if we already inserted a user document into our database, we must now specify the revision we're updating using the :_rev key:

```
(couch/with-db db
  (couch/put-document
    {:_id "user" :_rev "<revision number>" :username "foo" :pass "$dfsdf#23434"}))
```

When we retrieve a document from the database, it has both the :_id and :_rev keys populated, so make sure to preserve them for the next time you wish to save the document. Now let's look at how we get a document from the database.

---

5. https://github.com/cemerick/url

Retrieving a Single Document

Documents are retrieved using the get-document function, which accepts a string representing the ID of the document being retrieved.

```
(couch/with-db db
  (couch/get-document "user"))
```

We can, of course, combine multiple statements inside a single with-db statement. For example, if we wanted to retrieve the user, set a new username, and save the document, we could do the following:

```
(couch/with-db db
  (let [doc (couch/get-document "user")]
    (couch/put-document
      (assoc doc :username "bar")))
  (println (couch/get-document "user")))
```

Retrieving Multiple Documents

Sometimes we need to do a batch operation to retrieve multiple documents from the database. Clutch provides a function for doing this, called all-documents.

```
(couch/with-db db
  (couch/all-documents))
```

The preceding call returns the IDs and revisions for all the documents in the specified database. It is also possible to retrieve the complete documents from the database by setting the :include_docs key to true.

```
(couch/with-db db
  (couch/all-documents {:include_docs true}))
```

Additionally, we can restrict the bulk retrieval to a set of documents containing the IDs specified by the :keys keyword, as follows:

```
(couch/with-db db
  (couch/all-documents
    {:include_docs true}
    {:keys ["doc1" "doc2" "doc3"]}))
```

To do more-complex selections from CouchDB, you would typically create views to filter and return documents based on the application's needs. A view is analogous to a stored procedure in a relational database.

Deleting Documents

Finally, we delete documents by using the delete-document function. It accepts the document ID as a string and removes that document from the database.

```
(couch/with-db db
```

```
(couch/delete-document "user"))
```

That's all there is to it when using CouchDB from Clojure. Clutch makes it trivial to store and retrieve documents from the database, and more-complex functionality can be added to the database directly via its rich-views support. Now let's look at what's involved in accessing MongoDB using the Monger library.[6,7]

Using MongoDB

MongoDB is another popular document-oriented database. Unlike CouchDB, it favors consistency and partition tolerance as its primary goals. If you're not concerned with having global locks, then MongoDB is a fine choice.

Connecting to the Database

We'll use the Monger library for accessing MongoDB. Monger provides an idiomatic Clojure API for working with the database. It provides comprehensive support for the features MongoDB 2.2+ offers. As is the case with Clutch, we can use native Clojure data structures without having to worry about translating them into the MongoDB/BSON format. Finally, Monger defaults to a configuration that emphasizes safety and consistency. The latest version at the time of writing is [com.novemberain/monger "3.0.0-rc2"].

Connecting to the database is as easy as calling monger.core/connect!. When supplied no parameters, connect! attempts to connect to a local instance of the database using the default port. Alternatively, we can either provide a map with the :host and :port keys or fine-tune the connection using mongo-options. Let's see how this looks:

```
(ns mongo-example.core
  (:require [monger.core :as [m]])
  (:import
    org.bson.types.ObjectId
    [com.mongodb MongoOptions]))

;;connects to a local instance
(m/connect!)
;;connect to myhost.com on port 5001
(m/connect! {:host "myhost.com" :port 5001})

;;connect using custom options
(m/connect! (m/server-address "127.0.0.1" 27017)
            (m/mongo-options
                :threads-allowed-to-block-for-connection-multiplier 300))
```

---

6. http://www.mongodb.org/
7. http://clojuremongodb.info/

We can also set the default database using the *mongodb-database* var by calling the set-db! function, as follows:

```
(defn connect! [& [params]]
  ((partial monger.core/connect!) params)
  (monger.core/set-db! (monger.core/get-db "local")))
```

Setting the database with set-db! makes it implicitly available to subsequent queries.

Most of the interaction with the database is provided via the monger.collection namespace. Here we have functions to insert, select, update, and delete records. Let's look at each of these tasks.

Inserting Records

We use the insert function to insert new records in the database. The function accepts the name of the collection, denoted by a string and a map representing the document to be inserted.

```
(monger.collection/insert "users" { :first_name "John" :last_name "Doe" })
```

The function returns a write result, the status of which can be checked by using monger.result/ok?. The monger.result/ok? returns true if the write was successful.

If we wish to specify an ID for our document, we have to generate it using the org.bson.types.ObjectId:

```
(monger.collection/insert "users" { :first_name "John" :last_name "Doe" })
(monger.collection/insert
  "users"
  { :_id (ObjectId.) :first_name "John" :last_name "Doe" })
```

Next, we have the insert-and-return function. It acts exactly like insert, except it returns the inserted document as a map.

```
(monger.collection/insert-and-return "users"
  { :_id (ObjectId.) :first_name "John" :last_name "Lennon" })
```

We can also make batch inserts using the insert-batch function. This function accepts the collection name followed by a sequence of maps representing the documents.

```
(monger.collection/insert-batch
  "users"
  [{ :first_name "John" :last_name "Doe" }
   { :first_name "Jane" :last_name "Smith" }])
```

Selecting Records

Monger provides several functions for searching for records and returning them as Clojure maps. These functions are find-maps, find-one-as-map, and find-map-by-id.

The find-maps function can query for documents in the collection using a map that contains the key and value. Objects containing the key with the specified value are returned. All documents are returned if no parameters are specified.

```
(monger.collection/find-maps "users" {:first_name "John"})
```

The find-one-as-map function returns a single object matching the query.

```
(monger.collection/find-one-as-map "users"
  { :first_name "John"})
```

Finally, the find-map-by-id function accepts an object ID as the search parameter.

```
(monger.collection/find-map-by-id "users"
  (ObjectId. "514f455d03642f52431b5bfe"))
```

It's also possible to use the standard MongoDB query operators in search queries, as seen here:

```
(monger.collection/find-maps "products" { :price { "$gt" 300 "$lte" 5000 } })
```

Updating Records

We update records by using the update function, which inserts the record if it doesn't exist when :upsert true is specified.

```
(update "users" { :first_name "John" :last_name "Doe" })
;;update existing or insert a new record
(update "users" { :first_name "John" :last_name "Doe" } :upsert true)
```

Deleting Records

Finally, we can delete documents from the database using the remove function. When no match criteria is specified, all documents are removed.

```
;;remove ALL documents
(monger.collection/remove "users")

;; remove documents with the specified key
(monger.collection/remove "users" { :language "English" })
```

As you can see, working with document-oriented databases is quite straightforward. Depending on your application needs, you may wish to use a document store instead of a relational store, or a combination of the two. Whatever approach you choose, Clojure has you covered.

Writing RESTful Web Services with Liberator

In this appendix we'll cover how to use the Liberator library to generate our application end points.[1]

Using Liberator

Liberator is a Clojure library for writing RESTful services modeled after web-machine,[2] a popular service framework for Erlang. Its primary feature is that it puts a strong emphasis on decoupling the front end from the back end of your application.

Conceptually, Liberator provides a clean way to reason about your service operations. Each request passes through a series of conditions and handlers defined in the resource. These map to the codes specified by the HTTP RFC 2616, such as 200-OK, 201-created, 404-not found, and so on.

This approach makes it very easy to write standards-compliant services and to group the operations logically. It also means that your services will automatically use the appropriate HTTP codes associated with a particular response.

Due to its focus on the separation of the front-end and back-end logic, Liberator is a natural choice for writing many types of web applications. These include general-purpose services, single-page applications, and applications that might have nonweb clients, such as mobile applications.

---

1. http://clojure-liberator.github.io/liberator/
2. https://github.com/basho/webmachine

In this section we'll cover how to create a simple application that serves static resources, provides basic session management, and handles service operations.

We'll create a new application called *liberator-service* using a Leiningen template called *reagent-template*. This template is less opinionated than the Luminus template and therefore it provides a better starting point for Liberator-based applications.

```
lein new reagent liberator-service
```

Once the application is created, we need to add Liberator, Cheshire, and cljs-ajax dependencies to our project.clj dependencies vector:[3]

```
:dependencies
[ ...
  [cheshire "5.5.0"]
  [liberator "0.13"]
  [cljs-ajax "0.5.2"]]
```

Cheshire is a fast and easy-to-use JSON parsing library. We'll use it for parsing the requests from the client and generating the responses.

The application generated by the template contains a file called src/clj/liberator_service/handler.clj that contains the routes for the application. The home-page function generates the HTML using the Hiccup HTML templating library. The syntax is the same as the Reagent HTML templating syntax we covered previously.

Defining Resources

Liberator uses the concept of resources to interact with the client. The resources are simply Ring-compliant handlers that can be used inside your Compojure routes. These resources are defined using the resource and the defresource macros. We need to reference these functions in the liberator-service.handler namespace in order to start working with Liberator.

```
(ns liberator-service.handler
  (:require ...
    [liberator.core :refer [defresource resource]]))
```

Now we can replace our routes definition with a resource, as follows:

liberator-snippets/home.clj

```
(defroutes routes
  (ANY "/" request
    (resource
```

---

3.   https://github.com/dakrone/cheshire

```
    :handle-ok home-page
    :etag "fixed-etag"
    :available-media-types ["text/html"]))))
```

Note that we're using the ANY Compojure route for our resource. This allows the Liberator resource to handle the request type. Let's start the app by running the following command and navigating to http://localhost:3000/ in the browser. We should see the home page displayed, advising us to start Figwheel in order to compile ClojureScript.

```
lein run
```

Say we want to name the resource handler; we can use defresource instead:

liberator-snippets/home.clj

```
(defresource home
  :handle-ok home-page
  :etag "fixed-etag"
  :available-media-types ["text/html"])

(defroutes routes
  (ANY "/" request home))
```

The request in the preceding route is simply a map that's described in *What's in the Request Map*, on page 29.

A set of keys defined by the Liberator API represents each resource type for different types of actions that follow. A key can fall into one of four categories:

- Decision
- Handler
- Action
- Declaration

Each key can be associated with either constants or functions. The functions should accept a single parameter that is the current context and return a variety of responses.

The context parameter contains a map with keys for the request, the resource, and optionally the representation. The request key points to the Ring request. The resource represents the current state of the resource, and the representation contains the results of content negotiation.

Let's take a close look at each category and its purpose.

Making Decisions

Decisions are used to figure out how to handle the client request. The decision keys end with a question mark (?) and their handler must evaluate to a Boolean value.

A decision function can return a Boolean value indicating the result of the decision, or it can return a map or a vector. In the case where a map is returned, the decision is assumed to have been evaluated to true, and the contents of the map are merged with the response map. If a vector is returned, it must contain a Boolean indicating the outcome, followed by a map to be merged with the response.

When any decision has a negative outcome, its corresponding HTTP code is returned to the client. For example, if we wanted to mark as unavailable the route we defined earlier, we could add a decision key called service-available? and associate it with a false value.

liberator-snippets/home.clj

```
(defresource home
  :service-available? false
  :handle-ok home-page
  :etag "fixed-etag"
  :available-media-types ["text/html"])
```

If we reload the page, we'll see the 503 response type associated with the "Service not available" response.

Alternatively, we could restrict access to the resource by using the method-allowed? decision key along with a decision function.

liberator-snippets/home.clj

```
(defresource home
  :method-allowed?
  (fn [context]
    (= :get (get-in context [:request :request-method])))
  :handle-ok home-page
  :etag "fixed-etag"
  :available-media-types ["text/html"])
```

Since checking the request method is a common operation, Liberator provides a key called :allowed-methods. This key should point to a vector of keywords representing the HTTP methods.

liberator-snippets/home.clj

```
(defresource home
  :allowed-methods [:get]
```

```
  :handle-ok home-page
  :etag "fixed-etag"
  :available-media-types ["text/html"])

(defresource home
  :service-available? true

  :method-allowed? (request-method-in :get)

  :handle-method-not-allowed
  (fn [context]
    (str (get-in context [:request :request-method]) " is not allowed"))

  :handle-ok home-page
  :etag "fixed-etag"
  :available-media-types ["text/html"])

(defresource home
  :service-available? false
  :handle-service-not-available
  "service is currently unavailable..."

  :method-allowed? (request-method-in :get)
  :handle-method-not-allowed
  (fn [context]
    (str (get-in context [:request :request-method]) " is not allowed"))

  :handle-ok home-page
  :etag "fixed-etag"
  :available-media-types ["text/html"])

(defresource add-item
  :method-allowed? (request-method-in :post)
  :post!
  (fn [context]
    (let [item (-> context :request :params :item)]
      (spit (io/file "items") (str item "\n") :append true)))
  :handle-created (io/file "items")
  :available-media-types ["text/plain"])
```

We can also combine multiple decision functions in the same resource:

liberator-snippets/home.clj

```
(defresource home
  :service-available? true

  :method-allowed? (request-method-in :get)

  :handle-method-not-allowed
  (fn [context]
    (str (get-in context [:request :request-method]) " is not allowed"))

  :handle-ok home-page
  :etag "fixed-etag"
  :available-media-types ["text/html"])
```

Creating Handlers

A handler function should return a standard Ring response. Handler keys start with the handle- prefix. We saw a handler function when we used the handle-ok key to return the response in our resource.

There are other handlers, such as handle-method-not-allowed and handle-not-found. The full list of handlers can be found on the official documentation page.[4] These handlers can be used in conjunction with the decisions to return a specific response for a particular decision outcome.

For example, if we want to return a specific response when the service is not available, we do the following:

liberator-snippets/home.clj

```
(defresource home
  :service-available? false
  :handle-service-not-available
  "service is currently unavailable..."

  :method-allowed? (request-method-in :get)
  :handle-method-not-allowed
  (fn [context]
    (str (get-in context [:request :request-method]) " is not allowed"))

  :handle-ok home-page
  :etag "fixed-etag"
  :available-media-types ["text/html"])
```

Our resource now has custom handlers for each decision outcome.

Taking Actions

An action represents an update of the current state by the client, such as a PUT, POST, or DELETE request. The action keys end with an exclamation point (!) to indicate that they're mutating the application's internal state. Once an action occurs, we can return the result to the client using the handle-created handler.

Writing Declarations

Declarations are used to indicate the resource's capabilities. For example, our resource uses the available-media-types declaration to specify that it returns a response of type text/html. Another declaration we saw is etag, which allows the client to cache the resource.

---

4.   http://clojure-liberator.github.io/liberator/doc/handlers.html

Putting It All Together

Let's look at an example of a service that has a couple of resources that allow the client to read and write some data. The application will display a list of to-do items and allow the user to add additional items to the list.

The client will be implemented in ClojureScript and use Ajax to communicate with the service. The client code will consist of a few functions to retrieve, render, and save to-do items. Let's look at each of these in turn.

The first function renders the items in our list.

liberator-service/src/cljs/liberator_service/core.cljs

```
(defn item-list [items]
  (when (not-empty items)
    [:ul
     (for [item items]
       ^{:key item}
       [:li item])]))
```

Next we add a function called get-items to grab the items from the server as a string and a function called parse-items to parse it into a list. The parse-items function expects to receive data as a newline-separated string, generating a vector from nonempty items.

liberator-service/src/cljs/liberator_service/core.cljs

```
(defn parse-items [items]
  (->> items
       clojure.string/split-lines
       (remove empty?)
       vec))
(defn get-items []
  (GET "/items"
       {:error-handler
        #(session/put! :error (:response %))
        :handler
        #(session/put! :items (parse-items %))}))
```

Note the function is calling session/update-in! to store the result. This function is provided by the reagent-utils library. The session namespace contains a Reagent atom and provides several utility functions for managing its state.

The session provides a way to represent the global state for the application, such as the user information. It should not be used for any component-specific data, however. Since our application is extremely simple, it's a convenient way to track the to-do items.

If we receive an error, the :error-handler is invoked and populates the :error key in the session.

We also need to add a function for adding new items to the list. Let's call this function add-item!; its code looks as follows:

liberator-service/src/cljs/liberator_service/core.cljs

```clojure
(defn add-item! [item]
  (session/remove! :error)
  (POST "/add-item"
        {:headers {"x-csrf-token"
                   (.-value (.getElementById js/document "__anti-forgery-token"))}
         :format :raw
         :params {:item (str @item)}
         :error-handler #(session/put! :error (:response %))
         :handler #(do
                     (println "updating")
                     (session/update-in! [:items] conj @item)
                     (reset! item nil))}))
```

This function looks for the anti-forgery token on the page and sets it as the header, as we've done before. It also sets the :format key to the :raw value, indicating that we do not wish to do any processing on the data we send and receive. The success handler updates the session to conj the value to the list and resets the item atom to nil. Errors are handled the same way as for the previous component.

In order to use the add-item! function, we have to create a UI component; let's call it item-input-component and put the following code in it:

liberator-service/src/cljs/liberator_service/core.cljs

```clojure
(defn item-input-component []
  (let [item (atom nil)]
    (fn []
      [:div
       [:input
        {:type :text
         :value @item
         :on-change #(reset! item (-> % .-target .-value))
         :placeholder "To-Do item"}]
       [:button
        {:on-click #(add-item! item)}
        "Add To-Do"]])))
```

The component creates a local state to hold the value of the item as it is being typed in by the user and then calls the add-item! function to send it to the server.

Finally, we create the error-component that displays itself whenever the :error key is present in the session.

liberator-service/src/cljs/liberator_service/core.cljs

```
(defn error-component []
  (when-let [error (session/get :error)]
    [:p error]))
```

Let's update the home-page component to display the components that we just created.

liberator-service/src/cljs/liberator_service/core.cljs

```
(defn home-page []
  [:div
   [:h2 "To-Do Items"]
   [error-component]
   [item-list (session/get :items)]
   [item-input-component]])
```

Now let's update the init! function to fetch the initial list of to-do items from the server when the page loads.

liberator-service/src/cljs/liberator_service/core.cljs

```
(defn init! []
  (hook-browser-navigation!)
  (get-items)
  (mount-root))
```

Now we'll create corresponding resources to handle each of the operations. Let's start by adding a reference to clojure.java.io in order to read and write the to-do file and to ring.util.anti-forgery for handling CSRF.

```
(ns liberator-service.routes.home
  (:require ...
            [clojure.java.io :as io]
            [ring.util.anti-forgery :refer [anti-forgery-field]]))
```

Next let's change the home-page and add the anti-forgery-field to it. This is necessary to ensure that a fresh anti-forgery value is generated for each session. We also have to update the home resource accordingly.

```clojure
(defn home-page []
  (html
    [:html
     [:head
      [:meta {:charset "utf-8"}]
      [:meta {:name "viewport"
              :content "width=device-width, initial-scale=1"}]
      (include-css (if (env :dev) "css/site.css" "css/site.min.css"))]
     [:body
      (anti-forgery-field)
      [:p (str (anti-forgery-field))]
      [:div#app
       [:h3 "ClojureScript has not been compiled!"]
       [:p "please run "
        [:b "lein figwheel"]
        " in order to start the compiler"]]
      (include-js "js/app.js")]]))
(defresource home
  :allowed-methods [:get]
  :handle-ok (home-page)
  :etag "fixed-etag"
  :available-media-types ["text/html"])
```

The first resource responds to GET requests and returns the contents of the items file found in the root directory of the project. Note that when we're working with mutable resources such as files we do not wish to place them in the resources folder. Once the application is packaged as a JAR, then the resources become read-only. Therefore, we need to reference these from an external location.

```clojure
(defresource get-items
  :allowed-methods [:get]
  :handle-ok (fn [_] (io/file "items"))
  :available-media-types ["text/plain"])
```

In the resource, we use the :allowed-methods key to restrict it to only serve GET requests. We use the available-media-types declaration to specify that the response is of type text/plain. The resource then reads the items file from disk and returns its contents to the client.

The second resource responds to POST requests and adds the item contained in params to the list of items on disk.

```clojure
(defresource add-item
```

```
:method-allowed? (request-method-in :post)
:post!
(fn [context]
  (let [item (-> context :request :params :item)]
    (spit (io/file "items") (str item "\n") :append true)))
:handle-created (io/file "items")
:available-media-types ["text/plain"])
```

In this resource we check that the method is POST and use the post! action to update the existing list of items. We then use the handle-created handler to return *ok* upon success.

You'll notice that nothing is preventing us from adding a blank item. Let's add a check in our service to validate the request to add a new item:

liberator-service/src/clj/liberator_service/handler.clj

```
(defresource add-item!
  :allowed-methods [:post]
  :malformed? (fn [context]
                (-> context :request :params :item empty?))
  :handle-malformed "item value cannot be empty!"
  :post!
  (fn [context]
    (let [item (-> context :request :params :item)]
      (spit (io/file "items") (str item "\n") :append true)))
  :handle-created "ok"
  :available-media-types ["text/plain"])
```

Now if the value of the item parameter is empty, we'll be routed to handle-malformed to inform the client that the item name cannot be empty. Next time we try to add an empty user, we'll see a 400 error in the browser:

POST http://localhost:3000/add-user 400 (Bad Request)

If you click the Add To-Do button without filling in the item field, you'll see the following error:

As you can see, Liberator ensures separation of concerns by design. With the Liberator model, you will have small, self-contained functions, each of which handles a specific task.

Leiningen Templates

Once we create a particular type of application, such as our picture gallery app, we may want to write other applications that use the same structure. It would be nice to be able to create a skeleton app template that could be used for this task. This is precisely what we can do with Leiningen templates.

Throughout this book we've been primarily using the Luminus template for starting new projects.[1] Here we'll cover how a template works and how to make templates of our own.

What's in a Template

A Leiningen template is a collection of assets that are used to generate a particular project. The templates use the Stencil library to inject dynamic content, such as the name of the project, into the asset files when they're rendered.[2]

We'll take a look at a template project called *compojure-template* to see how it works.[3]

Since templates are Leiningen projects, they each contain a project.clj file.

compojure-template/project.clj

```
(defproject compojure/lein-template "0.4.2"
  :description "Compojure project template for Leiningen"
  :url "https://github.com/weavejester/compojure-template"
  :eval-in-leiningen true
  :license {:name "Eclipse Public License"
            :url "http://www.eclipse.org/legal/epl-v10.html"})
```

---

1. https://github.com/luminus-framework/luminus-template
2. https://github.com/davidsantiago/stencil
3. https://github.com/weavejester/compojure-template

It looks like a regular project file, except for the eval-in-leiningen key that prevents Leiningen from launching a separate process for the given project during the build time.

The template itself is found at src/leiningen/new/compojure.clj, and it looks like this:

compojure-template/src/leiningen/new/compojure.clj

```clojure
(ns leiningen.new.compojure
  (:require [leiningen.core.main :as main]
            [leiningen.new.templates :refer [renderer year project-name
                                             ->files sanitize-ns name-to-path
                                             multi-segment]]))

(def render (renderer "compojure"))

(defn compojure
  "Create a new Compojure project"
  [name]
  (let [main-ns (sanitize-ns name)
        data    {:raw-name  name
                 :name      (project-name name)
                 :namespace main-ns
                 :dirs      (name-to-path main-ns)
                 :year      (year)}]
    (->files data
             [".gitignore"  (render "gitignore")]
             ["project.clj" (render "project.clj" data)]
             ["README.md"   (render "README.md" data)]
             ["src/{{dirs}}/handler.clj"       (render "handler.clj" data)]
             ["test/{{dirs}}/handler_test.clj" (render "handler_test.clj" data)]
             "resources/public")))
```

The compojure function is where all the fun happens, and it's what gets called when we run lein new compojure myapp to create an application using this template. The function declares a map called data with some useful variables, such as the sanitized project name, that is used to render the assets.

The leiningen.new.templates/render function is used to generate the resulting files at the specified path. Each resource is represented by a vector where the first element is the name of the file to be generated and the second is a call to the render function with the name of the template file. The {{dirs}} tag is replaced by the value of the :dirs key from the data map.

We find the template files at the resources/leiningen/new/compojure path. These files don't need to have the same folder structure as the resulting project. As you can see in the preceding code, we specify the target path explicitly when we render each asset.

The template files use tags that match the keys in the data map, such as the {{namespace}} anchor, whenever dynamic content needs to be injected. This anchor is replaced with the value specified at that key when the resource is generated. Let's look at the handler.clj template file as an example:

compojure-template/resources/leiningen/new/compojure/handler.clj

```
(ns {{namespace}}.handler
  (:require [compojure.core :refer :all]
            [compojure.route :as route]
            [ring.middleware.defaults :refer [wrap-defaults site-defaults]]]))
(defroutes app-routes
  (GET "/" [] "Hello, World")
  (route/not-found "Not Found"))
(def app
  (wrap-defaults app-routes site-defaults))
```

Note that since Stencil uses {{ and }} delimiters, it can end up interpreting the contents of the template as tags. To avoid this, it's possible to temporarily change the delimiters as follows:

```
{{=<% %>=}}
(let [{{:keys [foo bar]} :baz} m]
  (println foo bar))
<%={{ }}=%>
```

Now that we've seen what a Leiningen template looks like, let's create a fresh template project by running the following command:

```
lein new template my-template
```

The resulting project contains the following files. Note that the package structure matches the name of the template that we supplied.

```
    ____.gitignore
|____.hgignore
|____CHANGELOG.md
|____LICENSE
|____project.clj
|____README.md
|____resources
| |____leiningen
|   |____new
|     |____my_template
|       |____foo.clj
|____src
  |____leiningen
    |____new
      |____my_template.clj
```

Once we've created our template, we can install it locally by running lein install. Then we can start using it instead of having to write the boilerplate for this kind of project. If we wish to make our template available to others, we can publish it to Clojars by running lein deploy clojars[4].

4.　https://clojars.org/

Index

Exercises and Teams

From exercises to make you a better programmer to techniques for creating better teams, we've got you covered.

Exercises for Programmers

When you write software, you need to be at the top of your game. Great programmers practice to keep their skills sharp. Get sharp and stay sharp with more than fifty practice exercises rooted in real-world scenarios. If you're a new programmer, these challenges will help you learn what you need to break into the field, and if you're a seasoned pro, you can use these exercises to learn that hot new language for your next gig.

Brian P. Hogan
(118 pages) ISBN: 9781680501223. $24
https://pragprog.com/book/bhwb

Creating Great Teams

People are happiest and most productive if they can choose what they work on and who they work with. Self-selecting teams give people that choice. Build well-designed and efficient teams to get the most out of your organization, with step-by-step instructions on how to set up teams quickly and efficiently. You'll create a process that works for you, whether you need to form teams from scratch, improve the design of existing teams, or are on the verge of a big team re-shuffle.

Sandy Mamoli and David Mole
(102 pages) ISBN: 9781680501285. $17
https://pragprog.com/book/mmteams

Clojure and Functional Patterns

Get up to speed on all that Clojure has to offer, and fine-tune your object thinking into a more functional style.

Programming Clojure (2nd edition)

If you want to keep up with the significant changes in this important language, you need the second edition of *Programming Clojure*. Stu and Aaron describe the modifications to the numerics system in Clojure 1.3, explain new Clojure concepts such as Protocols and Datatypes, and teach you how to think in Clojure.

Stuart Halloway and Aaron Bedra
(290 pages) ISBN: 9781934356869. $35
https://pragprog.com/book/shcloj2

Functional Programming Patterns in Scala and Clojure

Solve real-life programming problems with a fraction of the code that pure object-oriented programming requires. Use Scala and Clojure to solve in-depth problems and see how familiar object-oriented patterns can become more concise with functional programming and patterns. Your code will be more declarative, with fewer bugs and lower maintenance costs.

Michael Bevilacqua-Linn
(256 pages) ISBN: 9781937785475. $36
https://pragprog.com/book/mbfpp

Long Live the Command Line!

Use tmux and Vim for incredible mouse-free productivity.

tmux

Your mouse is slowing you down. The time you spend context switching between your editor and your consoles eats away at your productivity. Take control of your environment with tmux, a terminal multiplexer that you can tailor to your workflow. Learn how to customize, script, and leverage tmux's unique abilities and keep your fingers on your keyboard's home row.

Brian P. Hogan
(88 pages) ISBN: 9781934356968. $16.25
https://pragprog.com/book/bhtmux

Practical Vim, Second Edition

Vim is a fast and efficient text editor that will make you a faster and more efficient developer. It's available on almost every OS, and if you master the techniques in this book, you'll never need another text editor. In more than 120 Vim tips, you'll quickly learn the editor's core functionality and tackle your trickiest editing and writing tasks. This beloved bestseller has been revised and updated to Vim 7.4 and includes three brand-new tips and five fully revised tips.

Drew Neil
(354 pages) ISBN: 9781680501278. $29
https://pragprog.com/book/dnvim2

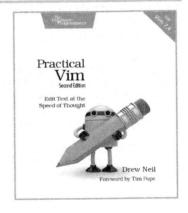

The Joy of Math and Healthy Programming

Rediscover the joy and fascinating weirdness of pure mathematics, and learn how to take a healthier approach to programming.

Good Math

Mathematics is beautiful—and it can be fun and exciting as well as practical. *Good Math* is your guide to some of the most intriguing topics from two thousand years of mathematics: from Egyptian fractions to Turing machines; from the real meaning of numbers to proof trees, group symmetry, and mechanical computation. If you've ever wondered what lay beyond the proofs you struggled to complete in high school geometry, or what limits the capabilities of the computer on your desk, this is the book for you.

Mark C. Chu-Carroll
(282 pages) ISBN: 9781937785338. $34
https://pragprog.com/book/mcmath

The Healthy Programmer

To keep doing what you love, you need to maintain your own systems, not just the ones you write code for. Regular exercise and proper nutrition help you learn, remember, concentrate, and be creative—skills critical to doing your job well. Learn how to change your work habits, master exercises that make working at a computer more comfortable, and develop a plan to keep fit, healthy, and sharp for years to come.

This book is intended only as an informative guide for those wishing to know more about health issues. In no way is this book intended to replace, countermand, or conflict with the advice given to you by your own healthcare provider including Physician, Nurse Practitioner, Physician Assistant, Registered Dietician, and other licensed professionals.

Joe Kutner
(254 pages) ISBN: 9781937785314. $36
https://pragprog.com/book/jkthp

The Pragmatic Bookshelf

The Pragmatic Bookshelf features books written by developers for developers. The titles continue the well-known Pragmatic Programmer style and continue to garner awards and rave reviews. As development gets more and more difficult, the Pragmatic Programmers will be there with more titles and products to help you stay on top of your game.

Visit Us Online

This Book's Home Page
https://pragprog.com/book/dswdcloj2
Source code from this book, errata, and other resources. Come give us feedback, too!

Register for Updates
https://pragprog.com/updates
Be notified when updates and new books become available.

Join the Community
https://pragprog.com/community
Read our weblogs, join our online discussions, participate in our mailing list, interact with our wiki, and benefit from the experience of other Pragmatic Programmers.

New and Noteworthy
https://pragprog.com/news
Check out the latest pragmatic developments, new titles and other offerings.

Save on the eBook

Save on the eBook versions of this title. Owning the paper version of this book entitles you to purchase the electronic versions at a terrific discount.

PDFs are great for carrying around on your laptop—they are hyperlinked, have color, and are fully searchable. Most titles are also available for the iPhone and iPod touch, Amazon Kindle, and other popular e-book readers.

Buy now at *https://pragprog.com/coupon*

Contact Us

Online Orders:	*https://pragprog.com/catalog*
Customer Service:	*support@pragprog.com*
International Rights:	*translations@pragprog.com*
Academic Use:	*academic@pragprog.com*
Write for Us:	*http://write-for-us.pragprog.com*
Or Call:	+1 800-699-7764